Praise for *Smart Baseball*

"I have known Buddy Bell a number of years, as a competitor, teammate, and friend. I don't know of anybody more qualified to write a book about this subject. I am so glad that someone has finally decided to write about it and to have it done by Buddy and his sons, makes it even better."

> —Mike Hargrove, manager of the Baltimore Orioles

"This book details how great players of the past, many of whom are Hall of Famers, prepared themselves mentally to excel at their sport. Anyone who has played baseball knows there is more to being successful than just talent."

> —Ray Fosse, American League All-Star
> and broadcaster for the Oakland As

"The mental aspect of the game is often overlooked. This book gives fans a different perspective into the great game of baseball."

> —Alan Trammell, manager of the Detroit Tigers

St.

Martin's Griffin

New York

SMART
BASEBALL

Inside the Mind of

Baseball's Top Players

BUDDY BELL and **NEAL VAHLE**

with **DAVID, MIKE,** and **RICK BELL**

www.stmartins.com

Library of Congress Cataloging-in-Publication Data

Bell, Buddy, 1951–
    Smart baseball : how professionals play the mental game / Buddy Bell and Neal Vahle with David, Mike, and Rick Bell.
        p. cm.
    ISBN 0-312-33334-X (hc)
    ISBN 0-312-33335-8 (pbk)
    EAN 978-0-312-33335-5
    1. Baseball—Psychological aspects. I. Vahle, Neal. II. Title.

  GV867.6.B45 2005
  796.357'019—dc22   2004057034

First St. Martin's Griffin Edition: March 2006

D 10 9 8 7 6 5 4 3 2

Contents

Acknowledgments

FIRST AND FOREMOST, I WANT TO THANK MY COAUTHOR, Buddy Bell, for his deep understanding of major league baseball and for his ability to express with clarity his knowledge and insights. Thank you also to his three baseball-playing sons, David, Mike, and Rick, for their thoughts and ideas on playing the game in the twenty-first century. It is important to acknowledge the contribution of Gus Bell, Buddy's father, who passed away in 1995. Gus provided the example and the inspiration for his son and grandsons to commit themselves to a career in baseball. His ideas about how to play the mental game filtered through to Buddy and his sons and are in this book. I owe a debt of gratitude to the many players, from Willie Mays to Sandy Koufax, whose autobiographies and biographies were essential to this work. Several friends of Buddy's from the world of major league baseball read the manuscript, endorsed our efforts, and helped move this project forward. Thanks go out to Sparky Anderson, Mike Hargrove, Todd Helton, Tim Kurkjian, Rocky Colavito, Ray Fosse, Charlie Maher, and Alan Trammell.

Additional thanks to those of my friends who read parts of

the manuscript and made helpful comments and suggestions: Walt Bentson, Dick Donaldson, Gary Feidel, Milton Friedman, Val Hornstein, Paul Johnson, Walter Le Conte, Michael Maday, Ted Mares, Chris McCluny, Barry Robbins, Arnie Scher, Rich Sigberman, and Curt Wells. Without the encouragement of Michael Murphy, author of *Golf in the Kingdom* and an authority on the connection between the mind and body in sports, this book would never have been written. I thank him for the inspiration to persevere.

Special thanks to our agent, Candice Fuhrman, who did so much to find the right publisher for this work. Thanks also to Marc Resnick, our editor at St. Martin's Press, for his professional competency and his knowledge of baseball. This work would be an imperfect product without the contributions of two excellent copy editors, Becky Maines and Lisa Smith. Thank you! Thank you!

To my three sons, Stephen, Tom, and Peter, and my daughter, Maria—who have made athletics an important part of their lives—my appreciation for their interest and support as the work progressed. Finally, for her patience and caring—and her editorial insights—I give grateful thanks to my wife, Nancy.

—Neal Vahle

Introduction

DURING THE THREE DECADES I HAVE BEEN INVOLVED PROfessionally in baseball, as a player, coach, and manager, the mental aspect of playing in the major leagues has been of great interest to me. The mental part of the game is so important. My success in the big leagues depended to a large extent on how I prepared myself mentally. Before each game, the mental preparation that enabled me to perform at a high level both in the field and at bat involved a lot of hard work. During the game, each pitch created a new situation, with several factors to be considered. A high level of awareness was required to avoid making mental mistakes. I don't ever remember being mentally fresh after a game. In fact, when we went off the field my mind was more drained than my body.

Clete Boyer, who in my opinion was one of the best defensive third basemen to play the game, was right on target when he said, "The thing about the game at this level is that there is very little difference in physical skills between the players; the real difference between them is upstairs. It is what is 'in your head' that makes the difference."[1] Mark McGwire, who seemed capable of hitting a home run every time he came to bat, was emphatic in pointing out the primacy of the mind. He voiced an opinion I agree with: "The one thing most people don't realize is that baseball is not physical, it's mental. Sure, you've got to have the ability, but you can overcome anything with the mind. The mind is so powerful."[2]

Yogi Berra, a smart baseball man who coached the Houston Astros when I played for them, pointed out that even though "everyone lifts weights and all the guys are much bigger and stronger, the mental part may be more important."[3] In recent years much emphasis has been given, as Yogi indicated, to the physical part of the game. Guys spend lots of time in the weight room, in the training room, in the batting cage, or in the bullpen. Ballplayers, even at the major league level, do not realize that they must give as much attention to the mental part of the game as they do to the physical. Time must be spent thinking about what they are going to do on a particular night or, for that matter, during a season. That's the smart way to play this game.

Willie Stargell, the Hall of Fame outfielder of the Pittsburgh Pirates, recognized that as players grew older, the mental part of the game became even more important. He said:

> Rarely does a player survive a long time on his physical capabilities. Sooner or later, a player's body tires or begins to wear out. That's when the mental side of the game takes over. The correct mental attitude can prolong a career several years. It can also relieve excess stress on a player's body and add productivity to his performance.[4]

In this book we explore the wide range of mental attributes that ballplayers use to play the game, including savvy and know-how, the power of concentration, competitive drive, self-confidence, mental imagery, leadership, having fun, hunches, and gut feelings. I have drawn on my own experience, that of my father, Gus Bell, a four-time National League All-Star who had a fifteen-year major league career, and that of my sons, David, Mike, and Rick. David played in the World Series with the Giants and now is with the Phillies. Mike has played for the Reds. Both Mike and Rick are currently in Triple-A.

We also present the insights of some of the game's greatest players, from Joe DiMaggio and Ted Williams to Orel Hershiser, Pete Rose, and Barry Bonds. You will get a chance to see what goes on inside the minds of highly skilled players before, during, and after the game.

SMART

BASEBALL

ONE

Savvy, Know-How, Smarts

My Experience and That of My Sons in
Becoming Smart About the Game

RALPH HOUK, A BIG-LEAGUE MANAGER I ALWAYS WANTED
to play for, made a telling comment when he described the
attributes of Moose Skowron, the first baseman on the great
Yankee teams of the fifties and sixties. Houk said, "Maybe he's
not what you'd call a brilliant man . . . [but he] was a smart
ballplayer."[1] Becoming a smart baseball player takes a lot of work
and no small degree of intelligence. It took me several years
to develop the savvy and know-how needed to excel in the
game. It is true, I did have an advantage. I grew up in a baseball
family. My father, Gus Bell, had a successful fourteen-year career
with the Pittsburgh Pirates, the Cincinnati Reds, the Milwaukee
Braves, and the New York Mets. I was born while he was playing in Pittsburgh.

The game was easy for me as a youngster playing Little
League baseball in Cincinnati. I simply went out and played and
relied on my natural talent. When I was fourteen years old,

things changed. I began playing with guys a few years older than I was. The game became hard, and I realized I had to do something about it. I had a passion for the game and already knew that I wanted to be a major leaguer. I began talking with my father—who, by the way, never pushed me into baseball—and my coaches. I sought their advice because I was aware that I had to become smarter about the game. I spent more time going to baseball games and watching the Reds on TV. But now I watched differently. I paid attention to how players positioned themselves on the field, and observed the different deliveries of the pitchers and different styles of pitching. In short, I became a student of the game. I learned by looking, listening, and asking questions.

When I was seventeen years old I signed my first baseball contract, with the Cleveland Indians. As I moved through the minors and into the major leagues with Cleveland—I was only twenty when I began my eighteen-year major league career—I worked hard to get to the point where nothing surprised me, where no situation on the diamond was unfamiliar. I got to know the pitchers and what I could expect from them, and I found out how to play the hitters. I came to grips with my own abilities—what I could and could not do. I did not lie to myself. I knew that those who succeeded at this game were smart baseball players. I knew that you could not show up at four P.M. the night of a game, put on a uniform, and go out and play winning baseball without a plan of action or a thought in your head.

My eldest son, David, is now thirty and plays for the Philadelphia Phillies. He appeared in a World Series in 2002 with the Giants and went to the American League play-offs two consecutive years with the Mariners. His experience growing up in a baseball family was somewhat similar to my own. My wife and I did not push him, nor his two brothers, Mike and Rick—who are both currently in Triple-A ball—into a career in baseball.

Without a doubt, however, growing up in a family where we paid a lot of attention to sports—not just baseball—affected all three of them. David explained how he got involved with baseball and began learning to play the game:

Our family is extremely close. Having sports gave us something to talk about and share, something in common. It was a great way to grow up. It was a huge part of our lives. When I was a kid I played the game because I loved it. I just enjoyed playing. I learned a lot about baseball just from being around it. I watched a ton of baseball both at the ballpark and on TV. My dad was great about having us with him. During the summer, we were at the ballpark almost every day. We spent hours and hours in the clubhouse around the players. During spring training, we all got out of school—my two brothers and two sisters and me—and went to Florida for a month. We went to the park every day. So it was a way of life. We saw a lot of baseball. I didn't sit through a game trying to figure out what the strategy was on the field or why the manager was making a particular move. I just enjoyed the game so much and loved it so much that I just watched and watched and watched, taking in everything, without thinking consciously that I was trying to learn something. At age seventeen, same as my dad, I signed a professional contract with the Cleveland Indians. Having been in a major league clubhouse many times and having seen how things were done there was big advantage for me when I became a pro. I knew how to act in the clubhouse. I knew how to carry myself. I knew what to do. I was around eighteen-year-olds who were away from home for the first time and had to learn all these things.

Having been in the major leagues for fourteen years, Gus Bell, my father, played an important role in my sons' development because he went to their baseball games while I was away playing for the Indians and Rangers. Here is what David had to say about him:

> I spent a lot of time with my grandfather [Gus Bell died in 1995 at age 67]. I probably spent more time with him than with my dad during high school. My grandfather was the most positive person I have ever been around. He knew how much I loved the game. He would talk about his career, tell stories about what happened, and talk about the camaraderie among the players. I would sit there listening to him and thinking "this is the best."

When the three boys were growing up I exposed them to baseball and other sports, but made every effort not to put pressure on them to follow me into the game. David describes what I did to help him. He said:

> Growing up, we never talked about the strategy of baseball or the mechanics of the swing. I did pick up things from watching my dad play. I watched every move he made on the field. It was so important for him not to push us, to be sure it was our choice. He just wanted us to enjoy the game. He taught us baseball through basketball. He was my coach in grade school and taught me how to be competitive and stressed the importance of working hard. As I got older I realized he used basketball to teach us about sports because he had played it himself and loved the game. After I signed a professional contract he thought it was okay to talk with me about how to play. We developed a more professional relationship, and I have called him when I needed help with my swing or was struggling and wanted advice.

Mike has been in professional baseball for eleven years. He played for the Cincinnati Reds in the year 2000 and currently is in Triple-A with the White Sox affiliate in Charlotte. In an interview with my coauthor, Neal Vahle, Mike said he has used me as a model in developing his style of play:

I learned the game by just watching my dad play with the Rangers and the Reds, and playing with my brothers Dave and Rick in our backyard. We saw so many games. We would sit there and watch my dad throw across the infield. When we were playing catch we would try to throw like him. We would watch him at bat and try to hit like him. A lot came from trying to imitate him. That goes for all of us. We would go to a Rangers game, and he would make a great play, and then we would go downstairs by the clubhouse or the parking lot and try to make the same play. We would then do it in our backyard—turning double plays, making up games like wall ball and home run derby. We didn't really have favorite players. Our dad was the only guy we cared about. We wanted him to get hits, to have a good game. As we got older, and my dad saw we were really interested, he helped us with the game. Many who saw him play tell me that I do everything exactly the same way he did. Our dad was our hero. I still want to be just like him.

Rick learned much the same way David and Mike did. Now twenty-five and playing for the Dodgers' Triple-A team in Las Vegas, he said:

Knowing the game came naturally to me. It happened almost subconsciously. I learned by going to games, watching my dad play, and hanging around the clubhouse seeing how players acted. When we were younger, my dad let us go out and play and have fun. He became more involved in our baseball careers when we got older. When he realized that we had a chance to do something and he knew we wanted to play, he stepped in and gave advice. Since I have been in professional baseball my father has been a huge influence. We talk about mental approaches to hitting. I talk to him on the telephone a lot, particularly when I am struggling.

Pitchers Who Developed Savvy and Smarts, and How They Did It

Everybody in the big leagues who has any smarts knows that to be successful you must have an in-depth knowledge and understanding of the game. Orel Hershiser, who won the National League's Cy Young Award in 1988 while pitching for the Los Angeles Dodgers, believed that his natural talent was secondary in his development as a major league pitcher. It was smarts and know-how that made the real difference. "It isn't the speed of my fastball that makes me successful," he said. "I need every trick in my bag to keep the hitters guessing, to keep them off balance. I'm not a junk baller by any standard, but I do take a decidedly mental approach to the game. I think, I study, I learn, I prepare, and I work at it." Hershiser saw his early successes as a pitcher as somewhat of a fluke. Those successes "in no way compared to my 23–8 season in 1988. The difference is knowledge, knowing why the results are successful. I'm not saying there wasn't talent in 1985. But I hadn't channeled it, dissected it, and studied it. The talent was raw and much of the success was luck."[2]

Hershiser described his evolution as a smart baseball player, tying it to a two-hit shutout he pitched in 1984 against the Chicago Cubs. While by baseball standards his effort was highly successful, he recognized that his mental preparation was still lacking. He reported:

During the summer of 1984, my first year in the majors, I pitched a two-hit shutout against the Cubs. . . . The media congratulated me on my performance. I should have been in heaven. This was, after all, why I played—a win, satisfied team-mates, and a happy manager. I had just delivered a beauty. But as I sat there, I was filled with an overwhelming sense of dread. I'll never forget how this felt. I should have been enjoying myself. Instead, I was scared to death . . . I didn't know exactly what it would take to repeat my performance. I knew I had thrown a great, two-hit shutout, but I wasn't sure how. And if I didn't know how, I was pretty sure I wouldn't be able consistently to do it again, except on raw talent or sheer luck. I knew I could not rest on my athleticism, skills, or experience. . . . I quietly made a resolution. . . . I was going to be the youngest, smartest major-league pitcher ever. And I wasn't going to *hope* that it happened to me. I was going to *make* it happen. Centering my mind on the details of preparation, day after day, week after week, was some-thing I could control. I would be a good student, studying and listening to everyone.[3]

I had a chance to observe Orel when he pitched for Cleveland in 1995 and I was on the coaching staff. A lot of what Orel said is right on. During games, Orel would sit on the bench between his starts, and focus on the game. He never missed a pitch. He would think along with the pitcher on the mound. He would know what the hitter was looking for. He was watching the defense. He was a real student of the game.

A lot of the game's starting pitchers do not have Orel's work habits and desire to master the details that can spell the differ-ence between winning and losing. On the days when they are not scheduled to pitch, they are not in the dugout watching the game. They can be found eating ice cream in the clubhouse, talking on the telephone, or watching TV. It's the reason why many don't develop the savvy and know-how needed to achieve their full potential.

Tom Glavine, now with the Mets after a long and successful career with the Atlanta Braves, is a pitcher who has mastered the details of his craft. He succeeds not because he has great stuff but because he has courage and savvy on the pitching mound. He doesn't try to do anything he isn't capable of doing. Former teammate Greg Maddux, himself a four-time Cy Young Award winner, described Glavine's mental approach to pitching in this way:

> [Tom] pitches according to what's unfolding in the game. He knows how to hold a lead, winning as many games 5–4 as he does 2–1, which is something you don't see often. With his mound smarts, he doesn't beat himself, but challenges the other team to beat him. The average pitcher in the league beats himself four or five times a year by making a poor judgment. . . . Tom hasn't made that mistake. Mostly, it's because he understands himself as a pitcher, knowing what he does and doesn't do so well.[4]

Maddux himself is probably one of baseball's most savvy pitchers. His fastball rarely exceeds 89 miles an hour, and he uses it almost exclusively. In fact, he counsels his teammates to spend more time controlling their fastballs and less on curves and sliders. His pitching coach, Leo Mazzone, said, "It is his number one priority. In his mind, if you can command your fastball and change speeds, there isn't a heck of a lot more you have to do." Even though his fastball has a lot of movement, he can usually hit a one-inch box from sixty feet, six inches away. He notices when hitters adjust just one inch in the batters' box after lunging at a changeup. His pinpoint control and his keen observation enable him to take advantage. Glavine, who played with Maddux for several years, said:

I think what separates him is he's so much better at recognizing what the last pitch dictated and gathering information from that than most guys are. Most guys say: "Oh, I threw a fastball in. Now I'm going to throw this." Why? They don't know. It might not have anything at all to do with the last pitch. I think that's what Maddux is good at. Seeing the hitter's reaction and using that information on the next pitch.[5]

Hall of Fame Dodger pitcher Sandy Koufax was one who succeeded not just on natural talent—and he had plenty of it—but from the know-how developed through dedication to the craft of pitching. For five years during the 1960s he was probably the most dominant pitcher in baseball. Here's how he described his mental approach:

I love it when it's going good, when the rhythm is with you and you're doing everything you want out there, and I love it when I've got nothing and I'm struggling to survive. Because that's what it becomes—survival. It's scuffling and sweating and trying a little of this and a little of that to hang in there until the rhythm comes back to you. When you have your stuff, you *should* win. But when you can end up winning, not on the strength of your arm, which is after all a gift from the heavens, but on the strength of your brains and your experience and your knowledge, it is a victory that you feel belongs peculiarly to yourself.[6]

Diamondback pitcher Curt Schilling, one of the most dominant pitchers in the major leagues, has accumulated an incredible amount of information on opposing batters. He has made a science out of their hitting styles and practices. Using a laptop computer, he spends the mornings of the days he pitches going over eight to nine years of material that he has researched. "I study history," he said. "I spend what some people might say is an inordinate amount of time preparing for my next start. There's a lot of technical advances that allow me to be better at what I do for a living. . . . There's a history between me and 90-some percent of the hitters I'm going to face on a given night."[7]

If I were managing a team and had to win a critical game, I would choose as my starter either Gaylord Perry or Ferguson Jenkins. Both are in the Hall of Fame. I played with them—Gaylord in Cleveland in the early seventies and Fergy in Texas in the late seventies—and I also played against them. As pitchers they had mastered the mental game. Those guys were so smart. They were always a couple of pitches ahead of the hitter. By that I mean that if the count was 0 and 1, they already knew what they were going to do when it was 2 and 1. They were setting guys up all the time. They knew every hitter, their strengths and their weaknesses. When I played against him, Fergy used to get me out all of the time. I could never think along with him. I would make easy outs or pop up. If I thought he was going to throw me a slider, he would jam me. If I thought he was going to throw me a heater in, he would throw a slider away. Against Fergy I would tend to overanalyze and think too much, and the more I thought, the worse it got. It all goes to show you that the brain can get in the way sometimes.

Perry and Jenkins were both fine pitchers. They had control over their bodies, and they could repeat their mechanics. By that I mean they used the same motion every time they delivered the ball. They could do what they wanted with the baseball. If they wanted to throw it away, they hit the outside corner. If they wanted to throw it in, they threw it in. Yet neither one had great stuff. They didn't have a Nolan Ryan–type fastball, nor were their breaking pitches out of the ordinary. It was their savvy, their knowledge, and their preparation that placed them a cut above other pitchers. They knew going into a game what they were going to do all the way through to the ninth inning. I knew a lot of guys with much better stuff who didn't achieve as much as these guys.

Fergy, for example, had his game plan made up before he got to the ballpark because he napped in the locker room before each of his starts. He had already prepared himself. He had shut off the analysis and the thinking part of the game, and was ready to play. He did something that all ballplayers must learn to do. They need to know when to shut it off, when to stop the information from coming in, and when to just go play and do instinctively what they have prepared themselves to do. More about this later.

While Perry and Jenkins got similar results on the pitching mound, their personalities were very different. Fergy was laid back and sensitive while Gaylord was a bull in a china shop. Yet they both could see ahead and had a tremendous memory. They could also slow the game down, which means they could retain their focus over long periods of time. In short, they could put it all together. Everything was in place. Many never get to their level because one of the key elements is missing. That's why they are in the Hall of Fame, and many very good players are not.

Hall of Famer Whitey Ford, who in his first thirteen seasons with the Yankees appeared in eleven World Series, had to rely on smarts and know-how because he was not the possessor of a 90-mile-an-hour fastball. When he came up to the Yankees in 1950 after three years in the minors, he still had a lot to learn about pitching. None of his minor league managers had been pitchers, and none of the teams had pitching coaches. Veteran Yankee pitcher and fellow New Yorker Eddie Lopat told him that he'd be seeing the same hitters year after year and he would have to find ways to get them out. "You have to get a book on these hitters," said Lopat. "Are they low-ball hitters or high-ball hitters? Who's looking for the curveball all the time. Who's a first-ball hitter."[8]

Lopat told him that hitters change, "and you have to learn to change with them. You might get a guy out with a high fastball one year, but the next year he may start hitting that pitch and you have to switch on him." Lopat told him that it was essential to "move the ball around. High. Low. Inside. Outside." Ford said that in the minors nobody worried about how to pitch to hitters or to think on the mound. Lopat was telling him new things about pitching, things "I'd never thought about before . . . I learned more in one spring than I had learned in three seasons in the minor leagues." As Ford's career developed he found that he learned a lot by watching opposing teams take batting practice. He made it a habit on the day he was pitching to sit in the dugout and watch them.[9]

Ford described an occasion when his watching the opposing team take batting practice made a major difference. Ford was a sinker ball pitcher with great control. "If I was pitching well, and in a good groove," he said, "I was keeping my sinker down and away, I would get fifteen to eighteen ground-ball outs in a game. The hitters would try to pull the sinker and hit easy ground balls to the infield." The Yankees were playing the Chicago White Sox and Ford noticed that "all their hitters were trying to go to right field, which wasn't their normal style of hitting." Ford then surmised that Paul Richards, the White Sox manager, who had a reputation as one of the most progressive-thinking managers in the game, had told his team "not to try to pull the ball against my sinker, to try to go with the pitch, and hit it through the middle." Ford countered by changing his pitching style. "I beat them that night," he said, "by throwing fastballs in and breaking balls in."[10]

Ford said that it wasn't unusual for teams to try to get up the middle on him. "That sort of thing happened quite often," he said. "I'd see these big left-handed power hitters like Jim Gentile and Norm Cash, who had trouble hitting me, and they'd be changing their style in batting practice, just trying to meet the ball and hit it through the box. So I would use that information to my advantage and simply change my style." Ford's Yankee manager, Ralph Houk, considered Ford to be one of the most savvy pitchers in the game. Houk characterized Ford's mental approach to the game in this way:

> He was a student. He made notes. He kept a book on the hitters, and he knew what he was going to do when he went out on the field. He knew what the hitters were doing, and what they were hitting, and where they hit it, and what the count was when they hit it, and what got them out the last time he faced them. He could set hitters up so good it used to amaze me. He'd go along and he wouldn't be striking anybody out, but now they've got a man on third base and nobody out—and Ford strikes out the batter, he doesn't let him hit the fly ball. He always had a pitch ready. He'd have the batter set up for the pitch, but he wouldn't use it until he needed it. He was great that way. He was great in making a batter hit into a double play. Or if a man had been hitting the ball up the alley between outfielders. Whitey would end up where the guy was hitting the ball to center. He'd just move the location of the pitch a little and the guy swings the same way and he hits it, but now it's an out. Whitey didn't overpower a lot of hitters, but it was amazing what he could do with them. He always knew what was going on. He was the best pitcher I ever managed, and there's no question about that. Real smart, real smart.[11]

Position Players Who Mastered the Thinking Part of the Game and How They Did It

Whitey Ford gave a lot credit for his success as a pitcher to his Yankee catcher, Yogi Berra. He viewed Berra as a highly intelligent baseball man. Ford said:

We all know what a tremendous hitter he was, but I don't think Yogi gets enough credit for being a smart catcher. I hardly ever shook him off. . . . Yogi called the game, and if I shook him off too much, I would hear about it from Stengel, or the out-fielders who had to chase the line drives. Mantle was the worst, always telling me, "Listen to Yogi." . . . Yogi knew the hitters, what they could hit, what their weak points were. And he knew what a batter looked for in certain situations. Yogi would fool them by calling crazy combinations. Say I threw a batter two curves for strikes. Now the batter is thinking, "There's no way he's throwing a third straight curve." So he looks for the fastball. Yogi would call for another curve.[12]

As I indicated above, I got to know Yogi when we were with the Astros. Yogi is so with it, and he's right on when talking about the mental part of the game. Because his grammar isn't always perfect, he is viewed by some as not too bright, which is not true. Jerry Coleman, a Yankee infielder for nine years who played with Yogi, gave a good description of Yogi's brains on the diamond. He said:

I think he was the smartest player I ever knew. He was smart enough to know how to play. And even more important, how to learn. He was able to learn from Bill Dickey. . . . Yogi had a handicap. He had the keenest baseball mind I ever saw, but he couldn't teach what he knew to others. When he was a player he didn't have to. The only ones he had to teach were [Yankee starting pitchers Allie] Reynolds and [Vic] Raschi. They were slow learners, but after a while they knew when they pitched the game Yogi called, they won. The pitcher and catcher almost always have conflict. He knew how to make the most of it. He would get on Vic. He called him "onion head." When he wanted a fast ball he would say, "Is that as hard as you can throw it?" It sounds school yard but it worked.[13]

Yogi himself commented on how he applied himself mentally so as to maximize his performance as a ballplayer. He said:

Baseball is a balance of physical and mental. Like anything, the mind and body are always lined. But since they say baseball is a thinking man's game, you have to use your brain a lot. Carlton Fisk, a real good catcher who was just inducted into the Hall of Fame, used to have a sign over his locker that said THINK. . . . I was always thinking when I played, even if I did say you can't think and hit at the same time. As a catcher I used to study the opposing hitters, their tendencies, their weaknesses, their strengths. To me, there was always something in the way a batter stood, the way he held his bat, to tell you what pitch he was looking for. . . . I always noticed the little stuff, it helps. . . . I really used my brain more than anything. As a catcher you scrounge for every edge. A thousand things happen in a game, little things, and you have to keep those things in your head. In the 1953 Word Series, I threw two runners out at third base on back-to-back bunts. People thought I stole the Dodger' signs. Truth is, I was watching how the batter's feet were pointed, and how our pitcher was keeping the ball where I wanted it. I could just tell the bunts were going to the left of the plate—and that's where they went.[14]

Hank Aaron demonstrated a high degree of know-how on the diamond, particularly as a batter. He believed that you could not overestimate the value of mental preparation in baseball. In the batter's box he constantly attempted to outsmart the pitcher. My dad talked about Aaron's savvy, and his ability to recognize a pitcher's strengths and weaknesses. Dad said that Aaron would eliminate those pitches that the pitcher had trouble getting over the plate. It made his job as a hitter much easier if he refused to offer, for example, at a pitcher's curveball until the pitcher could prove he could consistently put it in the strike zone. Aaron described his mental approach this way:

As a hitter, the mental aspects were especially vital to me. I was strictly a guess hitter, which meant that I had to have a full knowledge of every pitcher I came up against and develop a full strategy for hitting him. My method was to identify the pitches that a certain pitcher had and then eliminate all but one or two and wait for them. Usually I would wait for his best pitch, because I knew he would use it sooner or later. For instance, Bob Gibson was a fastball pitcher, so—depending on the situation—I might eliminate the slider, curve and changeup and just wait for the fastball. With a pitcher as good as Gibson, though, it wasn't enough just to guess the pitch. That much was obvious. The trick was to guess location. So, I might wait for a fastball low and inside. If I got it, I hit it. If I didn't get it I had to try to adjust. . . . To me hitting was a matter of knowing where the ball was going and when. Because of the way I waited for the pitcher's pitch, I often hit good pitchers the best. The good pitcher was the one who threw the ball where he was supposed to throw it. If Juan Marichal wanted to throw a fastball low and inside, he threw it low and inside, and if I was expecting a fastball low and inside, I was right on it. A lot of times I would hit a home run off a good pitch and when I got back to the dugout my teammates would say, "Man, that was a wicked pitch, how did you hit that thing?" Hell, it was what I was looking for. I never expected a pitcher to make a bad pitch. I respected the pitcher. . . . I respected the job they did, and I expected them to make good pitches. As a result, I might pop up a hanging curve

ball, because I was looking for a good curveball. That's why
I liked hitting against the Dodgers so much. Guys like Koufax
and [Don] Drysdale and [Johnny] Podres new exactly what they
were going to do with the ball, and if I could just think along
with them, I was ready. I guess the respect was mutual, because
Koufax and Drysdale were the ones who gave me the nickname,
"Bad Henry."[15]

Aaron's teammates respected his knowledge of the game.
Ralph Garr, who played with him on the Atlanta Braves, had
this to say:

Hank was just so smart about playing ball. A lot of people
seem to think black players have ability and that's all there is to
it, but it's just not true. I learned how to think on the ball field
from Hank Aaron. He was a scientific ballplayer, the most
knowledgeable baseball man I ever met. And if you talk to other
players on our team—guys like Dusty Baker and Clete Boyer
and Darrell Evans—they all tell you the same thing.[16]

Dusty Baker, who went on to manage the San Francisco Giants and the Chicago Cubs after playing with Aaron in Atlanta,
had these comments to make about his know-how as a baseball
player:

He knew the game better than anyone. He knew the umps,
which ones were high strike umps and which were low; he
knew every pitcher's sequence, knew where to play every hitter,
different on every pitch. One night in the dugout he said,
"Watch their left fielder. He puts his head down a little early
every time fielding ground balls. If I hit one to him, I'm going
to take off fast, slow down, then sprint." That night Hank hit a

routine single to left, and I look up and he's on second. He was amazing.[17]

I met Hank Aaron through my dad when I was in fourth or fifth grade. Even then I knew how special this guy was. He played the game with such ease.

Cal Ripken, Jr., of the Baltimore Orioles, is best known for his record-setting streak of consecutive games played. What always impressed me about the guy was his play through the first thousand games. He played through nagging injuries not just to keep the streak alive but because he knew his team needed him. He could easily have taken a day off, but he didn't. Ripken was a good hitter and he approached hitting the same way Aaron did. He went up to bat expecting to hit a particular pitch. He described his mental preparation this way:

> In the majors it probably didn't take long for me to get the reputation as a hitter who looked for pitches, more so than most hitters. Some people even call this guessing. I call it *figuring it out*, as my own experience was my guide. A simple example: If I got a base hit on a fastball my first time up, the second time I could safely look for something else. Sooner or later in that at-bat, I'd get it. The calculation gets much more complicated than that, and you also have to determine who's really calling the game, the pitcher or the catcher. The two positions can think very differently about setting up batters. It's part of the game I really enjoy.[18]

Hall of Famer Ty Cobb, one of baseball's great early talents, attributed his ability to hit consistently above .300 (his lifetime average over a twenty-four-year career was .367) primarily to his mental abilities rather than his physical skills. "The more I lived, the more I realized," he said late in his career, "that batting is a mental problem rather than a physical stunt. The ability to grasp the bat, swing at the proper time, take a proper stance, all these things are elemental. Batting, rather, is a study in psychology, a sizing up of a pitcher and catcher and observing little details that are of immense importance. It's like a study of crime, the work of a detective as he picks up clues."[19]

Cobb was sitting on the bench next to rookie Fred Haney in a 1922 game against the White Sox when he asked the young man whether he had been able to steal any of the catcher's signs. Haney said no and then sat flabbergasted as Cobb correctly called the next seventeen pitches. "The next ball will be a fastball. Now a curve." Haney thought it was no wonder that Cobb was a .400 hitter if he knew what pitch was coming. He wondered whether Cobb had some extraordinary psychic ability and asked him about it. "Son," Cobb said, "it isn't quite that simple. The tip-off came to me not from intercepting any signals, but from something I have learned about human nature. There is always a tendency in this business for a man to get too mechanical."[20]

The catcher for the White Sox that day was Ray Schalk, whom Cobb had played against for years. "Schalk was a great catcher," Cobb acknowledged, "but he is getting old now and he has let himself fall into a set routine. I have studied him for so long that I even know how he thinks. I merely keep pace with his mental processes and that's why I am able to call all those pitches correctly. I think along the same lines he does."[21]

Whenever, in his long and successful Japanese baseball career, Sadaharu Oh went into a batting slump, he would get together with his long-time hitting instructor, Hiroshi Arakawa. They would discuss, review, and analyze Oh's performance in the batter's box. "We went over the seven steps of my form: fighting spirit, stance, grip, back swing, stride forward, downswing, impact—take them apart and put them together again." Arakawa was particularly good at detecting the little things that Oh failed to notice. When they worked together to figure out the problem, a solution eventually emerged. "It was only a matter of time," said Oh.[22]

The good hitters find out as much as they can about the tendencies of pitchers. Pete Rose, who was one of the best hitters to ever wear a uniform, had a great career with Cincinnati as a part of the Big Red Machine in the 1970s. One of the things that impressed me about Pete, who was player-manager for the Cincinnati Reds when I joined the team in 1985, was the attention he paid to the pitchers. He was an avid student of pitching. He said:

> I study the pitchers. I don't believe I'm all that good a hitter against a pitcher the first time I see him. I want to know what he throws. I need to study that. They can tell you Orel Hershiser has a fine curve, which he does, but I need to see the windup, the delivery, the spin, the actual break of the ball. And when does he like to throw the curve? First pitch? Will he throw it when he's behind in the count? What about his fastball and his slider? If you figure out all the combinations—the order of pitches, the different speeds, the location, all the rest—batting can get to sound very complicated, like you need a degree in statistics to be a hitter."[23]

Rose also believed it was important to be thinking ahead, to know what pitchers he would face over the course of the next week. "Baseball isn't like football," he said, "where they give you six days to prepare for your next game. You get one day, part of a day, really, and if it's a doubleheader and you're playing both ends, you have about twenty minutes." It was important for him, said Rose, "to keep a feel for the flow." It was necessary "to know where you are, like when you're driving a car, and know what's coming around the corner." Rose studied "the rotations of the pitchers" for clues. In one series you might be facing the Dodgers with Fernando Valenzuela and Orel Hershiser, "two very different pitchers, and then in the next with Houston and Ryan and Scott."

It was helpful, Rose commented, to know when during the coming week you would be facing Nolan Ryan, one of the game's toughest pitchers. Rose described how he prepared for Ryan:

> He likes to throw that hard one near the letters, and when it closes with the plate the ball sails clear up and out of the damn strike zone. The pitch looks good coming in, you really think you see it, but the pitch turns out to be a ball. If you swing at it, just like a softball riser, you'll miss it, or at best hit under it. Pop fly. You have to tell yourself in the batter's box this is ol' Nolie Ryan throwing that hard sucker pitch. You have to keep that burning in your mind. Then you'll have the sense to lay off it. How does it help on Wednesday afternoon to know that you hit against Ryan the following Tuesday? It keeps a part of your mind going, keeps you fully aware.[24]

Rose said that it was valuable to think not only about today's game but those coming up down the road. "If you let yourself, if you're not afraid to work your body, work your mind, you can always do more than one thing, concentrate on more than one thing at a time." While Rose focused primarily on opposing pitchers, he also studied the mental makeup of opposing infielders and outfielders, looking for their weaknesses. He once told sports writer Earl Larson that "it helps to know the personalities of rival players in the league. And I feel I know most of them. What I'm saying is that if an outfielder offers to give me an extra base by playing one of my hits casually, I'll take it." Rose knew, for example, which outfielders sulked in the field after a bad plate appearance and didn't hustle after batted balls. When the time was right he tried for an extra base on them. According to sports writer Michael Y. Sokolove, Rose rarely guessed wrong. Of his 746 career doubles (second on the career list), quite a few came because he caught an outfielder napping.[25]

During twelve years in the majors Albert Belle had one of the great power careers. I had the privilege of being a coach for Cleveland while he was with the Indians. For eight seasons in a row he never fell below thirty home runs and a hundred RBIs. He was the first ever to hit fifty home runs and fifty doubles in the same season. The secret to Albert's success was the book he kept on pitchers. He wrote in the book during each game. The book was kept in a safe place in the clubhouse, where no one else could get at it. Albert didn't wait until after the game to write in it but went into the clubhouse after each at bat. If a relief pitcher came in, Albert would go into the clubhouse and consult his book. He did not show it to anyone. Albert believed that the book gave him a mental edge. It made him better than the pitcher he was facing. I believe that Albert was successful not just because he had the book but because he was so prepared in his mind. He was way ahead of the other players when it came to mental preparation.

Hall of Famer and Red Sox outfielder Ted Williams was known, both as a player and as a manager, for his in-depth knowledge of the game. As sports biographer Ed Linn observed, "It was mental dedication that marked him, the obsession with finding out everything he could about every pitcher he was going to face." As a rookie he pestered the veterans for information about opposing pitchers. When a new pitcher came into the league he would run around to find anybody who had played against him. Williams was a hound for data. Linn reported, "He had a perfectionist's eye for detail. He made a private study of the prevailing winds in all the ball parks. He knew the height of every ballpark's pitcher's mound. (They varied in his day). He could tell which batter's boxes sloped upward and which sloped downward."[26]

Williams studied the umpires as closely as he studied the pitchers. "The umpires make the strike zone," he said, so he made it his business to know which umpires called low strikes and which umpires called the high ones. Not only did Williams adjust to the umpires but he made it a point to stay on their good side. "He treated them like gods," Don Fitzpatrick, the Red Sox clubhouse man, remembered. Williams recognized that the umpires dealt not only with strikes and balls but with rewards and punishments: Give them a hard time and they will get you. He was even known for congratulating an umpire for calling him out on strikes. "What a dope I was to take it," he would say as he walked away from the plate after being called out on strikes.[27]

Linn reported that as Williams's career progressed he cultivated an ongoing relationship with the umpires and ultimately "played them like a virtuoso." During rain delays he would go down into the tunnel where the umpires hung out and swap stories with them. He'd let them tell their stories, and then he'd say, "Hey, how did so-and-so look in Cleveland?" They'd say, "You know, Ted, he got so-and-so out with this." Umpire Ed Runge remembered how Williams would come into the umpires' room saying that he wanted to get away from the press. "He didn't talk too much about pitchers with us," recalled Runge. "He always talked trades. Who would you trade for, that kind of stuff." Runge could see that in the process Williams was getting a complete scouting report on players' strengths and weaknesses.[28]

When queried by Linn about his buttering up of the umpires, Williams admitted it. "Absolutely true," he said. "Who knew better than the umpires who was sharp and who was losing his fastball and all the rest of it? Especially when a new pitcher had come into the league. They'd tell me, 'This kid is a real good pitcher and can thread a needle on the outside.' On somebody else, 'You won't have any trouble with him, Ted, he's nothing.'"

It's not surprising that when Williams became manager of the Washington Senators in 1969 he went to his old friends the umpires for information on opposing teams. He had been away from baseball for nine years. "I didn't know the personnel around the league," he said.[29]

As a player Williams shared his know-how with other players on the Red Sox. Shortstop Johnny Pesky, in particular, benefited from his advice when facing tough pitching. Pesky, who in August of his rookie season was leading the league in base hits, recalled an occasion when Williams's advice made a major difference. Pesky had gone 0 for 14 against Spud Chandler, a tough Yankee right-hander, who was pitching against the Red Sox that day. When Williams found out about it he sought Pesky out and said, "For chrissake, you're trying to pull him, and you're hitting ground balls to second base."[30]

When Pesky, a left-handed batter, came to bat in the eighth inning with the score tied 1–1, Williams, who followed him in the batting order, told him: "Johnny, he's going to throw that hard sinker, away from you. When you pull you're just going to hit a ground ball to second base. God damn it, listen to me. You've got to go up the middle or to left field. . . . You know goddamn well they're not going to walk you to get to me."

Pesky reported the sequence of events: "Ball one, strike one, ball two here comes that hard sinker. I go to left field, both runners score, and we're leading 3–1. I'm standing on first base and Ted's looking at me with his big shit-eating grin. Chandler in the meantime is stomping around the mound. . . . Chandler finally gets ready to pitch to Ted, then he steps off, he looks over to me and says, 'You little shit!' I say, 'Go fuck yourself.' He [Chandler] fires the first pitch to Ted, and it's a fastball right there (waist high over the center of the plate), and Ted hits it thirty rows in the bleachers. I'm in the dugout by the time he gets to third base. When Ted hit the ball, everybody in the dugout got up to see where it was going. He really crushed it. A crack. Teammates say, 'Geez, you got all of that, Ted.' "

When Williams got back in the dugout he started looking around and said, "Where's that horn-nosed little shortstop of ours?" He found Pesky and exclaimed, "God damn it, John, didn't I tell you how to hit Chandler?" Pesky responded, "Let me tell you something, Ted, he [Chandler] was so goddamn mad at me that he forgot you were the next hitter." Williams, winking at Pesky said, "I know, I know, and I was ready, wasn't I?"[31]

I consider Ted Williams to have been one of the greatest hitters of all time, and I would like to have had the opportunity to watch him play. My only contact with him came at a baseball banquet in Rhode Island in the early 1970s during my second or third year in the big leagues. The host seated me next to Williams. I was in my early twenties and really green and in awe of him. He started asking me questions about hitting, asking me how I would hit particular types of pitches. I was so frazzled that I didn't know what to say other than to mumble some things that didn't satisfy him. He said, "Don't you know how to hit?"

"Yes, I know how to hit," I said.

"Well, then answer me; tell me how you hit."

I didn't want the great Ted Williams to think I didn't know what I was doing in the batter's box, but words just didn't come out of my mouth. I was embarrassed and wanted to leave. It may seem strange, but that experience really helped me. I reflected on what happened, and from that day forward I wasn't intimidated by anybody, no matter how great they were. I didn't care what they thought.

In reviewing the ranks of those who played the game with high intelligence, it is important to give full credit to one of baseball's truly great minds, Hall of Famer and Yankee centerfielder Joe DiMaggio. The Yankee Clipper has often been described as one of baseball's most complete ballplayers. He excelled in all aspects of the game. He steeped himself in its nuances, and his deep knowledge was often a major help to his teammates. His Yankee manager, Joe McCarthy, appreciated his dedication. DiMaggio "really studied the game," recalled McCarthy. "He thought about it all of the time. That's what it takes to be great. You can't think about it when you get to the park. You have to prepare yourself mentally and physically. Joe had this marvelous sense of anticipation. That's because he studied the game. He never made a mental mistake."

Yankee pitcher Allie Reynolds remembered how DiMaggio's know-how and smarts contributed to string of Yankee championships. DiMaggio was not the kind who was continually offering his advice to other players, but he would give it when asked. "If there was a serious discussion about the game," recalled Reynolds, "Joe would get into it and give his opinion, and most of the time his opinion really helped win ball games. He knew an awful lot about pitchers and every hitter in the league. He really studied the game."[32]

DiMaggio probably best summarized the importance of shared knowledge in developing the savvy, know-how, and smarts needed to play the game when he said:

> Everyone who tries to play baseball or to teach it has to thank a lot of people for everything he knows. For everyone who is playing or teaching the game today is doing his work with the help of all the people who have been in baseball before him. Whenever anyone comes up with a smart play or devised an effective piece of strategy, the smart men of the game are quick to

pick it up, adapt it to their own uses, or pass it on to their own players or teammates. If anyone comes up with a good new wrinkle today, the smart men will have it on their ticket tomorrow.[33]

Mental preparation played an important part in the career of Hall of Famer Willie Stargell, who for twenty seasons was a fixture in the Pittsburgh Pirate outfield. It was the key, he said, to his success as a hitter. He prided himself on his ability to get hits when they counted, to be at his best when the pressure was on. "Hours before the situation arose for me to drive in the winning run," he recalled, "I was running thoughts through my mind on what to expect. I thought about each of the opposition pitchers, what they threw, how fast they threw, where they threw, and how often. I also used batting practice to try various methods of hitting I planned to use against the other team's scheduled starters and their top relievers. . . . By the time the situation arose for me to produce, I was ready. I had thought everything through in advance." Stargell's mental preparation undoubtedly gave him greater confidence in tight game situations. "I loved to hit with men on base," he said, "and the game on the line."[34]

Giants centerfielder Willie Mays, who, like me, had a ballplayer for a father, downplayed his extraordinary physical talents, believing that he succeeded because of the savvy and know-how he gained from becoming a student of the game and learning from some superb teachers. Mays had a strong desire to find out everything he could about the game. "I lived and studied it," he said. "There was something scientific in the way you caught a ball and then got rid of it. They didn't teach me much biology or mathematics in school, but I studied what you could do with a ball."[35]

Mays felt that too many sports writers and baseball people thought he had so much natural talent that his success came effortlessly. He disagreed. "Somehow, people thought that because I was a able to do a lot of things I just had a natural talent—as if

I had never worked hard to get where I did. When I'd hit a cut-off man in the right place, people would talk about my 'natural' vision, instead of realizing that I had planned before the ball was hit where I'd throw to." He studied the play of his opponents." All the analyzing I had done of other hitters helped me in the field, and my studies of pitchers' habits helped me at bat and on base. . . . A lot of thinking went into how I played and what I did."[36]

When the Giants moved from New York City to San Francisco and began playing in Candlestick Park, where swirling winds were extremely tricky and unpredictable, Mays had to change the way he played center field. It took a lot of observation, thought, and analysis to know which way to move when the ball was hit. About the winds at Candlestick he said, "The studying paid off," as he got to fly balls that other outfielders in the league were unable to reach.[37]

Mark McGwire credited his work with a psychotherapist and a counselor after a personal crisis in midcareer for making him stronger mentally on the playing field. It was in therapy that he became aware of how powerful his mind could be, and realized the impact of mental states on both baseball and life. He observed, "There are a lot of ballplayers playing this game strictly on ability. They don't use their minds. It's amazing to think I played this game for five years without using my mind." McGwire believed he would have been far less successful if he had not gone into therapy. "Without my counseling sessions, I would never have made it to where I am this day," he said "I'm so much stronger mentally than what people see physically."[38] McGwire is somewhat unusual in that regard: It is my impression that few ballplayers use psychotherapy as a tool for enhancing their ability to handle the stress. Many teams employ sports psychologists, and they do help players with the mental parts of the game.

The Contribution of Good Coaching

Mays's introduction to the fine points of the game began early in life. His father, an outstanding player for the mill teams in the Birmingham industrial league, began teaching him the game when he was a toddler. Mays said that he walked when he was only six months old, and that his father got him walking "after a baseball. Getting a baseball was just about the first thing I was able to do." His father put two chairs close to each other, and then put a baseball on one and walked him through. "See the ball," he said. "See the ball." He was then turned loose and told to go for the ball himself. "When he knew I could chase a ball, he gave me batting lessons. He handed me a rubber ball and a little stick maybe two feet long, and sat me in the middle of the floor. I'd play with the ball all day long, hitting it with the stick, then crawling or toddling after it across the room."[39]

Mays said that his father, who was only eighteen years old when Mays was born, wanted him to become a professional baseball player. He did not want Mays to work as he had in the steel mills. "When I was five years old he'd take me outside and bounce the ball on the sidewalk to me and yell 'Catch it,' and we'd do that for hours. He was quick, really quick, and got the nickname 'Cat.' " His father took him to many games. The young boy was allowed to sit on the bench next to the grown-ups. "There I'd hear them discuss strategy—how you'd play a right-handed pull hitter who was batting against a guy with a slow curve. Or how big a lead you could afford to take off first when you had a southpaw with a quick delivery on the mound."[40]

Mays felt that his father never pushed him into baseball. "He just exposed me to it and it happened all by itself from there." Mays was grateful for his dad's strong interest. "How many kids," he asked, "would have a chance before a game to be out on the field? I would run to first and slide, run to second and slide, then to third, then home. Sliding was simply a natural effort to me. I had seen my father do it many times and I had practiced it often. I thought my father was so good, I copied everything he did. I was just a kid, but I had the style, and some of the knowledge, of a grown-up ball player. I knew how to do things the right way."[41]

Mays had the benefit of excellent instruction as a teenager. One of the teachers who helped prepare him for the major leagues was Piper Davis, manager of the Birmingham Black Barons. "Piper," said Mays, "was like a father to me." Davis recognized Mays's talent when he was still in high school and recruited him for the Black Barons when he was only sixteen. The Black Barons were a part of the old Negro League that played in several East Coast cities, including the Polo Grounds in New York City. They drew several thousand people to their games.[42]

Mays said that Piper Davis taught him many lessons, but one of the most important involved how to survive in the duel between pitcher and batter. As a young player Mays was ripe for intimidation. He had hit a home run off Chet Brewer, one of the league's top pitchers. The next time up, Brewer hit him on the arm with a fastball. Pain went through Mays's entire body. "I was on the ground in tears when Piper bent over me and said, 'Don't let this guy show you up. You see first base over there? I want you to get up and then I want you to run to first base. And the first chance you get, I want you to steal second and then third.'" Mays said that he followed Piper's orders and stole second. "All of a sudden, as I was standing on the base, I realized what was going on. Piper made me show the pitcher that he couldn't hurt me by hitting me on the arm. Not only couldn't he hurt me, but that if he tried, I would show him up. That's how I learned against one of the best pitchers in the league."[43]

Like Willie Mays, I learned the finer points of the game from my father, and from a few very special coaches. My dad was the best coach I ever had. As I mentioned before, he stressed the mental part of the game rather than the physical. Having been a major leaguer himself, he often knew what I was going through. He always waited for me to come to him, and I went to him a lot because I knew he would be honest with me. He would not mince words and gave good, sound advice. He knew me better than anybody else, knew what I needed. I had some great coaches, but he was the all-time greatest. From working with my father I realized that I learned the most when I sought advice. I believe other players do also. They learn more when they seek out a coach for help rather than waiting for a coach to come to them.

San Francisco Giants outfielder Barry Bonds is another who has benefited from having a ballplayer for a father. Like me, he grew up in a baseball family. His father, Bobby Bonds, played the outfield for several major league teams, and his godfather, Willie Mays, played alongside his father. Both father and godfather were concerned that Barry, from an early age, learn to think like an outfielder. "Over and over again," recalled Barry Bonds, "they impressed on me the need to think about hitters, to study and learn them like tables in math. They taught me about who was running, who was pitching, what was happening in the game at the moment. You had to be ready for each moment, and each moment had to be taken for itself."[44]

Sports writer David Falkner reported that Mays and Bonds's father refined the teaching so that by the time Barry began playing in major league parks he was deeply schooled in the habits of batters, base runners, and pitchers. As a result, he was able to do things on the field that he might not have been able to do if he was simply a good athlete. "The game he plays," observed Falkner, "is subtle and smart, perfectly matched to his great speed and superb grounding in fundamentals." Throughout his career Bonds has relied on his father for advice. Until his father's cancer progressed to the point where he couldn't communicate, Bonds talked with his father daily during the season. "I've never played without my dad," he said. "My dad's always been there. I could take a bad swing on the field, and my dad could make a phone call in five seconds and tell me what's wrong."[45]

Working with an instructor who taught the strike zone was of immense help to Hall of Famer Duke Snider of the Dodgers. In Snider's case the teacher was none other than the team's general manager, Branch Rickey. When Snider was a rookie and sixth outfielder on the team, Rickey called him into his office and told him he would be a mainstay in the Dodger outfield when he learned the strike zone. Snider recalled that as a rookie, "any pitch that came within reach looked good to me, and I had a whack at it. In the dirt. Over my head. So I missed a lot.

"Mr. Rickey's remedy was to put me in the batting cage for three to four hours every morning with a pitcher and catcher and umpire. George Sisler, our batting instructor, supervised and Mr. Rickey himself was there every day watching my progress. My assignment was simply to watch pitches go by. All morning long. I was not allowed to swing. I was just supposed to call every pitch, ball or strike. It was amazing how wrong I was. But I learned." Snider gave Rickey a lot of credit. "I wouldn't have become the ballplayer I became if it weren't for Branch Rickey. Lots of people saw potential in me, but Mr. Rickey knew what to do about it."[46]

Snider still struck out a lot, and early in his career the strikeouts affected his confidence, which had a negative effect on his batting average. He credited Dodger shortstop Pee Wee Reese with giving him the advice that helped him avoid the self-criticism that limited him at the plate. Snider said:

He [Pee Wee Reese] could see how those K's kept eating away at me, so he came over to me one day and said, "Why do you let those strikeouts bother you so much? You're a power hit-ter, and any power hitter is going to strike out a lot because of those big swings you guys take. Why not just accept the fact that you're going to strike out ninety or a hundred times a year, espe-cially when you know you're going to get a lot of home runs and drive in a mess of runs for us? When you strike out, instead of getting yourself all mixed up in your head, just say to yourself, 'I still have another eighty-five.' Shrug em off like that.[47]

Snider reported that Reese's counsel helped him the develop "the stability" he needed to cope with the strikeouts. He imme-diately began to hit better. "By learning to shrug them off, fol-lowing Pee Wee's advice, I was able to rise above those K's and the next year finished among the leaders in nine of 12 offensive categories." He had 40 home runs, 130 RBIs, 120 runs and 199 hits.[48]

I had some great coaches: Joe Lutz, my Rookie League coach in Sarasota, Florida; Lenny Johnston, who managed the Class A Sumter, South Carolina, team I played for when I was eighteen; Don Zimmer, who had the best baseball mind I have ever been around in terms of knowing the game; and Rocky Colavito, who helped me a lot with my hitting when I got to the big leagues with Cleveland.

Joe Lutz had been a Marine drill sergeant, and he managed like one. His style would never have gone over in the big leagues, but it worked for rookies. We first-year guys needed what he had to offer. He was relentless on the fundamentals, on working hard, and driving you to the point where you could not go any further. He was always drilling us, demanding that we stay mentally alert. During games he would ask us what we would do during certain situations. He fired question after question at us. If we didn't pay attention or answer, he made us run laps around the field. He helped me appreciate the differing situations that arose during a game and the need to be mentally prepared. He did a lot to teach me the mental game. He made it clear that the only way you learned was by watching, listening, and asking questions.

Learning from Each Other

This may sound surprising to those unfamiliar with baseball, but in the big leagues, players learn more from each other than from their coaches. Their relationships with each other are much closer than their relationships with coaches; they are more comfortable with each other than with their coaches and spend time with each other away from the ballpark in social settings. Veteran ballplayers in the major leagues know a lot about the game and can be of great help to younger ones coming up. Graig Nettles was the third baseman for the Cleveland Indians during my rookie season when I was the centerfielder. I had the good fortune to watch him play, and he was the guy I learned a lot from.

It wasn't any one thing he said but a combination of things. He helped me get ready for each at bat and learn from it. He taught me a lot about how to play third base. He preached about the need to know the strengths of the hitter, the kind of stuff the pitcher had going for him, and the pitch selection, as well as the importance of being aware of the situation on the field. He helped me get my priorities straight, helped me know how to position myself before each pitch, and impressed on me the need to be aggressive to the ball. He said nothing about the physical or mechanical part of the game. It was all mental. He helped me see that faulty mental preparation was often the cause of a physical error on the field. You simply were not ready to make the play.

Probably as much as any other player, Graig Nettles helped me learn to play third base and understand the mental game.

When he was traded to the Yankees after my first season with the team, I became the Indians third baseman.

One of the smartest players I ever played with was Boog Powell, who had many great years with the Baltimore Orioles before coming over to Cleveland late in his career. Boog understood pitching. When he stood in the batter's box, he could predict with a high degree of accuracy what the pitcher was going to throw. Boog convinced me that 99 percent of the time during a game, a pitcher would give me pitches that I could hit. So, he said, "don't look for the bastard pitch, the ninety-five-mile heater on the black that you can't hit." He taught me not to give the pitcher too much credit. Boog stressed the importance of being realistic—of recognizing that sometimes in an at bat you have no chance because the pitcher makes great pitches. Nothing can be done about it, he said. You cannot, however, let a strike out affect your next at bat. You need to forget about looking foolish or making a big out because pitchers are not that perfect all of the time. If they were, nobody would hit above .200.

One guy who helped me a lot with my own hitting when I came up with Cleveland was Ray Fosse, a fine veteran catcher who was probably the most mentally tough player I ever played with. As a young player I had a particularly hard time hitting curve balls, and Mike Cuellar of Baltimore had a really good one. One night we were playing Baltimore, and Cuellar was on the mound. The only pitches he threw me in the strike zone were curveballs. I was looking for fastballs and didn't swing at his curve because I didn't think I could hit it. After the game Fosse said to me, "Why are you being so stupid? He's not going to throw you a fastball, so use your head. At least show the guy you have the ability to look for the pitch, even though you can't hit it. All he knows is that you are not swinging. The only chance you'll have of getting a fastball is if you show him that you are at least looking for his breaking ball." I took Fosse's advice and decided to sight on the curveball and at least offer at it, causing Cuellar to think differently about pitching to me. In future at bats, Cuellar occasionally gave me a fastball in the strike zone.

My relationship with veteran players like Fosse and Nettles was critical to my development as a player. I think it is imperative for young players to search out veterans like them and learn as much as they can. I have always told young ballplayers that it is *their* career, and if they don't take care of it, they won't be around long.

After spending thirteen years in the Dodger organization, Steve Garvey became a free agent in the early 1980s and signed with the relatively new expansion team, the San Diego Padres. An iron-man-type guy, a professional, and a great player whom I really admired, Garvey benefited, he said, "by listening to some pretty terrific teachers." He recalled the many conversations he had with Dodger hitters Manny Mota, Dixie Walker, Dick Allen, and Frank Robinson. "They all talked situations," Garvey recalled. "What does a pitcher do in this situation?" In the process Garvey developed what he called "The Book." It was not something written on a piece of paper.

The Book, he said, "is in your head. If you are going to be successful as a hitter you have to start to keep track of what a pitcher throws, his tendencies, his deliveries, his release point. It is a process you begin as early as possible in high school and college. If you see pitchers often enough—certainly in the minor leagues—the pattern is already set when you come up. It's just like being a salesman, you have to know your product, and you have to know the territory. A batter has to know the pitchers, and he has got to remember." Garvey recalled a play-off game against Montreal in 1981 when Expo right-hander Bill Gullickson was, as Garvey recalled, "busting the fastball in all day." The game was tied in the eighth when he came to bat. "I figured he was afraid of feeding me a fastball and would try to start me off with a slider, just to get ahead. He did, and I hit it over the left field wall. That's what I mean by The Book. You spend your entire career putting it together."[49]

Self-Evaluation as a Tool for Developing Savvy and Know-How

I think a key element in any player's mental makeup is his ability to make a correct evaluation of his own performance. I had an experience as a young player that helped me see the importance of self-evaluation. I was twenty years old and in my first year in the major leagues. The Indians were playing the A's in Cleveland and I was playing center field. Gaylord Perry was on the mound when the A's shortstop, Bert Campaneris, came to bat with the bases empty. Campaneris did not hit with power, and Perry thought I was playing too deep. He motioned me to move in. On the next pitch Campaneris hit a drive into deep left center field. I raced back to the fence, which was five feet high, and jumped up. The ball hit the top of my glove and dropped back into fair territory as I fell over the fence. I jumped back over the fence and held Campaneris to a triple. Campaneris did not score. As I ran off the field I was thinking I had made a pretty good play and saved a run. When I reached the dugout, Perry was standing on the top step. I thought he was going to shake my hand. Instead he said, "That ball has got to be caught." My first thought was, "You SOB, I saved you a run. I busted my ass getting back there after you pulled me in." I thought it unfair of him to react that way. After the game I reflected on the play and began to think, "I probably could have caught that ball." I was trying to justify not making that play. The more I thought about it, the more I realized I was making an excuse. It became clear to me as I reflected on that play that I did not want to accept anything less than the very best I could do. Thereafter I always made an assessment of my performance after each game, and in the process I became a good self-evaluator.

I believe that self-evaluation after a game is extremely important. If you have had a subpar performance, you need to figure out what happened. A lot of players get caught up in themselves and don't take the time after a game to reflect. They want to go home and forget about it. They are afraid to face what went wrong. They don't think about how they could have improved their play. These players don't last long in the big leagues.

Effective self-evaluation does not turn into self-criticism. Self-evaluation is objective and positive; self-criticism is negative and destructive. Those who criticize themselves beat themselves up, get down on themselves, think that nothing they can do is good enough. They deplete their energy and in the end wear themselves out. I have observed many ballplayers who are too self-critical. Too few ballplayers at the major league level have learned to evaluate their performances objectively.

We can learn so much from our experiences, particularly our failures—striking out, making an error, a base-running mistake, being out of position, not communicating with a teammate. The best players analyze what went wrong after a less than satisfactory performance. For me, self-evaluation became a key to my success as a player.

Injuries as a Catalyst for Learning the Game

It may sound surprising, but sometimes it takes an injury for a player to slow down, think about his performance, study the game, and improve his performance ability. Hall of Famer Joe Morgan, who has made a successful career in broadcasting since leaving the game, learned a great deal about the how and why of playing baseball after suffering a season-ending injury playing for the Houston Colt 45s during his first year in the major leagues. Instead of hanging around the clubhouse, he decided to use the time to study the game more thoroughly. He made it a project to go to each of his team's home games and take a seat behind home plate. He decided to learn by observing. He studied the pitchers, catcher, and infielders, and noticed the subtleties that he had missed while playing. He watched the moves pitchers made, "the imperceptible, easily overlooked tics of movement made by a catcher when pickoff moves or pitchouts were made." These telltale movements were valuable to him because they told him when he could steal bases. He recorded these idiosyncrasies in a notebook and referred to them throughout his career. After he recovered from his injury, all aspects of his game improved.[50]

A series of injuries while playing for the Oakland A's forced Mark McGwire to develop his mind and study the game. He learned about pitching and hitting while watching from the stands without worrying about hitting a home run or improving his batting average. His manager, Tony LaRussa, noted that McGwire's efforts really paid off. LaRussa said, "He started really studying the competition between the hitter and the pitcher and the catcher. For those of us who saw him as a young player, this move to be smarter is the thing that's most impressive. He's a really tough out, and he's a really good thinker."[51]

An injury spurred Dick Williams, when early in his career he was playing outfield for the Dodgers, to deepen his knowledge and understanding of the game. His efforts helped lengthen his playing career and facilitated his movement into the managerial ranks. A shoulder injury early in his career made it difficult for him to make throws from the outfield. Yet he was able to hang on and continue to play, though he was traded six times, and played four different positions in his twelve-year major league career. Williams had this to say about the impact of the injury:

There's a funny thing about injuries. They often force you to do things in a different way, your career takes a different direction, sometimes to a far better place than you ever would have reached if you stayed healthy. That's what I tell seriously injured players, because that's what happened to me. My injury forced me to watch, to listen, and to learn every tiny detail about this game, that once I could play in my sleep. Because if I ever wanted to play again, I could no longer be faster or stronger than anyone. Now I had to be smarter. I would sit on my butt in the dugout for nine innings and watch both the game and its players like I never watched them before. I studied opposing pitchers. I studied strategy. More than anything I studied human nature. And through it all, Dick Williams the player became something else. He became someone who thought before he acted. Someone who took nothing on the field for granted. Someone who wanted to leave nothing on the field to chance. From the vantage point that no other manager would ever have, I saw what it might take to manage a baseball team. It was then, sometime during the mid-1950s, that I decided that's what I wanted to do. To take my competitive fire, mix it with my knowledge of the dark side of the bench, and turn a team from a loser to my kind of winner. What could be more satisfying?[52]

Players with Natural Talent and Little Smarts

Ballplayers with great natural talent but without mental preparation, discipline, or willingness to learn and harness their talent limit their ability to play in the major leagues. They continue to come up short, wasting the physical gifts that should have provided the basis for a long and successful career. During his career Dick Williams observed several players who never developed the smarts needed to enable them to make the best of their talents. Dick Stuart, a home-run-hitting first baseman was one of these.

Stuart's problem was that his ego was out of control. He had what Williams called "a bad head."[53]

According to Williams:

[Stuart was] the poorest excuse for a caring baseball player I've ever seen. Once in Boston, with the bases loaded, Stuart got hit in the arm with a pitch. That would have sent him to first and scored a run, except that he wanted a chance at just one more RBI. So he complained to the umpire that the ball hadn't hit him—with a welt growing on the side of his arm as he spoke. The umpire couldn't believe a guy would intentionally cost his team a run on a bluff, changed his call, and let the selfish wonder stay at the plate.

Stuart eventually struck out. "I don't care if he did hit 75 home runs in two years with the Red Sox," said Williams. "He tried to hit nothing but home runs, and those players are no good for anybody."[54] Stuart was so focused on hitting that his fielding fell far short of what was expected of a major league first baseman. He earned the name Dr. Strangeglove, because his glove was, well, strange. He made a whopping 29 errors at first base for the Red Sox in 1963. Former Pirates boss Dick Groat observed that his biggest problem was lack of concentration. "Thinking about hitting instead of playing defense. . . . To Dick, fielding was a necessary evil." Once, during a Pirates spring training game, the stadium announcer said, "Anyone who interferes with the ball in play will be ejected from the ballpark." Pirates manager Danny Murtaugh said, "I hope Stuart doesn't think that means him."[55]

Jim "Catfish" Hunter, a pitcher without great stuff but a fierce competitor who got you out when he needed to get you out—he gave you the most comfortable 0 for 4 you ever had— described the foreshortened career of a physically gifted but bullheaded fellow New York Yankee pitcher, Ken Clay. Clay never made the leap from being a "thrower" to being a "pitcher." Hunter, who had that "feel" that all great pitchers have, was aware of the big difference between throwing and pitching. He often told Clay, who was a rookie, that if he, Hunter, had Clay's arm he would win twenty games every year. Clay wondered why he couldn't win twenty games himself if his arm was so potent. Hunter told him that he needed to learn how to use his great arm. "Clay was so clueless," said Hunter, "that he'd get out in the outfield before a game and throw long distance for hours. Naturally, that day he would get called upon to pitch (in relief) and wouldn't be able to get an usher out." Hunter's take on Clay was, "Great arm, great slider, bad brains. He wouldn't listen to anybody."[56]

Teammate and fellow pitcher Sparky Lyle observed the same problem with Clay. One Sunday afternoon he watched Clay warm up in the bullpen in preparation for a starting assignment the next day. "He must have been throwing for fifteen minutes," noted Lyle, "and he really aired it out, and as I was watching him, I was thinking that he was throwing too hard for too long." Lyle felt that his arm would be tired when he was due to pitch the next day. Lyle made a note in his diary the day after Clay's performance. He wrote, "Sorry to say I wasn't wrong about Kenny Clay. He wasted it all in the bullpen yesterday, and the Sox hit him for four runs in three innings. He told me when he got up to throw yesterday his arm felt sore and crummy, and he got worried and decided to throw it out, which isn't what you do. You have to have the discipline not to pitch, to wait. He had three whole days to rest his arm, but he didn't take advantage of them."[57]

Outfielder Willie Davis of the Los Angeles Dodgers was another player with outstanding physical gifts who lacked mental preparation and readiness. John Roseboro, who caught for the great Dodger teams of the 1960s, felt that Davis wasted a great talent because of an unwillingness to learn. Roseboro reported:

> Willie Davis could fly in center field, and he caught up to turn a lot of hits into outs. Willie should have been a better ballplayer. He thought he was. He was egotistical. I remember the first time he was interviewed in the clubhouse. A writer asked him if he thought he could hit .300 in the big leagues, and Willie said, "I think I'll hit .330." Some of us almost fell off our chairs. He has never hit .330 in his career. But he should have. Most of the time he hasn't even hit .300. He could fly. He should have been able to bunt his way to .300. One time I was asked to help him with his bunting and he told me he didn't need any help. "How many fucking bunts you beat out this year?" he asked me. I never tried to help him after that. Willie wasn't willing to work. He had extraordinary ability but he became an ordinary player.[58]

Hall of Famer Frank Robinson—probably the most intense guy I have ever been around; I played for him for three years—said that Davis never mastered some of the basic elements of the game. Robinson, a teammate of Davis's on the Dodgers, observed that "in game after game centerfielder Willie Davis would charge a ball hit out to him—and he was very quick getting to it—scoop it up, and, with a man on base, come up throwing. And time and time again the ball would sail over the cutoff man's head, allowing the base runner to advance."

The coaches would notice it, gripe on the bench, and tell Davis about it, but nothing seemed to change. Robinson said that Davis had all the tools to be a great ballplayer. He had "tremendous natural ability. I don't know if I've ever seen a player go from first to third faster than he did, and he covered an enormous amount of territory in the outfield. He could hit for average, had fair power, and could steal at least twenty bases every year." Robinson felt that the reason Davis didn't make the National League All-Star team until his eleventh year in the league was because "he wasn't a good baseball player. He didn't pay attention to basics."[59]

Robinson remembered a doubleheader played against the St. Louis Cardinals as "a perfect example of how Willie Davis's mind wandered." In the first game the Dodgers were down by three runs going into the ninth inning. Davis led off, and the count went to three balls and no strikes. The manager, Walter Alston, put the take sign on. Davis looked down at third-base coach Danny Ozark, stepped into the batter's box, and swung away, popping it up for an out. In the locker room between games, manager Walter Alston specifically asked Davis what he was thinking about. Alston said, "We're behind three runs, the count goes to 3 and 0, we give you the take sign—and you pop up the next pitch. That's the most ridiculous thing I've ever seen from you, Will, and I've seen a lot of mistakes from you. It's about time you got your mind into the ball game."

Davis, who was sitting next to Robinson during this lecture, turned to Robinson and said, "What the hell's wrong with that man?"

"What do you mean, Willie?" Robinson asked.

"Why did he single me out? Why's he getting on me," Davis replied.

"You mean you don't know what he's getting on you for?"

"No."

"Well, if you don't know, Willie, I'm not going to be the one to tell you," said Robinson.

Before the second game of the doubleheader Alston told the team that everyone would take pitches until they got the hit sign. Turning to Davis, he said, "Is that understood, Willie, do you understand?" Willie, according to Robinson, nodded his head. Alston emphasized the point by saying that he would levy a hundred-dollar fine on any player who swung before the hit sign was given. On the first pitch of the game Davis swung and popped the ball foul.

"Did you see that?" Alston cried from the dugout.

A chorus of players all said, according to Robinson, "Yeah, we saw it."

"That will cost him a hundred dollars," said Alston.

On the next pitch Davis swung again. "That's two hundred dollars," said Alston.

Robinson said that Davis never learned. He continued to miss signs and cutoff men throughout the rest of his career. "It seemed to be his style," said Robinson.[60]

Some major leaguers who are seemingly quite intelligent make stupid mistakes that jeopardize their careers. Herb Score was one of the most brilliant young pitchers ever to come into the major leagues. In 1955 he set an all-time record for strikeouts for rookies: 245. The following year he struck out 263 and had a win-loss record of 20–9. He had a major setback in 1956 when he was hit in the face with a batted ball and missed the whole 1957 season. He came back in the spring of 1958 and was his old self. "I was pitching as effectively as I ever did," he commented. Shortly after the season began he made a big mistake. He didn't take care of his arm. This is what he said happened:

> I was pitching in Washington. In the third or fourth inning my arm started to bother me. I didn't say anything. I figured it would work out. These are the mistakes you make when you are young. Then in the seventh inning I threw a pitch to somebody and it actually didn't reach home plate. I called out Bobby Bragan, the manager, and told him I thought I'd hurt my arm, and he took me out. The next day the thing had swelled up so much

I couldn't get it through the sleeve of my coat. It turned out I had torn the tendon in my elbow.[61]

He said he rested the arm for thirty days and then began pitching again, "throwing," he said with "a bad arm . . . a sore arm." In the process he lost his fastball, and was never the same again. "The last couple of years I pitched I was terrible," he lamented. "I just couldn't put it together any more."[62] Score's career might have been totally different if he had used good sense and taken care of himself.

Many players think that the more time they spend practicing, the better they will become. I don't agree. The important thing is to have a plan of action so that the time is well used. I got an important lesson in this regard when I was a teenager growing up in Cincinnati. I was practicing basketball in the backyard for about two hours. When I came in, my dad said, "You've been out there a long time. Were you working on something or were you just messing around?" I told him I was working on something. He said, "Well, what were you working on?"

I said, "Well, I was out there a couple of hours, I had to be working on something."

He got furious with me. He said, "First of all, if you were going out there and just having fun, that's fine. If you were just messing around, I can understand that. But if you are going out there to work for two hours, you had better have a plan. I don't want to hear that you are working for two hours without trying to get something done. That doesn't mean anything to me. I would rather you came in here and say you worked for five minutes, had a plan, and got something accomplished." I saw his point. Time doesn't really mean anything. I found that by having a plan to accomplish something specific every time I practiced, I got more done in less time.

I have seen too many ballplayers who think that practice for the sake of practice is a good thing, and that more time is better. When I was with the Texas Rangers there was a young player, an infielder whose name I will not mention, who would go out and take ground ball after ground ball after ground ball in practice. I said to him one day, "I don't see you working on your back hand. I don't see you changing your depth. I don't see you working on high hoppers. You are just taking ground balls. That's not going to help you." It seemed to me that he wanted everyone to see him taking all those ground balls so that they would get the idea that he really worked hard. The kid lacked smarts and didn't go far in baseball. At the end of the day, nobody gives a shit about how long you practice, but how well you play in the game. These two things don't necessarily go hand in hand. You need to make sure you are completely prepared for both practice and the game.

Ballplayers often make mistakes in handling the media, mistakes that haunt them on the playing field. Dodger shortstop Maury Wills described a post-game interview in which he was indiscreet. Broadcaster Vince Scully went deeper than usual into Wills's style of play and began digging into his thoughts and techniques on the diamond. "I gave away some of my secrets," said Wills, "and if anybody from the other team was listening, they could use that information to combat me."[63]

Wills also recalled an occasion in which he picked up valuable information while listening to a Scully post-game radio interview with Pirates ace pitcher Bob Friend. Friend had just beaten the Dodgers decisively and, as usual, had no trouble collaring Wills. During the interview Friend told Scully how he and fellow Pirate pitcher Vernon Law violated an unwritten law of baseball. Baseball's conventional wisdom dictated that when a pitcher got two strikes on a batter, he wasted a pitch. "A lot of times," Friend said, "when we get two strikes and no balls on a guy, we just throw a fastball right down the middle or on the corner. The guy is looking for an off-speed pitch outside the strike zone, so his bat isn't as quick. We throw the fastball and he either hits it on his fists, breaks the bat or just looks at it go by."

"And you do that consistently," Scully asked.

"All the time," replied Friend. "That's the way we pitch."

Wills was gleeful. "I'll be a sonofabitch," he said to himself. After learning about Friend and Law's approach to a two-strike count, Wills completely changed his strategy for hitting against them. "From then on I must have hit .350 against those guys," recalled Wills. "When Vernon Law or Bob Friend got two strikes on me, my bat was ready to move. Sometimes I'd invite an 0–2 count. I was getting two, three, and four hits a game off Pittsburgh all the time just on the strength of listening to the postgame interview."[64]

TWO

Staying Focused on the Present Moment

THE ABILITY TO CONCENTRATE, TO STAY FOCUSED ON THE here and now—in my opinion—is probably the most important ingredient in a ballplayer's mental makeup. Hitting a baseball that travels at upward of ninety miles per hour is a daunting task. It is equally difficult to pitch a baseball with velocity and movement to a precise location sixty feet away. High levels of concentration are required to do both. Wade Boggs of the Boston Red Sox got it right when he said, "The trademark of concentration is thinking of nothing."[1]

Practical Advice on How to Stay Focused

When I began playing baseball growing up in Cincinnati, my father gave valuable advice about how to concentrate in a baseball context. It was advice that stuck with me all through my baseball career. He said, "Never look past the ball." If you come up to bat thinking about hitting a home run or getting an RBI or raising your batting average, he said, you are not focused on the only thing that is important—the baseball. You will never be successful if you allow anything other than the baseball to enter your mind. If you get distracted, you might make contact, but it won't be solid contact. When he explained that to me, my concentration improved. Hitting the baseball became my sole focus. There was nothing else.

My son Rick acknowledged that staying focused on the baseball is not as easy as it seems. He said:

> It is a constant battle for me. At times in a baseball game you have a lull in the action. Sitting in the dugout it is easy to get caught up in what's going to happen later on in the game or in the next game. You have to focus on each at bat, each pitch. I force myself to concentrate. I remind myself that the only thing I can control is my approach to the next at bat. At the plate, if I am worried about getting a hit or my batting average, my focus is not on the baseball. If I look past the ball—by that I mean if I'm worried about where the ball will go—I will miss it by just enough. One thing I keep in my mind that I got from my dad is—don't look past the ball.

My son David, in his effort to stay focused at bat, has also taken my father's advice about never looking past the baseball. He said:

> The baseball is the most important thing in my mind while I am hitting. It keeps the fans, the score of the game, the slump I might be in, all the surrounding things— keeps everything out of it. Hitting becomes pretty simple. It narrows it down to just seeing the baseball. Then you have a chance. For some reason it is often easier for me to keep focused on the baseball in key situations rather than at the beginning of the game.

Ted Williams made essentially the same observation as my father when he said, "When you are concentrating on getting a hit, you won't see the ball as well. . . . But when you concentrate on seeing the ball, you'll hit it well, and then the hits will take care of themselves.[2]

My focus as an infielder improved when, as an eighteen-year-old playing for Sumter, South Carolina, in Class A ball, I was chewed out by Lenny Johnston, the manager, for not making a play on a ball at third base. A line drive hit the ground in front of me, bounced off a small rock, and glanced off my forehead. I thought it was a play I couldn't make, didn't attach much importance to it, and didn't expect criticism. Johnson thought otherwise and was angry with me. He told me that I wasn't in position to make the play. "You need to get in front of the ball," he told me. Johnson made me realize I wasn't fully prepared, that I needed to position myself better, be more aware of the type of pitch the pitcher was throwing and where the hitter might hit the ball. Johnson also made me realize that there are no excuses in this game. I concentrated better after that incident because I knew I had to take more responsibility for how I played.

David sees himself as a naturally intense person so, for him to improve his concentration, he had to find ways to relax. He said:

My ability to stay focused on the present moment improved when I realized that the more relaxed I was the better I could concentrate. When I stand at the plate I have to make every part of my body relax. It is something I have to do consciously. If I am thinking about too many things, I can't relax. If I can narrow my thoughts down to one thing—the baseball—then I can relax. Breathing is really important. When you breathe easy, you relax more. The easier your breathing, the more power you are going to have.

Like David, outfielder Eric Davis, who had a successful career with the Cincinnati Reds, indicated that his success at bat depended on his ability to stay relaxed and concentrated. He said:

> All experience in hitting leads up to this: The whole thing is recognizing the pitch fast, and do you recognize the pitch excitedly, or do you recognize that pitch relaxed? If you recognize that pitch excitedly, you're not going to hit it square very often. Not often enough. If you recognize it relaxed, you've got a better chance of crushing it often.[3]

I believe there is such a thing as being too relaxed, too nonchalant, too self-satisfied. I have seen this happen when, during a game, a batter gets hits the first two times at bat. He then gets too satisfied with his performance and, in the process, loses concentration. I have lost concentration because of a good at bat as well as a poor at bat. There needs to be a sense of urgency. There has to be some fear of failure so you won't miss anything. Otherwise you may not prepare yourself. While fear can be hurtful and detract from your ability to perform (more about this later) it can also serve as a motivator, help you focus on the situation, and therefore serve to improve your concentration.

Steve Garvey indicated that concentration could be made habitual if you worked at it. Garvey believed that ballplayers can learn to stay focused. "Concentration, like anything else," he said, "is a habit. Permit yourself to begin breaking that habit and you might as well look for another profession." Focusing on the present moment is all important. "Once you start separating yourself from the game," said Garvey, "you're lost. If you're twenty games back in the last month of the season or ten runs behind in the last inning, you've got to stay in the game." Garvey taught himself to block out all distractions. "It is one of my strengths," he said. "For two hours or three hours on a ball field, I'm in my own world. Nothing distracts me, nothing else gets in."[4]

Yankee shortstop Derek Jeter, a player who grew up fast in New York and became a team leader, described how he exerted control over his mind to maintain concentration. He said:

> I don't overanalyze it and I don't sit around and think about every detail so much that I can mess myself up. I'm not saying I'm not prepared, because I am. But I don't let myself become crazed and obsessed in anticipation of what might happen. I just let it happen, I embrace the moment and let the moment come to me.[5]

Sandy Koufax believed that mental discipline was required to improve concentration, particularly in the face of adversity— when a teammate made an error or an umpire made a bad call. "Once you begin to think in terms of what should have happened," he said, "you're in terrible danger of letting down. Concentration. *Con-cen-tra-tion.* You must forget the last game and the last inning and the last batter, because there is not a thing that you can do about them. The only batter you can get is the one standing up there at the plate with the bat in his hand. You can have the strongest arm in the world, but without total concentration, you will never be a winning pitcher."[6]

Hall of Famer Mike Schmidt, a great player who was businesslike in his approach to the game, indicated that his concentration improved when he quit trying to live up to standards set by the fans or media, and set his own standards. He said:

> I was able to alleviate outside pressure in part because I learned not to derive approval from fan or media reaction, or from any group reaction. A player who performs to satisfy his

own standards rather than those of fifty thousand people in the stands has a much better chance of succeeding. Fans can't help but expect too much. If they are booing you and you're completely plugged into them, responding to pressure, your hands and arms will get tighter, and you won't perceive things the way you want to. Only a hitter who can stay within himself can define his audience and his standards will relieve that kind of pressure and be able to go up to home plate loose and relaxed in the most difficult game situations.[7]

As a base stealer, Maury Wills of the Los Angeles Dodgers blocked out distractions through mental preparation in the clubhouse before the game. He sought time alone to get himself into a state of deep concentration. "I always felt I had a special job to do," he recalled, "a little bit more than a call of duty. In order for me to concentrate and to gear myself up, I had to be alone. . . . I even liked my locker to be off in a corner of the clubhouse. The clubhouse guys on the road would put me in a corner by myself. If they had a lot of lockers, they'd leave one empty next to me."[8]

I began focusing and getting myself ready to play in a manner somewhat similar to Wills. I would sit next to my locker before each game, preparing myself mentally. I didn't watch TV or play cards. I focused on the pitcher, thought about what I needed to do on the field, and broke everything down before the game started. I needed to get my mind ready; otherwise, out on the field the game would go too fast for me. In the 1980s the Philadelphia Phillies made it easier for players like me, who wanted to be alone before a game, by setting aside a special room called the mood room. It provided a quiet space for players to prepare mentally to play.[9]

David indicates that his level of concentration during a game is also based on mental preparation. He said:

The most important factor in enabling me to concentrate is preparation. If I have done all the smart work beforehand—know the starting pitcher and the relievers, watched video of my at bats against them, know how they have done in recent games, gotten in my swings—then it is so much easier to relax and let it happen. If I don't feel totally prepared, then it is a pressure situation. That's when I am tense, not sure of the outcome, and worried about where the ball is going to go. When I have done my homework, I can go out and play and live with the results.

When questioned by reporters during a seven-game hitting streak in 1991, first baseman Don Mattingly of the New York Yankees, the 1981 American League batting champion, responded by stressing the importance of concentration and describing the mental discipline needed in approaching each at bat. He said:

I don't look back, I really don't. I don't want to talk about what I did last Saturday because that doesn't help me tonight. I only care about tonight, or *today*, man. That's the whole deal. . . . I can't be worried about what's already past. I'm gonna help the Yankees win tonight. I'm gonna hit it hard tonight. I just worry about a one-game streak, then a one-game streak, then a one-game streak, then another one-game streak. I don't think about being hot for six or seven days. I just want to be hot tonight. It's just the same old story for me. One bat after another. Take 'em one at a time.[10]

Joe Torre, who caught for the Atlanta Braves early in his career, improved his concentration as the result of a conversation he had with Hank Aaron. Aaron told him that a hitter's level of concentration depended on his attitude toward each at bat. Torre recalled:

One day Hank I were talking about batting slumps when he made a comment that stayed with me ever since: "Each at bat is a new day." . . . When we find ourselves in a rut, "Each day is a new day" is a line worth remembering. When we take this philosophy to heart, what we're really doing is focusing on the present. We can learn from past failures and make mistakes, but we shouldn't get stuck there, either. The only way to reach our potential is to focus on what we must do now—this moment, this day—to perform effectively. . . . We lose our instincts and our smarts when we get caught up in outside distractions, past blunders, or worries about the future. We can't do anything about five minutes ago, much less last week. . . . On the other hand, we function at peak levels of efficiency when we focus relentlessly on the present.[11]

Willie Stargell, a Hall of Famer who for twenty years was the Pittsburgh Pirates regular left fielder, believed that the even-keel philosophy taught to him by his stepfather was critical in developing his powers of concentration. The key, he said, "was never to get too high or get too low. At either end of the spectrum, one loses a considerable amount of effectiveness." Stargell believed that it was important to stay in the gray area between the two extremes. "That's where one's most effective energy lies. . . . When things are going bad, don't get too discouraged, and when things are going good, don't get too excited." Stargell believed that by maintaining his composure, he was able to create consistency in his game, and to play good baseball year after year.[12]

Pete Rose believed that concentration improved if you stayed in the gray area that Stargell identified. "Baseball is peaks and valleys," said Rose. "You don't want to let yourself feel too high when you're on a peak because then you're gonna feel too damn low when the valley comes. You try to keep your emotions as even as you can, even though, if you have any sense, you recognize that it's an emotional game." According to Cincinnati Reds trainer Larry Starr, who watched him play for several years, Rose had an "incredible ability to focus." Starr, who had worked with many great players, observed that eventually almost all get distracted. "Eventually you see there are other things on their minds. One day they come to the ballpark and something's bothering them. Usually it's a problem at home. And it affects their play. . . . With Pete you never saw that. Nothing ever bothered him to the extent that he took it on the field with him." Sports writer Michael Sokolove saw in Rose this same ability to block out distractions. "The bigger the game, the more press attention, the greater the potential distractions, the keener was Rose's concentration."[13]

George Brett, a great player and the best hitter I played against, said that he learned a lot about concentration during a clinic that his Kansas City Royals team sponsored under the direction of Bill Harrison, a California eye doctor who had developed new approaches for improving concentration and relaxation. Harrison presented techniques for success-imaging and centering, all of which Brett felt were helpful. "We did things like spell words backwards while jumping on a trampoline, and doing jumping jacks with a strobe light on. Brett said several players tried so hard that they were unable to accomplish the tasks. Harrison told the team, "Don't try hard, try *easier*. It relaxes your mind, it relaxes your body." Brett said that when the crowd starts cheering during a close game, many ballplayers succumb to the temptation "to hit the ball off the scoreboard. They try *so* hard." Brett said that he learned, in part as a result of Harrison's teaching, to try easier. He learned not to overthink in the batter's box as many players are tempted to do. Brett improved his concentration by psyching himself down rather than up. "I don't key up," he said. "When you get too psyched up, the tension is too great. . . . I just try to see the ball and react."[14]

As a young New York Yankee pitcher, Jim Bouton often lost his poise with men on base and the game on the line. He tried harder by throwing harder. "It didn't take any thinking," he recalled, "just more muscle." The fear showed, not only in his ability to get the ball over the plate but in his appearance on the pitcher's mound. Veteran Yankee pitcher Whitey Ford made a telling remark to him between innings during a World Series game, when Bouton was tight, anxious, and distracted. "Kid," said Ford, "you're throwing nervous hard out there."[15]

Bouton knew that he needed to find a way to calm his nerves and focus his mind. His ability to concentrate and remained poised on the pitcher's mound improved dramatically when he applied ideas about balancing and centering contained in a book that had nothing to do with baseball, titled *Zen in the Art of Archery*. Instead of thinking about the mechanics of the pitching motion, which he had been doing, Bouton learned to block everything out and think about nothing. He said he got to the point where he could "just let it happen. I got out of my own way and let my knuckleball do its own thing. . . . I had forgotten that my unconscious knew a lot more about pitching than my conscious."[16]

Japan's great baseball star and legendary home-run hitter Sadaharu Oh kept his attention focused by applying the centering techniques he learned in the martial art of aikido. It was because of the work he had done with aikido that he was able to adopt an unorthodox but effective stance in the batter's box. He stood "flamingo style" on his back foot. This required great balance and the ability to manifest "ki," or centering energy, from a point just beneath his belly button. "Every motion I made,"

Oh recalled, "I concentrated ki in my one point and projected it downward into the ground and out through my forearms into the secret lengths of bat and sword." By this process he was able to keep his mind fully absorbed in the task of hitting.[17]

Orel Hershiser, who pitched for several years for the Los Angeles Dodgers, spoke animatedly about how important it was to stay focused on the next pitch:

> I don't allow my mind to stray far ahead. My one and only priority is the next pitch, not the no-hitter, not the shutout, not even the out. . . . The key for me is to forget about results and concentrate on execution.[18]

Hershiser described at length the regimen he had developed to get himself to the point where he could put full attention on each pitch. That regimen began long before game time; in fact, it started at home. He said that we might be surprised to learn that his wife, Jamie, played an extremely important role:

> Jamie is crucial to how well I do on the field, from simply keeping the house in order and making sure we're not in a tense moment at home, to making sure things run smoothly, to making sure people don't get at me on game day.[19]

The day before Hershiser pitched, as well as the day of the game, he spent time "getting into my 'zone,' my game mode." He wanted no interruptions, nothing that would affect his "train of thought." He wanted no pressure from the outside world. "For those two days, no matter what it was, Jamie took care of it. It's all on her shoulders. She knew that even though I'm there, she can't bother me." Hershiser says that he needed the time "to think and pray and listen to music and read my Bible." He reported:

Over the years I have discovered that I must find that serious, all-business, aggressive, almost mean side of my personality that allows me to compete at the big league level. That person is so intense he won't let one detail slip by and will bear down on every pitch. I can't be the happy-go-lucky, down-to-earth Orel when I go out to face the opposition. I have to be tough, and that means looking deep within my alter ego.[20]

Hershiser also had to be on guard against complacency. "Concentration on praise is a distraction that threatens the attitude I need. Complacency is death. Start thinking you've got it licked and you're finished." Hershiser also talked about how important it was for him to maintain balance. "There is a fine line," he said, "between being able to think about my game without starting to get wired, zoned, steely, quiet, intense. The game face is necessary, but for my sake, and the sake of my family, I put it off as long as I can. That benefits my game, too, because the game face that evidences I'm zoned is a drain on my system. It's vital in a game. Too early, it's debilitating."

Hershiser felt that by the time he left his house on game day for the drive to Dodger Stadium, he had become "two distinct personalities." The first, he said, "is the typical Orel who will greet friends and be light and happy and normal." Then his mental state began to change. He said:

At the same time, beginning to exist deep down inside me, is the other Orel Hershiser. That Orel has the ability to narrow his concentration to the regimen of game preparation. He can become aggressive, stubborn, focused, intense. He will miss no detail. He will even push his teammates to keep their heads in the game when necessary. When I'm the starting pitcher, that Orel might chastise a teammate who's not concentrating, not serious. That would seem totally out of place for the other Orel. But for this

Orel, the pitch, the next pitch, is all there is to him. Everything from that point will center around that.[21]

Between innings, when he is sitting in the dugout while the Dodgers are at bat, Hershiser keeps himself relaxed and concentrated by "yawning, praying, talking to myself and singing softly." During the later innings of the World Series game against the Oakland A's in 1988, in which the Dodgers had a three-run lead, the TV cameras caught Hershiser in the dugout with his head back, eyes closed, appearing as if he was meditating. When the TV commentator Bob Costas asked him after the game what he had been doing, Hershiser responded, "I was singing hymns to myself to relax and keep my adrenalin down, because every time I thought about being ahead, I got too excited to pitch." When asked what song he was singing, he said it was a praise hymn that had the following words:

> *Praise God from whom all blessings flow.*
> *Praise Him all creatures here below.*
> *Praise Him above ye heavenly host.*
> *Praise Father, Son, and Holy Ghost.*[22]

Hershiser's level of concentration evidently reached a peak during the 1988 season, when he led the Dodgers to a National League pennant and a World Series victory. Of the last 102 innings he pitched that year, 96 were scoreless. His ERA over that period was an incomprehensible 0.62. Teammate Kirk Gibson described the magnitude of that accomplishment with the following words of praise: "I don't know if we will ever again see the likes of what [he has] done. It may be that no other pitcher has ever stayed in that kind of groove for so long. He'll go down in history."[23]

Bobby Cox, the Braves' fine manager who has never gotten

the credit he deserves, contrasted the mental approach that works in football with that in baseball. He indicated that baseball players would be exhausted by the end of the first month of the season if they played with the emotional intensity required in football. Baseball, he said, "is not like football, where you can take your aggression out on a guy six inches from your nose. Baseball is a real skill sport. You don't want to be so fired up you can't perform."[24]

Rituals as an Aid to Concentration

While I didn't find rituals to be particularly helpful, many ballplayers use them as a means of deepening their level of concentration. David doesn't use them either, but he has noted that a lot of guys go through a ritual or routine as they get ready to bat and it works for them. Rick, however, does use a ritual when he is in the on-deck circle waiting to bat. He said:

> I like to use a ritual when I am on deck. For example, I flick the weight bat with my wrist. I do it a certain number of times. I will stick with that until I make an out. Then I change the ritual. A lot of guys use the sign of the cross. I haven't tried that, but I might some time.

Dodger shortstop Maury Wills considered the little mannerisms or rituals that ballplayers go through an important aid in maintaining focus. "The way a guy goes up to home plate and takes his swings, tugs at this and that, adjusts various parts of his body, makes the sign of the cross. . . . They help the hitter get his concentration," said Wills. Even the way a player puts on his uniform makes a difference. "I would say that most athletes put on their uniform top before their uniform bottom. . . . It is a ritual. Some people do certain things the same way. Or maybe they wear a piece of lucky clothing."[25]

Red Sox shortstop Nomar Garciaparra steps out of the batter's box after each pitch, kicks the dirt with each toe, adjusts his right batting glove, adjusts his left batting glove, and touches his helmet before getting back in the box.[26] Mike Hargrove, who, after his major league career, managed in Cleveland and Baltimore, went through so many time-consuming elements in his batting ritual that he was known as "the human rain delay."[27] Former Mets reliever Turk Wendell had an eccentric ritual. While on the mound, he wore a necklace made from the teeth of animals he had killed.[28] A lot of Catholic ballplayers, particularly those from Latin America, make the sign of the cross before every at bat. Catcher Pudge Rodriguez does so before every pitch.[29] All through his long career, Wade Boggs ate chicken before every game. He began it as a rookie when he noticed a correlation between multiple hit games and poultry plates. His wife reportedly has more than forty chicken recipes.[30]

Like many ballplayers, former Red Sox outfielder Carl Yastrzemski went through a ritual in the batter's box that enabled him to eliminate distractions and keep his mind focused, particularly between pitches. "I was constantly talking to myself," he said. "I never stopped . . . I knew every single time, whether I swung at a pitch or not, if I was ready to hit, whether there was something else I should have done differently. Did I jump out too hard on it? Not enough?"[31]

Yastrzemski said that Yankee pitcher Mel Stottlemyre often heard him talking to himself at the plate and kidded him about it. Yaz knew that Stottlemyre was probably right because in his own mind he was thinking something like "gotta be quick, gotta be quick," but he never realized he was saying it so loud. "Then again," he remembered, "I was so intent on concentrating and repeating these instructions to myself that I probably did talk out loud but never knew it. Corrections, adjustments, complaining to myself. They were what I always did."[32]

Yaz recalled a game against the Twins in Boston's Fenway Park in the final days of a wild pennant race in 1967 in which it was particularly difficult to concentrate. "The stands were loaded," he recalled, "with people standing up and cheering before the game began. There was a level of intensity I had never seen or felt before. . . . The noise factor was monumental all day. Each time a player's name was announced, the volume almost hurt. As I got up out of the batting circle, it grew even louder, still rising as I stepped into the batter's box. Finally, it would tone down, but it wouldn't stop, and you almost wanted to say, 'Shut up, let me think.' " [33]

Yaz believed that the rituals or mental habits developed over the course of his career got him through that particularly difficult day. "I'd take a pitch, and go through my ritual, step out of the box, hitch up, touch my helmet, my belt, my shirt. I'd pull on my pants, unconsciously. I guess what I was really doing was buying an extra second or two to talk to myself. Maybe I was talking out loud, as Stottlemyre insisted." He had developed the ability, he said, "to block everything out, the noise, the situation, and 35,000 screaming people." He got himself into such a deep state of concentration that, even though when he looked into the stands he could see fans yelling, he was unaware of any sounds. "I didn't hear them," he recalled.[34]

As for me, rituals were never a big part of my game. David didn't use the kind of rituals described above. But he considered his work routine before a game as a kind of ritual. He said that he would take a lot of swings during batting practice, hit off a tee, and hit soft toss (a form of batting practice).

The Mobilizing Force of Anger

Some people can use anger to their advantage and others can't. I learned to use anger to improve my focus early in my career. When I was a young player I had trouble driving in runners in scoring position. I wanted to do it so badly that I would lose focus. I was trying to relax at the plate, because I thought it was the right thing to do. My hitting coaches had told me that I would hit better if I was relaxed. It wasn't working for me. I told my dad and he said: "Does relaxing in the batter's box feel natural? Does that feel normal? Is that the way you want to be?" I told him that I felt squeamish when I tried to relax. My body felt like it was in different pieces. I didn't feel at one with my body. He told me to use my natural aggressiveness to my advantage. He said, "Just be angry. Get mad at the ball. Don't back off. Be really aggressive." He said that being angry and aggressive would focus me on what I was doing in the batter's box. I took his advice and became a much better hitter. Thereafter I used anger to my benefit. Being angry was by design. I felt better when I was angry, when my teeth were clenched. I could see the ball better when I was angry. It made me more competitive. When I was angry I moved faster, had more energy, wasn't worried about things, and played better.

Anger doesn't work for everybody. In fact, anger hurts a lot of guys. Their minds become unclear and they lose concentration. They get too wired and the game speeds up too much for them. They lose touch with what is important. Most guys whose anger is out of control don't last long in the big leagues.

When I was with Cleveland we had a pitcher by the name of Jerry Johnson who just could not control his anger. He had great stuff and was a good person. If things went well for him, he was okay. However, if the opposing team started getting hits off him, he got so pissed off that he couldn't pitch. His anger crushed him. You had to take him out of the game. He was a competitive guy, but he couldn't recover. He couldn't turn the page. I have been around a lot more guys like Johnson whose anger was destructive than guys like me who could use anger for positive purposes.

Anger worked for me because I kept it within bounds. I chose to get angry because it was consistent with my personality. I was simply being myself. Before I let myself get angry I was trying to be cool. It didn't work for me. Some guys think that it is good to get angry and they try to fake it. When something goes wrong on the field, they come back to the dugout acting like they are pissed off. You can tell when guys aren't really comfortable with anger. They are lying to themselves, and somehow think they can fool people. Watching them, I find myself feeling embarrassed.

David's approach to anger is much the same as mine. Here is how he describes it:

> I think anger has played a much more positive role in my game than a negative one. If you are passionate about the game and want to do everything you can to win—and things aren't going well—you are going to get mad. If you don't, you are incredibly good about being calm, or you don't care enough. It has got to bother you. You are going to get upset. You let it out. You throw something. You let it go instead of letting it build up inside you. That might be what it takes to get you going again. So anger has its place.
>
> There are times when anger can help motivate you. I have felt pumped up after having a run-in with an umpire or a guy on another team. The rush of adrenaline you get when you show your anger and let your feelings out is pretty incredible. The best way to use anger is to channel it. You make an out and

you are furious with yourself. You are letting the team down and you are letting yourself down, and you want to throw something. If you can somehow take that energy and say okay, I am going to use this energy in the next at bat, that's when things start clicking for you. That's when you become a much better player—when you can channel that negative energy into something positive.

It took me some time to learn how to use anger. Anger can get out of hand and hurt guys, especially in baseball, where you can have six hundred at bats during a season. If you throw something or cuss every time you make an out your anger doesn't get you anywhere. It can be a long season for guys who get frustrated after every at bat. Earlier in my career I spent too much negative energy on being angry. I let it get to me when I was in the minor leagues and struggling, and wanting so badly to get to the major leagues. As I got older and smarter I learned to turn it into something positive.

One of the best players I played with—who used anger effectively throughout his career—was Todd Stottlemyre, who pitched for several seasons in the big leagues. He pitched like he was mad. He had that look on his face. Anger is what drove him. It made him successful. If he had been a position player, playing every day, I don't know how he would have done it. He would have worn himself out, he was that psyched up.

Some players think they need to show anger to prove to their team members that they care. They make outs and force themselves to show negative emotions. They make a mistake in the field and throw something in the dugout. I don't respect that kind of behavior.

Mike uses anger when it serves him. He knows that there are occasions when anger helps him concentrate and deal with negative thoughts. He said:

When I am really going good at the plate, I am happy and relaxed. My mind lets my body work right. There is no need to be
angry. I use anger when I am in a slump or not going good and
being negative. When I am thinking, "I hope I get a hit, I hope I
can," I know I must do something quick to change the mental
picture. I use anger to stop the negative voice. I call the pitcher
every name in the book. I use self-talk—"I am going to kill the
pitcher, I've got this guy." It helps to get me pissed off, to get my
mind off being passive and negative. When I use the anger technique, I need to breathe, breathe into my gut. I don't use anger
all of the time, only when it is necessary.

Many players have used anger the way David, Mike, and I
have used it to enable them to play better baseball. It is not
surprising that, given his combative personality, Frank Robinson used anger very effectively on the playing field. Pitcher
Don Drysdale, who faced Robinson regularly in the course of
his career, said that "if there was one guy who seemed to hit
better when he was angry, I'd nominate Frank Robinson. He
seemed to make better contact than the rest when he was boil-
ing." Robinson, according to sports writer Michael Sokolove,
believed that teams played better if they took a "rugged approach" to the game. Sokolove saw Robinson as "a notori-
ously tough player who stood right at the top of the plate,
daring pitchers to hit him."[35]

Jim Pagliaroni, a catcher for the Boston Red Sox during the
Ted Williams era, described how Williams got himself ready to
hit. Williams would take early batting practice, before the fans or
press arrived. He would wave his bat at the batting practice
pitcher and start screaming at the top of his voice, "My name is
Ted fucking Williams and I am the greatest hitter in baseball."
Williams would take a vicious cut at the ball and hit a line drive,

and say "Jesus H. Christ couldn't get me out." He would then hit another drive and say, "Here comes Jim Bunning [ace Detroit Tigers pitcher], Jim Fucking Bunning, and that little shit slider of his. He doesn't think he can get me out with that shit."[36] By the end of batting practice Williams would have raised his anger level to the point where his mere presence in the batter's box would intimidate opposing pitchers.

Baseball immortal Ty Cobb, noted for his combativeness on and off the field, appeared in the batter's box, "with his neck thrust out, his body crouched over the plate, showing them an angry, determined, scornful, fighting face." A teammate of Cobb's on the 1922 Detroit Tigers team, Fred Haney, watched Cobb at the plate on numerous occasions, and said he fired himself up as he waited in the on-deck circle. "The muscles in Ty's face were tense," Haney recalled, "his bright blue eyes blazed; his forehead furrowed into an intense frown. He was working himself up into a fury—a fierce determination to dominate the pitcher, to hit the ball." By the time Cobb stepped into the batter's box, Haney said, you could almost see sparks in the air. Cobb seemed to be telling the pitcher, "I dare you to pitch to me, I dare you."[37]

Darryl Strawberry, according to teammates, had a mean streak in him, an inner combativeness that helped his hitting in the years he played for the New York Mets before being traded in 1992 to the Los Angeles Dodgers. In the off season before joining his new team, Strawberry became a practicing Christian. The feisty, aggressive Strawberry suddenly became mellow, peaceful, and laid back. As the season progressed his batting average and home-run production slacked off, never equaling his performance with the Mets. His new manager, Tommy Lasorda, could not understand what was happening. "This guy hit 37 home runs last year," Lasorda growled as the season wore on and

Strawberry continued to languish at the plate. "Did he forget how to hit?"[38]

The *San Francisco Chronicle* reported in early July of that season that Brett Butler, the Los Angeles center fielder and an outspoken Christian, took Strawberry aside during a pregame workout in Montreal and told him that Christians didn't have to be that mellow. "Brett told me," said Strawberry, "that I had to start getting mean. I have not had any anger or frustration for a long time. When I get frustrated, I see the ball better. I have better concentration. I didn't have that now and I don't know why."[39] Catcher Gary Carter, who was with the Mets when Strawberry had his best years, and who was now a Dodger teammate, agreed that the problem was in Strawberry's laidback attitude. "You know what I don't see any more," said Carter. "I don't see that anger in his swing. I don't see that feeling in his bat speed. In New York you could watch him from the dugout when he swung, and it would go 'whoosh.' I don't see that anymore."[40]

Dodger pitcher Don Newcombe, one of the first black pitchers in major league baseball, had a tendency to get lackadaisical on the pitching mound, particularly if his team had given him a lead. Jackie Robinson, the Dodger second baseman, was particularly aware of his teammate's proclivity to lose focus, and he dogged him about it. "I was pitching one day in Pittsburgh," recalled Newcombe. "I had an eleven-run lead. I let up a little and loaded the bases." A dangerous long-ball hitter, Ralph Kiner, was coming to the plate and Robinson came over to the mound to bawl Newcombe out. "If you don't want to pitch," shouted Robinson, "go back to the hotel. Get the heck out of here." The speech stirred Newcombe. "I got so mad I struck out Kiner and got out of the inning." The next day Robinson told Newcombe, "The only time you pitch good is when you get mad. From now on I'm going to keep you mad." Newcombe acknowledged that Robinson was right. "Whenever I needed it," said Newcombe, during the years they played together, "he got on me."[41]

Al Leiter of the New York Mets was also well aware of the need to channel anger on the pitching mound. In the spring of 2002 Leiter was given responsibility for helping pitcher Shawn Estes with his attitude on the mound. Estes, who came in the off season to the Mets from the San Francisco Giants, had a reputation of having a strong arm and a less than strong mind. Leiter noted that "there were issues that his head might not be right." Leiter hoped to instill some anger into Estes's pitching. "I want him to be pissed off when he goes out there to pitch," he said.[42]

Willie Mays recalled how late in his career he fed on the fury aroused by opponents who no longer respected his ability to hit. Suffering from exhaustion and in a slump, Mays had just gotten back in the Giants lineup after being hospitalized for five days. In the third inning of a game against the Braves, with runners on second and third, the Braves' manager, Billy Hitchcock, decided to walk the Giant's hot-hitting third baseman, Jim Ray Hart, to get to Mays, who was next in the batting order. Mays was apoplectic. "They were loading the bases to pitch to me! That never happened before. I was furious and embarrassed, but raring to go. . . . I couldn't wait to get up to bat with the bases loaded. Did I concentrate? Make me look bad, huh? I smacked a single past first base and the runs were enough for victory."[43]

Don Drysdale, one of the great Dodger pitchers of the 1950s and 1960s, recognized that he survived for almost fifteen years in the major leagues because he was intimidating on the pitcher's mound. He reveled in his reputation "for being a mean bastard." "Baseball," he said, "was a game of intimidation. . . . I always believed that it was them or us, and nothing was going to stand in my way. Take no prisoners, and if you were going to lose, take down the son-of-a-bitch who beats you—make him feel the cost of victory."[44]

Ron Santo, who was the Chicago Cubs third baseman during the years Drysdale was pitching for the Dodgers, considered him to be as "tough a competitor" as he had played against in the major leagues. Writing in 1993, Santo said that Drysdale was "an intimidating sort, not the kind of pitcher you find these days around major league baseball. He thrived on pitching inside. Now, I'm not talking about brushing you back occasionally, I mean he threw at you. His philosophy was that the plate was his, and you as a batter were in his space. He wanted you off the plate, period. He wanted to establish the outside of the plate in the umpires' minds."[45]

Drysdale acknowledged that over the course of his career he had developed a Dr. Jekyll-and-Mr. Hyde personality. He was seen as a guy "who was an SOB on the mound, but a pretty decent drinking companion afterward." As the old saw goes, he recalled, "I was the same guy who would brush back his grand-mother to win a game one minute, and then sing songs at a base-ball writers' banquet the next." He didn't take his anger out at home. "I wasn't one of those guys who woke up mad on the day I pitched. I wasn't a bear around the house or anything like that. I didn't wake up in a bad mood, growling at my wife." His mood changed, however, when he left home. "When I got to the ballpark, which was my office, and put that uniform on, I guess I worked myself into a frenzy. I had a pretty good temper—and I still do on occasion—but I basically kept my red-ass per-sonality at the ballpark. It all locked in when you saw that first batter staring out at you from the plate."[46]

Drysdale could be particularly ferocious and intimidating if he felt that the other team's pitcher was knocking down Dodger batters intentionally. He said:

I had the belief that for every one of my teammates who went down, two players from the other team would go down. Or, if two Dodgers were knocked down when I was pitching, four opponents would bite the dust. I thought that was a nice orderly way of doing things. I didn't like to save my retaliation pitches for the lousy hitters, either. If I felt moved to knock down the opposing pitcher, I would. But that was only one. I still had another to go, and I preferred to hold that one for a big guy in the lineup. . . . It was like Russian roulette, but the general rule of thumb was, "hit 'em where it hurts." Don't waste your time with a guy who isn't hitting his weight.[47]

Major league baseball no longer allows pitchers to intimidate hitters the way they were able to when Drysdale, Gibson, Newcombe, and Gossage were in their prime. Umpires now crack down on pitchers who purposely brush back a batter. Bob Gibson believes that, as a result, major league baseball "lacks the competitiveness that baseball used to be all about." He said:

By looking closely at just one issue—pitching inside—it can be easily perceived how financial considerations have dominated the scene. Owners are against inside pitches because they threaten to nick their million-dollar investments. The whim of the owners of course trickles down to the umpires, whose warnings to pitchers lead the batters to believe that they are well protected at the plate. Nowadays, the umpire can eject a pitcher for throwing at a batter even *without* warning him first.[48]

Roberto Clemente recognized that anger helped him play better baseball. "When I get mad," he once admitted, "it puts energy in my body. . . . If I would be happy, I would be a bad player." Criticism in the press often fired him up. His biographer, Phil Musick, noted that "from the moment he saw himself referred to in cold, unmistakeable type as 'the Puerto Rican Hotdog,' his body was eternally charged." As his career progressed and he led the Pittsburgh Pirates to pennant-winning seasons, his popularity with baseball writers grew, and he was not often subjected to the negative comments that aroused his ire. When he wasn't found wanting by the press, "when the [critical] documents could not be found," Musick said, "he resolutely fueled himself on imaginary adverse criticism."[49]

While many ballplayers use anger to their advantage, it is important to remember that anger hurts more ballplayers than it helps. Hall of Famer Mike Schmidt put into perspective the adverse impact of angry outbursts on the ability to perform. He said:

> Out-of-character displays of temper can disrupt your concentration, and your game, and you won't be as productive. Igniting a quick temper with an incident here or there can throw your game out of whack. . . . If you tend to get thrown out of games or break bats, you shouldn't get high on the fact that you're known as a guy with one of the hottest tempers around. That kind of reputation can lead the opposition to believe that they can get to you and your game.[50]

Slumps and How to Deal with Them

Slumps affect everyone who plays the game. Slumps for hitters seem to follow a predictable course. It happens this way. You make an out and then you try to make up for it in the next at bat. You are going to try to do better, even hit a home run. Then the last at bat creeps into your mind, and the trouble begins. You screw up the next at bat, and the next and the next because you are trying to make up for your previous failures. You make two, four, or eight outs in succession, and then you become obsessed. You lose concentration because too many things creep into your mind—your batting average is falling, you're not helping the team, you can think of nothing positive. You are distracted, become mentally soft, don't want anyone to know that you are not mentally tough. You begin thinking that the problem lies in your physical ability. You can't do it anymore and your career is over. You are unwilling to allow for the fact that it might have to do with your mental state. You are in a slump.

Joe DiMaggio provided a wonderful description of the emotional progress of a batting slump. It began, he said, with "simple wonder." It continued through "prolonged bewilderment, dawning realization, horror, grim determination, helpless rage, [and] self-pity."[51] Loss of confidence, DiMaggio believed, caused slumps. As self-confidence slipped away, hitters tightened up and began to press. Pressing, to DiMaggio, meant being "overanxious, impatient and abrupt." DiMaggio acknowledged that there was no "pat cure" for a slump, and "almost any way out of a slump is about as effective as any other." He believed, however, that if a ballplayer was able to step back mentally and view the situation from a broader perspective, slumps would end sooner. He said:

> If a ballplayer in a slump could console himself with the thought that once out of it he'll probably hit like a house-a-fire, it would help his frame of mind, but I've never met a ballplayer who could reason that way. There's always the horrible thought that maybe this is the end, that the pitchers are on to you at last, that you're really all washed up. It is not a frame of mind which lends itself readily to consolation.[52]

Yogi Berra was correct when he observed that slumps were a normal part of part of the game, something that all were affected by at one time or another. "Everybody has slumps," he noted. "Hitters and pitchers struggle for no reason. Your good moods suddenly become bad moods. Who knows why? As Catfish Hunter used to say, 'The sun don't shine on the same dog's ass all the time.'" Berra felt that a slump was prolonged by trying too hard to break it. He said, "I've seen guys do different things to snap out of slumps. They experiment. They change their stance. They grip the bat tighter. They think too much. They take bad advice. They often make things even worse." Berra's formula for breaking a slump was to focus the mind on positive thoughts:

> The big thing is not to change who you are. Think positive. Don't . . . press . . . More than anything, you have to have a good frame of mind to break a slump. As you see, I didn't even like to call a slump a slump. I just temporarily wasn't hitting.[53]

The worst slump I ever had occurred in 1985 during my last year with the Texas Rangers. I had been in the big leagues for thirteen years, was thirty-four years old, and until then had been a pretty consistent player. I had gone through slumps before and handled them pretty well, never getting to the point where I doubted my ability to play. The slump began in August when the team fired the manager and decided to stress youth and cut down on salary. I was told they were going to trade me. It took six weeks before they could work out a trade. During that time I went into a funk. I was a zombie. I felt like I was a player without a team. I couldn't concentrate, or do what I needed to do to prepare myself to play. My batting average dropped to something like .219.

When a trade went through to Cincinnati, my hometown, I was happy. I was finally coming home to play. But the slump deepened. I seemed unable to focus. I had been a good player, an

All-Star, and now I was a bad player. I was tight and tormented. I went to my dad and told him I was embarrassed, afraid to make an out. I was thinking of retiring because I couldn't hit anymore. My dad didn't accept my excuses. While he was compassionate, he was not kind to me. He knew what I was going through because he had been through it himself. He told me something that alleviated the fear. He said, "Since you are already trying to make an out, go out and hit the ball to the shortstop. It will help you stay down on the ball and it will keep you from over-swinging." In a crazy way it made sense to me. I instantly came out of the slump, drove in 25 runs in September, hit home runs, and batted over .300.

Baseball's very best players, even the legendary Ty Cobb, go through slumps. The scenario for Cobb often went as follows: For three or four days he would hit the ball right on the nose, but straight at some fielder. He just couldn't buy a hit. Since he would be hitting the ball squarely, but with no luck, Ty would tell himself that he shouldn't give the problem any serious thought. But with every day's failure, he saw his batting average tailing off, and he started worrying. He said:

> That's mistake number one. Now that I'm thinking about my slump, I'm also starting to think about how to overcome it. This is when my trouble begins. In my effort to overcome it, I'm changing my stance, my swing, and my stride, and this further handicaps my timing. When I first went into the slump I tried my best to keep from worrying. I killed off the desire to press by gripping the bat with my hands spread apart. This helped me to control the bat better. It also kept me from going after bad balls, which always happens when you're pressing. So my best bet for ending a slump is not to worry and go right on batting in my regular style.[54]

Cobb had a mental toughness that I believe all major leaguers must have to maintain concentration. As Cobb indicated, every at bat should be approached in the same way. It should not matter what happened before or after, or last week or last month. You have to be mentally tough to block all distractions and stay focused on one thing. I can spot players who are not mentally strong, because after going 0 for 2 in a game, they start to press. They feel a sense of urgency. When they've gone 0 for 3, they feel really strapped. Mentally tough players do not allow their minds to be overcome by worry or fear. They are able to move forward, respect their opponent, but not give them too much credit. Pete Rose was a guy who was mentally tough. It didn't matter whether he was 0 for 3. He approached each at bat the same way.

Slumps sometimes occur right after a player is traded. It happened in 1969 to Joe Torre after being sent by the Braves to the Cardinals. He succumbed to the temptation to show the Braves that they had made a good trade. He tried to do more than it was possible for him to do and paid the price by falling into a slump. He said:

> I put tremendous pressure on myself, wishing to impress everyone on the club (which included several superstars, such as Lou Brock, Curt Flood, Bob Gibson and Steve Carlton), and live up to the high hopes fostered by the trade. I had been traded for the hugely popular Orlando Cepeda. I learned from that experience that trying to wow everyone while making impossible demands on yourself is a lethal combination—it only makes you tighten up more. You don't realize that that mind-set is totally counterproductive until later, with the luxury of hindsight.[55]

Torre noted that a ballplayer must play within the range of his ability. When a player learned to "stay within himself" he would no longer try to do more than was possible. Torre said:

There's a baseball cliché that sums this up. *Stay within yourself*. Like many clichés, this one happens to be true, but it also contains deeper wisdom that you can apply beyond baseball. You've probably heard baseball commentators suggest that a batter at the plate or a pitcher on the mound must stay within himself. It means that he should not try to do more than is possible; that he knows what pitchers he can hit or throw and does not move outside his range of ability; that he remains patient, focused, and grounded in the moment.[56]

Cal Ripken, Jr., provided a graphic description of the damaging effects of trying too hard to succeed. In mid-June of the 1990 season, his batting average had dropped to .209. Mired in a dreadful slump, he felt that his career was in jeopardy. He said:

> I was as frustrated as I've ever been. I was at rock bottom, thinking I might be through. I mean, it wasn't a matter of being tired. I just wasn't myself at the plate. I had developed bad habits, trying to do too much, and the more I fought it physically, the more it became a mental problem. The more you fail, the more you search, the farther away you get, the more doubts creep in. The mental part is worse than the physical. You start to feel alone, as if you are the only one who has ever gone through it. . . . Mentally you start to question yourself . . . Is this the trend that will continue for the rest of your career?[57]

Ripken credited the Orioles manager, Frank Robinson, for giving him the support he needed. "Robinson called me into his office," said Ripken, and "addressed my mental state of mind." Robinson shared his own experience with slumps and told Ripken how he got out of a particularly deep one:

He told me about 1965, when he was 0 for 22, with nothing but lazy fly balls and easy ground balls, totally convinced that he'd never get another hit, much less two in the same game. . . . He told me about how he'd been described in Cincinnati as an "old thirty" when he'd been traded from Cincinnati to Baltimore. He told me how he'd used that remark to motivate himself with great success. (Robinson won the Triple Crown that year.)[58]

Ripken said that Robinson gave him "a new perspective on the highs and lows, not just of a season, but of a career. Slumps were an expected part of every season." Robinson helped him, said Ripken, "believe that I wasn't necessarily finished as a hitter."

Encouragement from a respected Hall of Famer helped Carl Yastrzemski get out of a slump. He recalled that after coming up to the Red Sox from the minors, he played far under his ability. "I was trying to hit a home run every time up. A base hit didn't mean anything. It tore me up inside, tore me up to the point that I almost threw my career away." The situation came to a head in Detroit when he faced two of their toughest pitchers, Frank Lary and Jim Bunning. Yaz said he "couldn't even get a loud foul. I was breaking my bats by having them sawed off by the pitchers. They'd throw inside, and I'd swing at a bad pitch. The ball would hit the trademark and—*bing*—split in half. That's how the pitcher sawed you off."

After the game he sat in the locker room with his close friend and teammate Chuck Schilling and started to cry. "I felt that everything I had ever worked for was gone. I doubted myself. I told Chuck I didn't think I could play in the big leagues." Yaz's average had dropped to .220, and he was being platooned against left-handers or benched entirely. The Red Sox brought in Ted Williams to work with him, and it made a big difference. "He didn't say anything technical about hitting, but he pumped me up mentally. 'You look good swinging,' he said. 'Think the count. Be aggressive.'" Yaz said that he went on a hitting tear, with 22 hits in 46 at bats, a .478 clip.[59]

Graig Nettles believed that the best way for teams to get out of a slump was to accept the fact that slumps happen. They are a part of baseball. He described a time during the 1983 season when the Yankees were in a slump. The team had not been coming up with the big hits when they needed them, with men on base. Manager Billy Martin had called a team meeting and told the club to "stop pressing." Nettles said that the team listened, but it was hard for this kind of message to sink in. "When you get up to the plate your own thoughts go through your mind, and you decide you don't want to leave it up to the next guy. When you press you say to yourself, 'I have to do everything myself, because no one else is doing anything. If I can get hot, then I can carry the club, and we'll win more games.'"

Unfortunately, Nettles said, "The game of baseball doesn't work that way. To win you usually need three or four guys hitting at the same time. If I get on a hot streak I could carry the club for a week or two, but my streaks come when I'm relaxed and swing easy, not when I'm going out trying to carry the club." Nettles said that players needed to accept the fact that they, as individuals, could not take on the responsibility for getting their team out of a slump.[60]

A good description of how negative thought and anxiety produce slumps was provided by Hall of Famer Duke Snider. Snider tracked the emotional roller coaster he went on during the slump he fell into during the 1949 World Series between the Dodgers and Yankees. He was still a young ballplayer, only twenty-two years old. It was his second year in the major leagues and his first World Series:

My humiliating failure against Allie Reynolds and the rest of the Yankees may well have had its start not on the playing field, but in all the hoopla before. . . . I slid, without knowing it, into my old habit of thinking too much . . . by the morning of the first game I was doing a good job of turning myself into a basket case. . . . As we got ready to leave for the ball park for the first game, the inside of my mouth felt like cotton. . . . My hands were clammy. I was short of breath, and I hadn't even left the hotel. When I walked onto the field at Yankee Stadium and gazed upward at the house that Ruth built, my blood pressure took another spurt upward. . . . When they introduced the players and we took our spot along the foul line near home plate, my knees felt like rubber. But I felt confident I would perform well. I had always had success in pressure situations. I wanted it badly—I wanted it too badly. History has recorded that the Yankees defeated us in five games, but it doesn't record the agony I went through. I had insured my own failure by putting too much pressure on myself. Reynolds tied me up completely in that first game and set me down on three strikeouts and a pop-up. . . . I was worried about myself. It was the first game, but the nerves and insecurity of not knowing how I'd do in the next game sealed my fate for the rest of the Series. It may have taken the Yankees five games to defeat the Dodgers, but it took them only one game to beat me. After the second game I was tied up in knots. Pee Wee [Reese] and Jackie [Robinson] could see I was becoming a candidate for a strait jacket but nothing they said helped me relax. By the time the series was over I wanted to pack my .143 batting average and get out of town as fast as I could. . . . I was the goat of the Series with that batting average, zero runs batted in and eight strikeouts in only five games—all this from the number three hitter in the lineup.[61]

Pitchers as well as hitters are prone to slumps. They go through periods when they can't seem to get anyone out, even though physically there is nothing wrong with them. Jim "Catfish" Hunter, normally a very relaxed and laid-back player, who brought the easygoing spirit of rural North Carolina with him to the pitching mound, found himself uptight and trying too hard after becoming a free agent and signing a large contract with the New York Yankees. He got off to a rough start, losing his first four games. He was being hounded by reporters because of his big salary and slow start, and began arriving at the club-house earlier and earlier for games to avoid the reporters. One day as he was dressing for the game he walked over to teammate Lou Piniella and said, "I'm through trying to strike out twenty guys every game."

"What do you mean, Cat?" asked Piniella.

"I've been overthrowing. I've been trying to earn that big money on one outing. I haven't been pitching like myself. I have been throwing every pitch as hard as I could."

"You have to relax," said Piniella.

"That's it," replied Hunter. "The next start I'll be my old self, even if I get my ass whipped. I'll pitch the way I've always pitched." Hunter did exactly as he said he would do. He stopped overtrying, settled down, and pitched the way he had for the Oakland A's, and finished with a 23–14 won-loss record, leading the league in wins as well as innings pitched, and an ERA of 2.58.[62]

Like Hunter, "Goose" Gossage slumped as soon as he moved from the Angels to the Yankees. He signed as a free agent with New York in 1978 after several successful years in California. He immediately blew several save opportunities. "I stunk up the joint," he said. He wanted to show that he could contribute and began to press:

> I committed the cardinal sin of trying too hard. Instead of re-
> laxing and staying within myself and allowing my natural ability
> to take over, I began to press. Instead of throwing with freedom

and fluidity—just cutting loose—I tried to force good pitches.
I overthrew, which only made matters worse.[63]

Gossage reported that the Yankee catcher Thurman Munson
used humor to get him to relax. Gossage described a game in
which he was brought in to pitch with the winning run at the
plate. Munson came to the mound and said, "Well, Goose,
you've given up home runs to lose games, and thrown wild
pitches. You've lost on base hits and you've got beaten on errors.
You've done it all. What have you got planned for us today?"[64]
On another occasion Munson came to the mound as Gossage
arrived from the bullpen, slapped the ball into Gossage's glove,
and asked, "Okay, Goose, how you going to lose this one?"

Gossage replied, "Get your ass back behind the plate and we'll
find out, won't we."[65] Munson, Gossage said, "kept me loose by
getting on my case."[66] Gossage noted that Munson and the
other Yankee veterans had a way of staying relaxed by making
light of game situations, and playing as if they were on a sandlot,
and not in front of fifty thousand fans.[67]

Tom Seaver, who pitched successfully for several years with
the Mets and Reds, believed that mental discipline was the key
to success in breaking a slump. The best way to stay positive, he
advised, was to "remember the good things . . . [and] ignore the
bad."[68] He said:

Slumps are very difficult things to try to decipher or decide
which way to go to get out of them. . . . The thing is to discipline yourself mentally, to build on what's positive and dismiss
what's negative. . . . Let's say a club is hot and has been winning.
If you can use that winning to help you keep winning, fine. But
you've got to be disciplined enough mentally where if you're in
a losing streak, and you lose today, you forget it immediately. And
when you go out there tomorrow you forget what happened to-

day. But if you win today, you go out there remembering what happened today. It sounds impossible to do, but it's not if you are well disciplined.[69]

Sandy Koufax, who dominated hitters for five years in the early 1960s, recalled that, as a rookie, he felt he needed to look good in every game, in every inning, and on every pitch, or he'd be taken out of the game. As a result he often tried too hard and began to press. It had a snowballing effect. "When you press," he said, "you're afraid to let anyone hit the ball, because if they hit the ball it can go out of the park, or at least in between a couple of fielders. The one way you can be safe is to strike everybody out." There was a problem here, however. Koufax continued, "There is one built-in limitation the rules makers placed upon the strikeout, a limitation which very frequently eludes strong-armed pitchers. You cannot strike anybody out until you have two strikes on him. You don't care about that, though. You're going to throw the third strike past him three times."[70]

Koufax said that when you start thinking this way, things fall apart. "Everything suffers," he noted, "when you press. Your control suffers, your stuff suffers, your fastball doesn't move, your coordination and timing are bad. Things then can go from bad to worse. So you walk a couple of men and now you get angry. . . . You're not doing the job. The back of your neck begins to glow, and now you're pitching out of both fear and anger."[71]

Joe DiMaggio recalled that ballplayers were often given to bizarre, outlandish remedies to cure a slump. Herb Pennock, whom he considered to be one of the greatest southpaws who ever pitched, and one of the most intelligent players the game ever produced, tried to get out of a pitching slump by letting bees sting his ailing left arm. Pennock did it, DiMaggio said, "on the theory of an amateur doctor who told him that bee venom would revitalize it. It didn't, of course, but the quack was around a few days later telling Pennock the reason the remedy wasn't effective was that he used domesticated bees; wild bees would positively do the trick." Pennock told DiMaggio, "You know, I was so desperate that I considered going out to the woods and looking for wild bees."[72]

Dealing with the Fear of Failure

Fear of failure is big in baseball. It is so easy to lapse into negative thinking, and be afraid to make a mistake or make an out. So many bad things happen if you make an out. Ballplayers must learn how to shift attention from the negative to the positive. That's what mental toughness is all about. As I said before, those who are mentally tough have disciplined their minds to the point that they do not allow negative thoughts to creep in. They block out all the fear, all the anxiety. In the face of adversity they are able to keep their minds focused on the positive.

Goose Gossage developed a particularly effective way of dealing with negative thoughts and handling fear. He said:

> When negative thoughts tried to elbow their way in, I would step off the pitching rubber and say to myself, "No, I don't have time for you right now. I am going to put all your negatives in a little black bag, rip it up and set it aside." That kind of self-dialogue helped me a great deal early in my career . . . I stress that a major component of being mentally tough is remaining focused on the task and expecting good results. Once you start thinking about how things can go wrong, they will. Why? Because you've lost your focus by allowing negative thoughts to creep in.[73]

Gossage indicated that "doing the job [of being a closer] successfully is such an exercise in positive thinking."[74]

Tim Worrell, who at age thirty-six won the job as closer in 2003 for the San Francisco Giants after a career as a middle reliever, said that it was his ability to eliminate the negative from his mind that enabled him to succeed. He said:

> At the beginning of my career . . . I was looking at things that could be bad instead of things that could be good. Out of spring training, the reason they picked me as a closer is, I could get my butt kicked one day and come back the next and forget about it. It's experience and age. It's not my stuff because the whole bullpen has better stuff.[75]

Barry Zito, the young Oakland A's pitcher who won the Cy Young Award in 2002, is aware of how damaging negative thought can be, and how many ballplayers are unwilling to recognize their impact and take action to deal with them. He said:

> A lot of people, if you try to tell them they create their reality through their thoughts, they don't want to know that; they don't want to think that what they have in their world is because of their thinking. They want to think it's because of fate or because some people were gifted and other people weren't.[76]

Joe Torre was well aware of how players' minds often focus on the negative, and how damaging that can be. "Those of us prone to negative thinking," he said, "must recognize that this mindset is our biggest obstacle to progress. . . . If we don't maintain a realistic, positive perspective our job performance will get impaired."[77] At the same time, Torre indicated that it was unwise to "rid yourself of every ounce of tension or fear." You should recognize, he said, "that you can be afraid, admit your fear and still function at a high level of effectiveness." For those who had great difficulty in handling their fears, Torre believed that psychotherapy, was a useful tool. He stated:

> If you are constantly afraid, it helps to talk about it. In recent years some of our players spent time with sports psychologist Frank Pirozzolo, who's worked with the Yankee organization. I know other baseball teams have also used psychologists. It gives players a chance to talk out their anxieties, to deal with things going on in their personal lives that might be getting in their way. Talking with a psychologist helps these players compartmentalize their worries so they can get out on the field and focus on the present. They don't get rid of their fears, but they can set them aside when it's time to perform.[78]

Hall of Famer Reggie Jackson believed that the fear factor was minimized if a player understood his limitations and did not try to do more than he was capable of doing. "You hear a lot in baseball about guys giving 110 percent, or some such nonsensical thing. I don't want guys giving me 110 percent, because that means they're trying to do things they can't do, especially when the pressure is on." Jackson preferred to be with players "who understand their limitations and capabilities, and play within them." He believed that overtrying damaged a player's ability to give his best. "In specific situations at bat or in the field," he said, "I don't want guys trying too hard. I want them doing what is necessary."[79]

Former Dodger manager Tommy Lasorda noted that during a losing streak many teams find themselves believing that more effort is required. Lasorda described the snowballing effects of a losing streak on a team. "A losing streak," he said "feeds upon itself. Each loss makes the next game that much more important, putting additional pressure on the players. They stop being aggressive because they're afraid to make a mistake, changing the way they normally play and making it even tougher to stop the losing streak."[80]

Former Cubs third baseman Ron Santo believed that the greatest impediment to a third baseman's concentration was fear of being hit by line drives from right-handed power hitters. "You need a strong chest to knock down those line drives," he observed, "and a strong head to stay in the game." Santo said that the third baseman "has to concentrate more than any other position in the field." With a fastball pitcher on the mound, third basemen are "going to get a lot of balls pulled your way. . . . If you have fear, you are going to be doomed." Santo noted that during the course of his career fear drove many potentially good young third basemen out of the position.[81]

Maury Wills believed that potential base stealers were often stopped by the fear of being picked off or thrown out. He said:

> In order to be an outstanding base stealer you have to eliminate fear of failure. It's like being a safecracker. You can't be down there on your knees turning around every second to see if somebody's looking. Confidence and self-belief are antidotes to fear. You have to have the confidence that if you get picked off in the first inning of a World Series game, you can still steal in the ninth inning when it means the game. It's like falling off a horse. You have to get right back on. It's better to get picked off first base being aggressive than to be thrown out at second for being too conservative at first. You have to study the pitcher and see what you think is the key and then you have to believe it.[82]

Wills recognized that it took a certain amount of faith and daring. A lot of players are doubtful and hesitant. As a result, he said, "they get psyched out. They get to thinking about safety first and start hugging the base."

Bob Welch described how he let fear of failure dictate his actions on the pitcher's mound in a game with the Oakland A's against the California Angels in May 1994. He walked three batters at the end of the batting order, including the pitcher, and then gave up three straight singles. After the game he described what had gone through his mind:

> I started to back myself into a corner and I couldn't get out of it. I started thinking, "I can't give up another run." And then I tried to strike everybody out. I walk one guy, and I think I can't walk the next guy. And then I do. I am throwing the ball as well as I can throw, but what keeps getting in the way is my head. . . . I tried to do things that had nothing to do with pitching. . . . I was so fired up and then I let everybody down.[83]

Welch recognized that to deal with fear and pitch successfully he had to have better control of his mind.

"The Thing" is the name that has been given to a mental rut that some ballplayers have gotten into during the course of their careers. Suddenly, for no apparent reason, they lose the ability to throw the baseball with accuracy. Infielders who have thrown to first base a million times can't hit the first baseman. Catchers can't throw the ball back to the pitcher, and pitchers are as likely to throw the ball over the catcher's head as hit the strike zone. It has happened to a lot of players. The most well known are second basemen Chuck Knoblauch and Steve Sax, and pitchers Rick Ankiel and Steve Blass. My son Mike experienced it in spring training of 2001 with the Rockies when I was the manager. He had signed as a free agent after having played in the big leagues with the Reds the year before. It happened to him after he attempted to add catching to the repertoire of positions he could play. He recalled:

> The Rockies called me at Christmas and asked me if I wanted to learn to catch. I worked on it during the winter and in the first weeks of spring training. When the hitters started taking live batting practice, I suddenly could not remember how to throw. I could not hit the pitcher. You usually just throw and not think about it. Now I focused on trying to let the ball go at the right time. I tried to battle through it, struggle through it. Nothing worked. I was a mess. It zapped me of energy, everything.

Mike described how he learned to overcome "The Thing" and deal with the underlying fear that caused it. He said:

> I began working with Rob Svetich, a Rockies coach. He had experience with players who had developed The Thing and was confident that he could help me beat it. He introduced me to a technique called self-talk and gave me pamphlets to read describing it. Self-talk and affirmations are the same thing. The idea is to stop the negative thinking that comes from fear of throwing the ball away or fear of being embarrassed. I can't do it, I can't play, I can't throw—these are the negative thoughts that must be dealt with. You start with a key word or a command such as "stop" or "quit," or "stop right now." Then you make a shift in consciousness through the use of an affirmation such as "I can play" or "I am as good as anyone out there" or "I know I can, I've done it a thousand times." You say these words with enthusiasm and conviction. You may need to yell at yourself. You do not plead, ask or live in hope. Never think or say to yourself, "I hope I get a hit, I hope I can do this."
>
> When I started using self-talk I said an affirmation maybe a

thousand times a day. By the two-hundredth time I started believing it. Self-talk—or affirmations—did it for me. It cured me of The Thing. Now I use self-talk whenever I catch myself dropping into negative thought or when I am struggling. It calms me down and helps me relax. When I use self-talk I feel like I can do anything. It is the biggest part of the game for me. I am mentally stronger because of it. Some guys have to hit more, throw more, or take more ground balls. I need to get myself mentally prepared. Self-talk does that for me. I have the physical ability. When I am mentally confident, prepared, and relaxed, I can play. Everything works.

Barry Zito also uses self-talk or affirmations as a way of preparing himself mentally to play. Zito said, "I will take a goal and I say it as it were in the past tense. . . . [I] wear the mood that [I've] already achieved the thing [I'm] trying to accomplish."[84] Inside the bill of his cap when he pitches is an affirmation which says, "Be still and know." After he pitched a 2–0 game against the Yankees in late May 2003, the *New York Times* reported: "He frequently pulled his cap, but not because he was sweating or uncomfortable. Zito was reading positive messages—reminders to trust himself, that he writes on the bottom of the bill of his cap."[85]

Zito said that affirmations were particularly helpful when he was not performing at his best. He said, "When I am really struggling, I'm doing a lot of mental work. In the four days going into my pitching start, . . . I'm listening to affirmations, and sometimes it just gets locked in." Zito's commitment to the use of affirmations is so strong that he uses them regularly in daily life. "My biggest thing," he said, "is putting up signs in my room reminding me who I am. I use affirmations that I say while I am driving or that I put on an audiotape."[86] Zito credits the writings of the twentieth century American spiritual philosopher

Ernest Holmes, who created a philosophy called "Science of Mind," with inspiring him to work with affirmations.

Disrupting an Opponent's Concentration

Ballplayers recognize that concentration is so important that during the course of a game teams try to disrupt their opponent's concentration. A pitcher may be distracted by base runners threatening to steal or by players yelling at him from the opposing dugout. Hitters may be distracted by infielders repositioning themselves prior to the pitch or by the actions of the catcher. When catching, Yogi Berra continually tried, through conversation, to get a hitter's attention and get his mind off the at bat. He confessed:

> American League hitters said I was always trying to "psych" them. . . . I know I made a lot of hitters think. Some of them were good at thinking. Al Rosen for one. He played third base for the Cleveland Indians. I used to go out to talk to Allie Reynolds, our pitcher. . . . When I would come back from talking to Allie, I would say something to the umpire, like "thanks for not coming out and listening to what we were talking about. It was private." And then I would say to Flip [Rosen's nickname], "The Chief [Allie's nickname] wants to throw you a fastball. I'm going to call for a curve. Be looking for a breaking ball." If it made him think, it made our job easier. So I did it. . . . I knew that when the hitter said, "Yogi, shut up," I was doing good.[87]

When I played against the Yankees, catcher Thurman Munson talked incessantly to me throughout the whole at bat. "What's going on? How you been?" Called me Gus's son. "Hey, Gus's son. What's going on." I finally had to turn to him and say, "Shut up, Thurman, I'm trying to hit." Which reminds me, the toughest thing for me about being Gus Bell's son was the scrutiny, the expectations, and the comparisons. There also was the envy. People thought I was born with a silver spoon in my mouth. In some ways it is a no-win situation. My three sons no doubt have to deal with the same challenges.

Getting into the Zone

Baseball becomes a lot of fun when you get into a groove, into the flow of the game where everything clicks, and the game slows down. The good players in the majors are all proficient at hitting, throwing, and catching. What separates the best players from the good players is the ability to slow the game down. Once the game speeds up, your mind has to work faster and more clearly. To slow the game down you need to be able to eliminate distractions. You need to think fast to slow the game down. As your mind slows down and your concentration deepens, you get locked in, get into the zone. You are no longer conscious of the crowd. You don't hear anything. It is like being in a sound-proof room. You are so focused that it is like being on the diamond all by yourself.

My first experience of getting into the zone came when I was twenty years old in spring training during my rookie year. The Indians went on a trip to play other teams and I was left behind in camp at Tucson because I was scheduled to begin the season in Triple-A. Three of the team's outfielders got hurt on the trip and I got a call in the middle of the night to meet the team in Yuma for a ten A.M. B squad game. Yuma was four hours away and I got there just as the game started. They put me in the outfield, though I had never played it. I went 4 for 5. I was then asked to play in the afternoon in a regular A squad exhibition game against the San Diego Padres. I again went 4 for 5. The next day they still didn't have enough players so they asked me to start. I went 3 for 4 and hit the home run that won the game. I was in the zone in all those at bats. I saw everything so clearly. All that I was focused on was seeing the ball and doing something with it. I was playing like I did when I was in the backyard at home when I was kid. I wasn't afraid of making an out. I stayed in zone for the next ten days. As a result, I made the Indians' opening day roster.

Now I said to myself, "How the hell am I going to stay here? God, for just one night give me that feeling back." I struggled a lot during my first year in the big leagues. I found myself searching for the way I saw those pitches during training camp. All through my career I searched for that feeling. I got in the zone more often as my career went on. It was the result of my experience. I was smarter. It became easier to push the distractions out of my mind.

Rick Wolff, who worked with the Cleveland Indians as a sports psychologist, noted that the phenomenon of being in the zone has been studied for some time. "What we find happens," he said, "is a performer becomes so focused on the task that the rest of the senses become oblivious to outside distractions."[88] David has provided a good description of what it is like to be in the zone:

> It is a feeling of playing in a game and being so focused that you don't hear the crowd. You see better, you hear only what you need to hear and nothing else. The game slows down so much that everything becomes clear. You can't wait to get up to the plate or out on the field. It is such a powerful state that you want to take advantage of it. Being in the zone means being fully in the present moment. When your teammates are in the zone you can see it in their eyes, hear it in the things they say; you can tell it out on the field. Every good player goes through times when he is in the zone.

Ballplayers have different experiences of getting into the zone. David's probably are not unique. He said:

> It is amazing the things that may trigger an experience in the zone. It may be one at bat, one pitch. "There it is, I found it." One little thing may trigger it. Maybe making a big out, or doing something negative. Then suddenly it clicks. You may be struggling. No matter how hard you try, you can't get a hit. Then, all of a sudden you feel one thing in your swing that you have been searching for and that's all it takes. You have a shift in consciousness that brings you into the zone, and you can't wait to get back up there the next time. The bigger the game the easier it has been for me to get in the zone. I don't know why. It could be the adrenaline or the nervous energy. I am not sure.

Mike experiences a big difference in the quality of his play when he is in the zone. He said:

> There are times when you go to the plate and know you are going to get a hit or hit a ball hard. You believe it. Your body works perfectly together. You are not tense, or straining to hit the ball. Everything just happens together, perfectly. Sometimes I go up there and I feel that there is no way this guy is going to get me out. The ball looks slower, it looks like someone is playing catch with me, it is that slow. That doesn't happen all the time. It happens when you are going good. When I feel good at the plate I can slow the ball down. The same thing happens on defense. When they hit you a ball, it is slow; it looks like someone rolled the ball to you. On the other hand, when you are struggling, you can't get the glove down fast enough.

Rick's experience of being in the zone is similar to David's and Mike's He said:

When I have been in the zone, I am locked into what I am doing at the plate. Everything feels slower. You get back to the dugout and you want to get back up to the plate again because you don't want it to end. You don't want the feeling of everything being so slow to stop. You don't want to lose that feeling because it doesn't happen that often. You don't want things to speed back up because that's when the game gets harder. I have also experienced being in the zone playing third base. At third, there are tough angles for making throws. You may have to come in on the ball and throw across your body on the run. When things slow down, all you can see is the first baseman. The feel of the ball and where you are going to release is just perfect. You don't notice the runner. You don't notice anything but the first baseman and where you are going to hit him, which is right on the chest.

David points out that you can stay in the zone for only so long. He explained:

It is hard to stay in the zone. You have a limited capacity for staying in it. It can wear you out. You are so focused and so concentrated that you run out of energy. Even though when you are in it, it doesn't feel like it is taking a lot of energy. Staying clear for a long period of time is difficult.

Rick agreed, stating that he found it physically and mentally draining to be completely comfortable at the plate and in the field for long periods of time. David said that for him, getting into the zone often came unexpectedly. It wasn't something he could program. Rick said that, although you can't consciously move yourself mentally into the zone, through mental preparation you can get yourself into a space where you are more likely to experience it. He said:

Things slow down because you put yourself in a position to slow things down. When you take ground balls before the game, you try to get a feel for it. It helps if you keep after the ball with your feet, rather than being flat-footed or on your heels. You need to be at your best to get in the zone. But the final part just happens. You do everything to give yourself a chance, but it doesn't always carry over. If there were a set of techniques, guys would be using them in every game. Getting into the zone is still somewhat of a mystery to most of us.

David played with Barry Bonds during the 2002 season, when the Giants went to the World Series. He thought that Bonds had an extraordinary capacity for getting into and staying in the zone. He said:

The better the player, the longer they can stay in it. Barry Bonds is a perfect example. When he hit 73 home runs during the 2001 season he was in it for the whole year. When I played with him in 2002 he spent most of the year in the zone. For him to do what he does, everything has to be clear to him—only swinging at strikes, not reacting to a bad pitch, and never making check swings. He is probably the best example of someone who has been in the zone for two years. And that's amazing. A lot of other things go into his success, but an important part of it is his ability to focus and concentrate.

Giants first baseman J. T. Snow, who has played with Bonds for seven years, also has seen Bonds get into the zone on a regular basis. "He can slow the game down and get into the zone every day," said Snow. "The new guys on the team, Jose Cruz, Neifi Perez, Ray Durham and Edgardo Alfonzo are amazed by how he does it."[89] First baseman Andres Galarraga, who has played with Bonds for two years during his own long and productive career, marveled at Bonds's ability to stay focused, particularly during a season in which his father, Bobby Bonds, was dying. "It's unbelievable," said Galarraga. "As soon as the game starts he concentrates at such a high level."[90] Hall of Famer Orlando Cepeda, who had several great years playing first base for the Giants and goes regularly to Giants games, also commented on Bonds's ability to concentrate. "What amazes me is how Barry has been playing, with his mind on his father," said Cepeda. "It's incredible that he's able to concentrate on a baseball game."[91]

Many players have experiences of getting into the zone. Don Baylor, who had a career season and was chosen as the league's Most Valuable Player while playing for the California Angels in 1979, described a game in April against the Oakland A's in which he was in the zone:

On April 21, everything seemed especially connected, the will, the desire, the effort, the training. Before our game against the visiting Athletics, I had been out in the batting cage next to the left field bullpen. Fans were hanging over the wall watching. . . . I felt real locked in on my swing and the fans seemed to sense that. It was one of those particularly hot California days, but still I wanted the extra work. The bat just felt too good in my hands to put down. When the game started Bob Lacey, the A's left-hander, threw me a little slider down and in. The pitch looked just like the balls I had seen in batting practice. Big and fat, as if it were sitting on a tee, begging me to hit it. Almost every pitch looked that way. I crushed a first-inning grand slam. The ball landed right on the netting covering the batting cage where all those fans had been watching me less than two hours before. I usually do not watch my home runs, but I stood there for a few seconds, mostly thinking about the hard work that day and all the days before, and how maybe it could all translate into something really big.[92]

Joe Morgan reported he was in a trancelike state in the batter's box in a game in Milwaukee in July 1965, his rookie year. A very peculiar thing happened:

> We played an extra inning game against the Braves. In my first at-bat I homered against Tony Cloninger. I homered in my second at-bat as well. When I hit the second home run, I had a weird and uneasy feeling running around the bases. . . . In these first at-bats, I was seeing the ball differently. Instinctively, I had cut out a lot of preliminary hand and head movements at the plate. Suddenly I saw the ball as I have never seen it before. It was as though the ball came at me in slow motion. I have since learned, by talking with a lot of different athletes, that that happens at particularly high levels of concentration. Magic Johnson, for example, has said that, when moving at full flight, he saw everyone else on the court moving in slow motion. Ted Williams . . . all through his career was able to slow the baseball down to the point where he could actually pick up the spin on it. That's what happened to me.[93]

As a rookie in 1982, Cardinal outfielder Willie McGee made one of the great catches in World Series history. He took a three-run homer away from Gorman Thomas of Milwaukee with a leaping, twisting catch against the left centerfield fence. McGee described how time slowed down as he ran for the ball:

> At the point of contact I was in the right position—to where I could go back and be under control. Because I was set up right and knew what I was looking for, I saw the ball good all the way. I got a good jump. I knew where the fence was at all times. I knew where I was going. I was in control all the way, and then something amazing happened. I still see it and feel it to this day

every time I think about it. The last five steps or so, it seemed like everything went into slow motion. I have no explanation other than I was under control. It couldn't have happened if I was all out. But there it was. The ball was up there real slow, my body was slowly moving toward it. It was amazing. When the ball was hit, I saw myself breaking. I knew where I had to run to—and when I jumped it was like I was somebody else watching me do this in slow motion. I was this other person who knew exactly when I had to jump, where I had to jump, and where the fence was. I saw it all happen before it actually happened. And then, after I came down with the ball, there was this total silence. I became aware of this silence only afterwards, when I was walking back to my position, and I heard somebody in the stands behind me whack a glove or something on the railing.[94]

Hall of Famer Reggie Jackson was probably in the zone during hot streaks when, as he said, "you just want the pitcher to hurry up and throw the ball." Before the sixth and deciding game of the 1978 World Series against the Los Angeles Dodgers, Jackson could feel a hot streak coming on during batting practice. "The ball looked like a volleyball to me," he remembered. "I hit maybe forty balls during my time in the cage. I must have hit twenty into the seats—upper deck, bull pen. It didn't matter. . . . The players around the batting cage were amazed and so were the writers."[95] Then during the game, on three consecutive pitches off three different pitchers, Jackson hit three home runs, winning the game and clinching the Series for the Yankees. Teammate Sparky Lyle called it "one of the greatest exhibitions of hitting in baseball history. Lyle, who felt that Jackson was egotistical and "at times hard to take," agreed that in the big games, Jackson had it all together. "He can get way up," said Lyle, "and hit the hell out of the ball. . . . I can't figure out how he does it, but he does it. . . . If Reggie could concentrate all year long like he does in the play-offs and the Series games, his records would be unbelievable."[96]

A player doesn't need to be Hall of Fame caliber to experience the zone. In June 1995, utility infielder Mike Benjamin of the San Francisco Giants, whose career average was below .200, compiled a major league record of fourteen straight hits over three games in three days. The *San Francisco Chronicle* reported that he was in "a trancelike realm."[97] Benjamin said, "I really haven't been able to explain it. All I know is it seems like you have all the time in the world to hit the ball." Sports psychologist Rick Wolff assumed correctly that Benjamin would not keep it up. "It's curious that he's done this," said Wolff, "and just as curiously, he'll stop hitting. That's not to put a hex on him, but that's been the nature of his career."[98] Benjamin was traded by the Giants the following year, presumably because of his low batting average.

Atlanta Braves catcher Javy Lopez was no doubt in the zone during a hot streak in the spring of 2003. By June he had hit 18 home runs, this after hitting only 11 during the entire 2002 season. After hitting 4 home runs during a two-day stretch he said, "I've never been in a streak like that in my life. . . . It's hard to explain the feeling at the plate. Everything I see, balls away, balls, I'm seeing everything right in the middle."[99]

Pitching for the Philadelphia Phillies over the course of a long career, Robin Roberts prided himself on his ability to block out everything around him on the field, anything that might distract him. "I don't think anyone was ever able to concentrate in a baseball game any better than I was," he recalled. "I stood out there in total isolation, just throwing that ball as well as I could. Nothing bothered me." Driving home with his wife after a game against the Dodgers in which there were thirty-five thousand people in the stands, he asked, "Was there a big crowd tonight?"

"It was jammed," she replied.

Roberts was so focused on the game that he never noticed. "Not once," he recalled, "not warming up, not pitching, had I ever looked at the crowd. Nor did I ever hear them. That's how intensely I concentrated." Roberts apparently had a unique talent for getting himself into the zone.[100]

Roberts talked about a game against the Dodgers in which he recalled only seeing the catcher's mitt. "I concentrated to the point where I didn't even see the batter. I saw only the catcher." Roberts's teammates, particularly the younger pitchers, didn't believe that it was possible for a pitcher to disregard the hitter. "They thought I was kidding," he recalled. "I couldn't convince them." He acknowledged that it was hard for anyone to believe it possible or even "to imagine that kind of concentration." Yet he believed it was essential, especially for fastball pitchers. Fast-ballers, he pointed out, "must concentrate that way because if you don't follow through all the way it takes just a little bit off your fastball."[101]

While experiences of being in the zone are not uncommon among ballplayers, no one associated with sports psychology seems to know how to guide players into this altered state of consciousness. Rick Wolff asked the question, "How do you get into the zone?" His answer is indicative of the mystery that surrounds the subject. "If I knew that," he said, "I'd be a million-aire many times."[102]

THREE

Competitive Drive

Natural Ability Is Not Enough

MANY MAJOR LEAGUE BALLPLAYERS THINK THAT THEIR natural ability alone will get them to the promised land. They fail to realize that talent gets you only so far. You will not succeed in the big leagues without strong desire, determination, willpower, intensity, a sense of urgency, and a willingness to work hard and push yourself to the limit. Tommy Lasorda was right when he said, "It's not always the strongest who wins the fight, nor the swiftest that wins the race, nor the best team who finishes first, but the one who desires victory the most."[1]

Many ballplayers have just enough competitive drive to get themselves on a major league roster. They don't have the desire or determination, however, to be really successful. Competition for me comes down to this: Who is willing to take the extra time to plan a workout? Who is willing to organize their time so that they can be better prepared? Who is willing to take batting practice until their hands bleed, if that's what it takes to figure it out? Who is willing to do what it takes to win?

David has also observed a lack of competitiveness in some very talented players. He said:

> Those who have the skill level, but don't get to the big leagues, often lack competitive drive. Guys have different personalities and some are not as competitive as others. It is weird to think of it that way, but talented, great players who make it in the major leagues and don't play at their skill level may also be lacking in competitiveness.

Cal Ripken, Sr., who had a long career both as a player and manager, also observed many players in professional baseball who had the talent but lacked the competitive drive. In his view, talent was not as important as desire. He said:

> I saw a lot of guys come through the minor leagues who were blessed with all the ability that you'd want to be blessed with, but lacked the desire to play the game. They lacked the dedication to work at the game. And they didn't make it to the big leagues.[2]

Hall of Famer Duke Snider recalled the case of Dodger first baseman Wes Parker, who, despite being a "gifted player" and "a highly intelligent man," lacked the competitive drive needed to perform at a consistently high level. Parker told Snider, "I have trouble devoting myself 100 percent to baseball. I have my investments in the stock market to think about. I like to date. I enter bridge tournaments with my father. I just can't seem to give myself completely, day in and day out, to baseball."

Snider noted that during one season Parker changed his attitude and it showed in his performance. Snider said:

> A few years later he told me he was going to give himself 100 percent to baseball. He did, too. He didn't date as much, and he

cut down on the other outside distractions, and—you guessed it—he had his best year ever. But the next season he told me, "I can't do that again." So he didn't and, he never equaled that one stellar year when he forced himself to concentrate on his profession.[3]

My success in the big leagues was in part due to a strong desire to compete. I think I may have been born with it, although my father did a lot to bring it out in me. So did my high school basketball coach, Jerry Doerger at Moeller High in Cincinnati. Doerger was a "get after it" kind of guy. He would never let us feel like we were doing enough. There was no such thing as being satisfied with our performance. He never wanted us to feel giddy, or too thrilled with our success. He just kept pushing and pushing. He made you feel like you were never inferior, that you couldn't be beaten. He kept me on edge, instilled in me a sense of urgency. If it hadn't been for him and the competitiveness that rubbed off on me, and the energy I got from it, I would not have achieved as much as I did in baseball.

My father my taught me to recognize the difference between physical pain and an injury that required rest and recuperation. I was a better competitor thereafter. I was in high school at the time and got what I thought was a hip pointer playing basketball. The pain stayed with me into the baseball season and affected my performance. I had given in to it. My dad wanted to know what was wrong with me. I told him that it hurt. He asked if I knew the difference between pain and injury. He said, "I don't want to hear that you are hurt if you can play. If you are really injured and can't play that's fine." He told me that if I would forget about the pain I would heal quicker. I trusted him and put it out of my mind. I wanted to let him know that I could compete. The pain went away and I began playing up to my ability.

Though I retired as an active player in 1989, I still enjoy competition. When I play golf, I've got to be playing for something. If I play by myself, it is not nearly as rewarding as when I play with somebody who is my equal. I play much better because of the competition. If we are playing for money, I play even better. While golf satisfies my desire to compete now, competition was much more fun when I was playing on a major league team. If I win at golf, I ride home alone and have no one to celebrate with. In the locker room after a great baseball game there are a lot of people celebrating. When you play on a team you have people to lean on, to push you, to appreciate you. I think it helps make you more competitive.

David is very quiet, but extremely competitive and about as mentally tough as they come. He describes his competitiveness this way:

> I have always been competitive and have had a strong desire to succeed and do the best I can. That came pretty easy for me. It is something inside you. You can't always see it. Something deep down inside tells you that you are going to do whatever it takes. You are going to work at it. There is a determination, a love of the game, a passion for it. You know that nothing is going to stop you.

David is right when he indicates that in a team sport like baseball you are responsible for helping your teammates compete. He said:

> A team sport is more challenging than an individual sport because you not only have to make yourself better, but you need to help your teammates improve as well. You must do it if you want your team to win. I feel like I am a better competitor now than early in my career because I have tasted winning, and I now

know what it takes. I think I am more competitive because I am smarter about it now, and do more things to help my team on the field.

Ballplayers Whose Success Is Based on Their Competitive Drive

I played with guys who were great competitors, who succeeded more on competitiveness than on natural athletic talent. Jim Sundberg who caught for the Texas Rangers, was one of them. He caught every day in the heat of Arlington, and on the same day after he had an operation for hemorrhoids. Ronnie Oester, a second baseman for the Rangers, is another. He laid it all on the line, gave up his body, dove for every ball. If you ever got in a fight with him, you would have to kill him because he wouldn't stop. He wasn't the most talented guy, but because he was so competitive, he got the most out of his ability.

Pete Rose is an example of someone whose competitive drive was so strong that he succeeded with far less natural talent than most players. He was probably one of the greatest competitors of all time. When the game started he was as determined as anyone I have ever been around. The game itself was so important to him. He never let up. Nothing distracted him. He had one thing on his mind—to get a hit off the pitcher. He never gave in to the pitcher, and he was never, ever intimidated by anybody. Nobody could get into his head. He was so on top of things. Even at the end of his career, when the competitive drive begins to fade in most players, Pete still had the energy, the fire, and the determination. His level of desire was so strong. Those who were around Pete saw the same things I did.

Joe Morgan, who played with Rose for several years in Cincinnati, never saw him let up: "Every game was the seventh game of the World Series. He had this unbelievable capacity to literally roar through 162 games as if they were one single game. . . . Full speed ahead, helmet off, hair flying. . . . He gave his heart and soul to the game; he epitomized its fierce competitiveness, its joy, its beauty."[4] Dodger first baseman Steve Garvey, who played against Rose in the National League for several years, said that it was Rose's willpower that made the difference. "Rose succeeded out of pure determination," said Garvey, "and getting every ounce of ability from his body every time out."[5] Tom Seaver, who pitched for Cincinnati in the last years of Rose's career, considered Rose to be in a class by himself. "There was no one else like him in the years I played." Though over the course of his career Rose got more base hits than any player in the history of baseball, Seaver saw Rose as "a guy who couldn't run, couldn't throw, had no real postion, had no power." Yet his contribution was enormous. "You couldn't win without him," said Seaver.[6]

Seaver considered Rose to be "a throwback, a fellow who could have played on the same field with Wee Willie Keeler and John McGraw, with Ty Cobb and Honus Wagner. He gave fans a chance to imagine what the game was like in baseball's dead-ball era, and he gave kids with average ability the message that with hustle and hard work, you could make it in the modern era."[7]

Sparky Anderson, who was Rose's manager in Cincinnati, saw the same thing that we players saw. "The best way and the only way to explain Rose," said Anderson, "is he's the one greatest competitor I have ever seen. I have never seen one in baseball like him. He's the only player I have ever seen with total tunnel vision. Every single day he would drive. He was obsessed with it. That's the best way to describe him—an obsession with competing."[8] It made up for what he lacked in natural athletic talent. Anderson said that "the man didn't really have any tools at all. He wasn't a fast runner. He wasn't a good thrower. He wasn't a great fielder. He didn't have that much power. Yet he could beat you in more ways than any other player I ever played with or managed."[9]

It was Rose's competitiveness that separated him from other players and made him truly great. Anderson said:

> I saw a man compete like no one ever imagined a human being could compete. He takes no quarter and gives no quarter. In fact, if he had one of those steamrollers used to pave roads, he'd run right over you and not worry about it. He expects the same from you. That's the way he plays the game of baseball.[10]

Anderson had great admiration for Rose because he did so much with so little talent:

> I admire him more than anyone I've ever been around because he never should have attained the greatness he did. He attained it through sheer determination. It's a tremendous tribute to say that he really did not have that much talent.[11]

The baseball literature is full of stories of guys like Sundberg, Oester, and Rose who got there because they were fiery competitors. Billy Martin was one of these. He exhibited a doggedness and absolute determination to win that characterized his performance as a Yankee second baseman and as a manager for several ball clubs, including the Yankees. In 1953 the Yankees won their fifth straight pennant and World Series under manager Casey Stengel. As he had in the 1952 Series, Martin played an important role, getting key hits in critical situations. Stengel acknowledged Martin's contribution, stating, "A lot of the reason [for the Yankee victory] was the fresh kid at second base. He really learned how to play, and he kept that fire under 'em all year."[12] Cleveland Indians general manager Frank Lane paid Martin the ultimate compliment that could be given to an opposing player when he said, "Martin is the kind of guy you'd like to kill if he's playing for the other team, but you'd like ten of him on your side. The little bastard."[13]

Ty Cobb saw in Martin a lot of the feistiness that had been responsible for his own success in major league baseball. "If I were managing a ball club," he told a San Francisco sports columnist after learning that Yankee top brass were unhappy with Martin's off-the-field behavior, "I'd certainly do everything within my power to keep from losing a player like Martin. He's a winner. I think of him as a throwback to the old days when players were supposed to fight for every advantage. Sure there are better hitters, better fielders, but for fight, spirit, and whatever it takes to win a game, Martin is something special."[14] Martin moved into the managerial ranks soon after his playing career was over, and brought with him the same intensity and competitiveness that he had shown as a player. The Minnesota Twins were one of the first of several teams he managed. Pitcher Jim Kaat remembered him as having "a fiery personality. . . . He ran a fiery club. We were always in the games."[15]

In his first stint as Yankee manager Martin drew praise from almost all his players. Lou Piniella, who played outfield for Martin, thought he was "as lively a bench manager as there was in the game." He had "a certain flair, a certain hype. He exuded confidence, and the players on his ball clubs exuded confidence about him. You could tell there was something different about him."[16] Relief pitcher Sparky Lyle, who played for Martin as a Yankee from 1974 to 1976, saw all the competitive qualities needed for success as a manager. "Billy had that fieriness," said Lyle, "he had that competitiveness that oozed all over him."[17] Lyle indicated that before Martin took over the helm in 1976 the Yankee team did not have "the drive" to make it a winner. "I think if Billy hadn't come the team would not have been capable of doing things we now can do. Before he came we knew we were good, but it was Billy who taught us how to come from behind and win." The team came to believe they were winners, and could play "hard-ass ball. We have a scrappiness, and its from him that we got it."[18]

One of the game's all-time fierce competitors was second baseman Eddie Stanky, who played on championship teams with both the Dodgers and Giants in the 1940s and 1950s. Stanky was a force to be reckoned with, not because of his athletic talents, but because of his uncanny ablity to make key plays that provided the margin of victory. His Dodger manager, Leo Durocher, loved him because he always gave 100 percent. He was, said Durocher, "one of the scratchy, diving, hungry ball players who come to kill you." Dodger general manager Branch Rickey made a comment on Stanky's competitiveness that has become a part of baseball lore. Said Rickey: "He can't hit, he can't throw, he can't run, and he can't field. All he can do is win games."[19]

Ballplayers with Both the Talent and Desire

All of the players who have achieved greatness in baseball, all of the Hall of Famers, have had both natural talent *and* strong competitive drive. Teammates as well as those who played against them have testified to the way they competed.

Joe DiMaggio was certainly one of the game's great talents as a hitter and fielder. He was also a strong competitor. Even though he gave the appearance at the plate and in the field of a man who had ice water flowing through his veins, the competitive fires burned brightly in him. "When I was playing ball," he said, "there would be sixty thousand people in Yankee stadium and I would burn inside because I wanted to hit the ball so badly. I wanted to be the greatest I could be. I burned in my belly to be the best there was."[20] Charlie Keller, who played beside him in left field for several years, said, "There was one thing about Joe that nobody ever came close to. That was the kind of competitor he was, how he took responsibility for winning or losing, how he got the big hits in the big spots."[21]

Hank Aaron's competitive drive often enabled him to play when other less determined players would not even have dressed for the game. San Francisco Giants manager Dusty Baker, then a young teammate of Aaron's, said that the thing he always remembered about Aaron "was his ability to play with pain." Baker saw Aaron, on many occasions, limp into the clubhouse before a game and "barely make it to his locker. Then he'd sit down with his newspaper and not even look up as everybody else came in and got dressed."[22]

Baker believed that mentally Aaron was in the process of handling his injuries. "I believe he was thinking away the pain," said Baker. "He'd sit there for the longest time, and his eyes wouldn't even move. Then it would be time for the game to start, and he'd get up like there was not a thing wrong with him. He'd pound the ball and run the bases like a kid. Then, when the game was over, he'd come limping back into the clubhouse like he was on his last legs."

Baker said that Aaron strongly believed that a player had a duty to be out on the field. "He preached to guys like me," said Baker. "He'd say, 'Now you got to play a hundred and fifty games a year, so pick your spots. You can miss two games a month. Just two a month. So pick the days you're gonna be hurt, or you're gonna rest, or you're gonna have a drink or two. The rest of the time, be out on the field.' "[23]

Aaron's friend and teammate, Ralph Garr also had great respect for Aaron's recuperative powers and his ability to play with pain. Garr recalled an instance during the National League playoffs against the New York Mets when Aaron came into the clubhouse with a severely cut hand and it appeared that there was no way he could play. The night before, he had come home late after an evening of drinking with his ballplayer friends at Niekro's bar in Atlanta. He didn't have his key so he got into the house by sticking his fist through a window. It had taken several stitches to close the wound. Garr reported what happened in the clubhouse. "When I saw him come in with that hand all cut up, I was scared to death. I thought, Oh no, Hank's messed up and now he's not gonna be able to play in the play-offs. I asked him about it and he said, 'What you gonna do, Ralph?' I said, 'Man, it's impossible to play ball like that.' He said, 'Don't worry, Ralph. It'll work out all right.' I didn't believe it, though. Then he calls in the team doctor, goes into the back room and takes a couple shots of novocaine in his hand, puts on a black glove and goes out and hits .357 against Seaver, Koosman, and Gentry. From that day on I said no man alive could ever compare with Hank Aaron. That was the thing that made me realize that he wasn't like the rest of us."[24]

Hall of Famer Frank Robinson was probably the most intense, competitive guy I have ever been around. He played with a chip on his shoulder. He didn't like anybody and nobody liked him. He played in spite of injuries that would have kept a less determined player on the bench. As a minor leaguer he knocked himself out twice crashing into fences going after fly balls, but both times he stayed in the game. On another occasion he was hospitalized overnight after being knocked out by a fastball that cracked over his left eye. "I was back in the batter's box two days later," Robinson recalled. "I had to show everyone how much I wanted to play this game. . . . This black man was a battler and a winner, and he was going to the big leagues."[25]

After becoming a major leaguer he continued to recover quickly from injuries. He once received a cut on his arm that took thirty stitches to close. "We were playing the Mets," Robinson recalled, "and I was on first. The ball was hit to the shortstop, who threw to the second baseman, Ron Hunt. He caught the ball at the base, pivoted and went into the air. When he came down, his spikes punctured my left bicep. Doctors said I wouldn't play for a month, but I was back in ten days."

Robinson had gained a reputation as a hard base runner, showing no hesitation about slamming into opposition infielders. "The baseline," he said, "belongs to the runner, and whenever I was running the bases I always slid hard. If the second baseman or shortstop was in the way coming across the base trying to turn a double play, I hit him hard. . . . I wanted infielders to have that instant's hesitation about coming across the bag at second."[26] He wanted infielders to know that Frank Robinson was throwing 195 pounds of "I don't give a damn about my body" at them. Robinson explained his attitude: "There are only 27 outs in a ball game, and it was my job to save one for my team every time I possibly could. I had learned to play the game that way under George Powles back in Oakland, and I believed everyone should play the way I did—which was simply to win any way you could within the rules." Robinson got into a fight with Braves third baseman Eddie Mathews during the first game of a doubleheader after a particularly hard slide into third. Mathews smacked him in the nose, drawing blood, and when Robinson fought back, Mathews hit him again on the mouth. Mathews was thrown out of the game, and Robinson went into the clubhouse. He saw that his right eye was beginning to swell closed, his nose was still bleeding, his lower lip was cut, and his thumb was jammed.[27]

The Reds manager, Freddie Hutchinson, didn't expect Robinson to play any more that day, even though there was the second game of the doubleheader still to be played. Robinson told Hutchinson, "I can play and I'm gonna play." He recalled, "I had to play. I couldn't let a little beating keep me out of the lineup." So despite his injuries he was in the lineup. Here's how he did it. "I had a pocket full of gauze swatches," he said, "and a couple of times while at bat, I had to call time and stuff one up my nose to stop the bleeding. The fact that the vision in my right eye was so blurry worried me most, but that proved to be no problem. I had a walk, was hit by a pitch, hit a single, a double, and a two-run home run. I also made a good catch on a drive that cleared the box seat railing down the left field line. I leaped and caught the ball, and held it as I flipped backward into the seats." The batter had been Eddie Mathews. "Thank you very much," said Robinson.[28] The Braves won the game 4–0.

On the mound Bob Gibson of the St. Louis Cardinals was probably as fearsome as any pitcher in the game. Hank Aaron considered Gibson, a Hall of Famer, to be "probably the best black pitcher in major league history."[29] His single season earned run average of 1.12, established in 1968, has not been matched and probably never will be.[30] Lonnie Wheeler, a sports writer who coauthored a book with him, stated that in the pitching fraternity he was the alpha and omega of competitors. Wheeler said:

> If Gibson's speed was memorable—and it was—his fierceness was legendary. . . . That impression was created by the chilling expressions cloaking his face when he turned for the sign; by the rear ends he reddened when batters failed to show proper respect for his inalienable right to a part of the plate . . . and by the will to win that came through palpably in every grunt and grimace.[31]

Here is how Tim McCarver, the Cardinal catcher, described Gibson's competitiveness.

> I never saw anyone as compelled to win as Bob Gibson was. Gibson hated to lose, and because of that, he hated the competition. Hated them. I was driven to win, but not like Bob Gibson,

not with his intensity. His desire to win and succeed influenced me and all of our teammates. We revered him as a teammate. The guys on the club understood his competitive drive—to the extent that we could, anyway—and created a tension for all of us. At the same time, he loosened us up, too, because when he wasn't pitching, he was one of the funniest men on the team. But it was his competitiveness that set him apart. Clearly that was what made him reside on the next level of athletes.[32]

Richie Ashburn, a fellow Nebraskan who hit for a high average playing outfield for the Philadelphia Phillies, undoubtedly spoke for other batters who faced Gibson during his long career. Ashburn said:

> Gibson and I share the same loyalties to the State of Nebraska, and we had nothing against each other, but when the game started I always had the feeling I was standing there as the Grand Dragon of the Ku Klux Klan. He was the toughest pitcher for me. Like Koufax and Marichal, Gibson dominated, but he did it longer and did it with a vengeance that savaged the hitters. His pitches were devastating. His fastball was the equal of Maloney's and Ryan's and his slider had no equal. And more's the pity, Gibson was mean on the mound. He had a menacing, glowering intensity that more than occasionally deepened into a sneer. His intimidating demeanor, his lack of concern for the welfare of the hitter, combined with his almost unhittable pitches, put Gibson in a class by himself.[33]

Joe Torre, who was Gibson's catcher during his days as a player in St. Louis, remembered how Gibson was determined never to allow a batter to get the upper hand. Torre reported an incident concerning Dodger first baseman Ron Fairly, who got more than his share of hits off Gibson:

Ron Fairly hit Gibby about as well as anybody did. He didn't hit him hard, but seemed to be able to drop in a lot of base hits against him. One night Fairly came up and banged base hits against Gibby in his first two times at bat. Then Gibby got a single, and as he's standing on first base, Fairly saunters over and says, "God man, Hoot, you've got such good stuff I don't see how anybody can hit you." Gibson didn't even look at him. He just said, "You asshole." I'm catching, and the next time Fairly comes up he glances back at me and says, "I'm not going to like this at bat am I?" He took one in the ass at that time.[34]

Gibson himself acknowledged that he intimidated batters. He said:

I don't deny that I played with a chip on my shoulder, operating on the assumption that there was a pointed edge to anything anybody on the other team had to say to me. Everything I did on the field was calculated to gain the upper hand, and I always figured that the other guy had the same agenda. Nobody got the benefit of the doubt from me in the heat of a ballgame.[35]

Hall of Fame pitcher Bob Feller believed that it was his competitive drive that differentiated him from other ballplayers, and enabled him to play when he was experiencing significant bodily pain. "People have played baseball with more ability and success than I had," said Feller, "but nobody has ever played it with more competitive zeal. I had that fire in the belly every time I went out there, and when it was a crucial game, that fire burned even hotter."[36] Feller described an incident in his career that demonstrated his tenacity and strength of will. In 1951 he had a freak accident in a whirlpool bath in the Cleveland Indians clubhouse. He picked up a hose to fill a tub of water when the nozzle came loose and doused him with hot water. He was scalded, he said, from his chest to his knees. He was so badly burned that the trainers didn't expect him to play for weeks. "The next day," said Feller, "I showed up at the ballpark, put on my uniform and was ready for another game."[37] The coaching staff was apparently appalled at Feller's rashness and did everything but order Feller to go back home.

Feller was determined to play. "The team was off to a winning start and I was doing my share. This was no time to give in to something like scalded skin unless you're incapacitated, and I wasn't. Maybe it hurt like the devil, but so do a lot of other things. I wanted to pitch, so I was at the ball park. It was that simple." Feller missed one pitching turn and then beat the White Sox on an eight-hitter. After the game Feller said that the trainer got half sick pulling the cotton wrapping off his raw flesh, and he noticed that "not a whole lot of my teammates felt like watching the fun."[38]

Desire, willpower, and a highly competitive spirit enabled Cincinnati Reds second baseman Joe Morgan to play in an important game against the Mets despite a high fever. Morgan arrived at the ballpark one day running a temperature of 104 degrees. The trainer took one look at him and went to the manager, Sparky Anderson, and told him that Morgan was in no condition to play. Anderson called Morgan into his office and told him that he was scratching him from the lineup. Morgan raised no objection, but when he arrived back at his locker he saw a sleeping bag rolled out, a pillow, two aspirin, and a glass of water. There was a note from a teammate buddy that said, "Take two of these and get over Koosmanitis."[39] (Jerry Koosman, the excellent New York Mets pitcher, was scheduled to be on the mound against the Reds that day.)

Morgan knew his teammates wanted him to play. It was an important game against a team that was in the pennant race with them. Morgan went back into the manager's office and demanded to be put back in the lineup. "It wasn't just a demand," recalled Morgan. "I was just crazy." Anderson at first refused, but when Morgan remained adamant, he relented. Morgan played and played well. He got two important hits that helped win the game. As far as the high temperature was concerned, his desire to play and his competitiveness made him forget he was sick. "A temperature of 104?" he smirked. "I'll get over it tomorrow."[40]

The winner of four Cy Young awards, pitcher Steve Carlton had all the physical tools of a good pitcher—an unhittable slider, a great fastball, and pinpoint control. Joe Morgan observed, however, that the most impressive thing about Carlton was his mental toughness. "He was pure warrior," said Morgan. "He never gave in." Morgan believed that Carlton's inner strength and competitiveness were in part due to his long-time participation in a martial arts training program. It fostered the warrior spirit that Carlton brought to the pitching mound.[41]

The will to win was one of the qualities that made pitcher Larry Dierker of the Houston Astros one of the best pitchers in the American League in the 1970s. Jim Bouton commented on a game Dierker pitched that showed his ability to handle adversity. He had pitched a no-hitter going into the ninth inning, but the Astros hadn't scored, and so the game went into extra innings. He remained in the game into the thirteenth, when he was pulled for a pinch hitter. Houston scored two runs and it looked like Dierker would at least get a victory for his efforts. However, weak relief pitching in the bottom of the thirteenth cost Houston the game. Jim Bouton saw the game as a "tremendous performance by Dierker. Every inning he got up he knew he not only had to get them out in the bottom of the inning, he had to get them out in the next inning too. It's like climbing a mountain. Struggling to the top, then realizing there are two more peaks to climb." After pitching a game like that, Bouton said, "and getting zero for it," Dierker didn't bitch or complain or berate anyone. "He just sat in the locker room and listened to the game go down the drain, and never so much as flinched." Bouton said that Dierker was much admired by his coaches for his mental toughness and determination. His former manager on the Houston Astros, Paul Richards, once remarked with approval, "He's a cold-blooded, fish-eyed son of a bitch."[42]

For many years relief pitcher Goose Gossage possessed all the requisite qualities of a great closer. He had, recalled manager Lou Piniella, "the heart of a lion. He loved pressure. He wanted the ball in the big spot. He could intimidate a hitter just with a stare, then throw the ball in at incredible speeds. He'd come into a game in a tight spot, take the ball from the manager without conversation, start warming up, and knew he was telling the other team, 'There's no way, no way at all, you can beat me.' Few did." Piniella, who played left field for the Yankees in the years Gossage pitched for the team, had vivid memories of "Goose snarling as he walked out of the bullpen past me in left field to get at those hitters."[43]

Gossage acknowledged that he was "off the charts in intensity," constantly trying to intimidate hitters. About his approach to pitching he said:

> I had developed a controlled rage on the mound. I'd work myself into a lather entering the game. Just to get my game face on I'd cuss out Danny Colletti, the Yankee Stadium attendant who drove me in from the bullpen. If I didn't feel mad enough warming up, I'd call out the catcher and verbally abuse him. Ron Guidry still laughs at the memory of the time I came in from the bullpen and Graig Nettles walked over from third base to remind me of the game situation—runners on base, the num-

ber of outs, and my responsibilities on a sacrifice bunt. I got into Graig's face and shouted, "I don't tell you how to do your fucking job! Don't try to tell me how to do mine!" Nettles, keep in mind, was one of my closest pals. Guidry's recollection shows the over-the-top intensity I had on the mound.[44]

Jackie Robinson was one of the most competitive athletes who ever played the game. His teammates, as well as those who played against him, have testified to his competitiveness. Their comments indicate that he was in a class by himself. He set the standard for what it means to compete successfully under pressure:

Ralph Branca: "Jack was the best competitor I ever saw on a ball field. He could intimidate the opposition and never felt we were out of any ball game. It seemed at times he could almost will things to happen."[45]

Roger Craig: "He played the game with reckless abandon. If he got on first, you knew he would make second; if he got on second, you knew he would make third. . . . When I think of Jackie now I think of him as a great player and a great man, but also as somebody who was so competitive, so intense. Jackie was like a great fighter getting ready for the heavyweight championship of the world before every game.[46]

Don Newcombe: "It was a thrill playing on the same team as Jackie Robinson. He was such a tremendous competitor. I had a tendency to let down a little some days, to lose my concentration. Jack would come to the mound and get all over me. He would call me every name you could think of. I would get pretty angry at him, and I would take it out on the hitters. . . . [Jackie Robinson] was like an alley fighter, he wanted to win so bad. He wanted to win at everything: baseball, cards, shooting pool, everything."[47]

Duke Snider: "Jackie Robinson was the keenest competitor I

ever saw in baseball. I remember one game we were playing against the Cubs in Chicago. Sam Jones was pitching and he was throwing hard, and we weren't hitting him. Jackie came up, and he threw a close pitch, and Jackie started jawing at him, calling him gutless and screaming he would beat him by himself. Jones got real hot and he hit Jackie with the next pitch. Jackie just got up laughing and jogged to first base. That's all Jackie needed to turn a game around again. 'I'm gonna steal, I'm gonna steal,' he's yelling at him. Sure enough he steals second. 'I'm gonna steal third, I'm gonna steal third.' Then, in a flash, he has third stolen. By now you can fry an egg on old Sam's face, he's so mad. 'I'm gonna steal home, I'll steal home,' and he makes one of those breaks, and Jones bounces the ball in the dirt. Jackie scores and we win the game by a run. Jackie's as fiery a competitor as I ever saw. He fought for everything he got. . . . He was such a great competitor, such a hard-nosed player. Jackie Robinson taught me mental toughness. I don't think you can play this game, take the pressures, unless you are mentally tough. If I had that, I owe it to Jackie Robinson. Nobody was tougher."[48]

Leo Durocher: "If I go to war I want Jackie Robinson by my side. What a competitor. What a fighter. Sure we had our feuds, because he wanted to win and I wanted to win. It was never racial. That garbage didn't mean anything to me. I had no trouble with him in Brooklyn when we wore the same uniform. I had a lot of trouble with him when I went over to the Giants and we wore different uniforms. A lot of things have been written about me and Jackie through the years and not all of them are true. They said I threw at him, and I had Alvin Dark go after him on a slide. That was part of the game, just trying to win. How about Jackie knocked my little second baseman, Davey Willams, out of a baseball game with a body block. That was part of the game, too. Jackie Robinson was tough and hard-nosed and a complete player, and I admired the hell out of him."[49]

Buddy Kerr (Giants shortstop): "In the early days we used to knock him down a lot, not because he was black, but because he was new. Who didn't go down in those days. Then after a while, Ott [the Giants manager] told us to forget it. 'I think it is the worst thing we can do,' remarked Ott. 'The guy is fearless.' It was a little different after Leo took over. Jackie went down again, but I never thought it was very smart. The guy was just a tough hitter, and he simply couldn't be intimidated."[50]

Richie Ashburn (Phillies outfielder): "He was an absolutely fearless player at the plate and on the bases. There was no way to intimidate him. You just hoped that if the pitcher knocked him on his ass, he wouldn't hit a line drive at him next time."[51]

Harry Walker (Cardinals outfielder): "Jackie was always fired up in a game. It was great to play against him because he made you play your best. What was interesting from the standpoint of drawing fans was that Jackie drew fans from all over the league in those days, but the other colored players didn't. Even when Willie Mays came into the league in 1951, he never drew fans the way Jackie did. Willie wasn't as hungry as Jackie was. He didn't play with that same fire, day in and day out."[52]

Robin Roberts (Phillies pitcher): "He was among the greatest ballplayers and competitors I ever played against. . . . Sometimes he looked a little stiff and awkward out there—he was not a graceful performer—but what a base runner, what reflexes, and what a competitor! And he was tough. Nothing describes him better than just plain tough. . . . He was fun to play against because he made the game so exciting. His base running was incredible. One time I picked him off first, and he thought he was safe. He got into a big argument with the umpire about the call. The next time up he got a base hit, got to third on another hit, and then stole home. That made up for the bad call for him."[53]

Joe Garagiola (Cardinals catcher): "Jackie had an inner conceit as a player. He drove pitchers and catchers crazy. He would actually yell at the pitchers, 'I'm going, I'm going. Do anything you want, pal, you can't stop me,' Then he would go and steal the base. When he got on, it was like the Jackie Robinson hour, he would so dominate the play while he was on. Everybody would be caught up in his antics—the pitcher, the catcher, all the fielders, the bench, everybody in the ballpark. He was the most intimidating player on the bases I ever saw."[54]

Don Zimmer: "Jackie had an inner fire about him like nobody else, but how he was able to contain it while being subjected to all that racial abuse when he first came up I'll never know. In later years, once he was established, he was able to retaliate—in the best way he knew how, with his God-given abilities. One of the best examples of that was a game we played against the Giants. Sal Maglie, who hated us and showed it on many occasions when he'd knock us down with pitches, was pitching for the Giants. Maglie's favorite targets were Furillo, Campy, and Jackie. On this particular day, his first pitch to Jackie was a high inside fastball that just missed Jackie's head. What happened next was something I never saw before or after. Jackie stood there at the plate and started screaming at Maglie: "You dago bastard! You couldn't hurt me if you hit me! If you throw at me again I'm gonna bunt down the first base line and knock the shit out of you!" Sure enough, Jackie bunted Maglie's next pitch down the first base line and beat it out easily because Maglie never left the mound."[55]

Robinson's performance in the critical final game of the 1951 season, when the Dodgers needed a win to gain a tie with the Giants in the pennant race and force a play-off, is indicative of the true competitive spirit of this great ballplayer. It was in a game in Philadelphia against the Phillies, and it turned out to be a see-saw battle. Tied 8–8 at the end of nine innings, the game went into extra innings. In the top of the thirteenth Philadelphia outfielder Eddie Waitkus, a left-handed pull hitter, came to bat with two outs and the bases loaded. Robinson, playing second base, was playing deep. Waitkus rifled a line drive to Robinson's right that looked like a sure base hit. Robinson ran and dove full out. According to Maury Allen, Robinson's biographer, "He caught the ball stretched out, fell to the ground hard, and caught his right elbow in the pit of his stomach. He was woozy for several minutes and finally walked off the field with help from shortstop Pee Wee Reese and the Dodger trainer."[56]

Robinson was still wobbly as he sat in the dugout, decided he couldn't play any longer, and got up to leave for the clubhouse. Reese stopped him and said, "We need you."

Robinson said, "I don't think I can help the team."

Reese, who had been through many tough games with Robinson, knew better. "If you can't," said Reese, "I don't know who can." Robinson returned to the bench and then struggled to get out to second base for the bottom of the thirteenth inning. In the top of the fourteenth Robinson came to bat with the score still tied, to face the Phillies' ace pitcher Robin Roberts, who was pitching in relief on this final day of the season.

Roberts remembered the situation. "The one thing I didn't want to do was give him a ball he could pull." He proceeded to pitch him on the outside corner. On a high outside fastball, a pitch that could have been lined to right field for a single, Robinson, according to Allen, "snapped that quick bat, caught the pitch in full flight and drove it over the left-field wall for the game-winning home run."[57] Deliriously happy, his Dodger teammates hoisted him onto their shoulders. Robinson's wife, Rachel, remembered that Robinson also treasured those moments. "What happened that day," Rachel recalled, "always ranked as one of Jack's biggest thrills in baseball."[58]

Years later Robin Roberts commented on Robinson's heroics that day. "He won that great game off me in the fourteenth inning in 1951 after knocking himself out catching that line drive. I think that was the best example of the competitor he was. Not too many guys would have survived that shot he gave himself in the stomach." The Reverend Jesse Jackson also remembers that game. "He was knocked out," recalled Jackson, "and then he came back to hit the game-winning home run. It was such a marvelous performance under pressure, so much a part of the legacy of Jackie Robinson."[59]

Veteran Ballplayers Who Lose Their Competitive Drive

The competitive spirit diminishes as ballplayers age. Careers in baseball do not last forever. At some point it becomes harder to prepare. You can't do what you did physically five years ago. You've been doing it on brains for a long time. Now preparing takes up the majority of your day. Your body is working differently. Baseball becomes more a job than a sport. You get injured and don't recover as quickly. You begin going down and you can't perform at the level you once could. You find that you can't run with the kids anymore. You don't have the energy you once had. Your brain starts to go sour because of the time it takes to prepare. You get discouraged. The game ultimately beats you down, so you decide to go do something else. It's sad, but it's real, too. That's what happened to me after twenty seasons as a professional ballplayer, eighteen of which were in the major leagues.

Hank Aaron recalled that at age forty-two, after breaking Babe Ruth's career home run record, he began losing interest in the game. "I wasn't hitting the ball well. Instead, I was finding that a ballplayer ages fast when he loses his motivation. I was sluggish and inconsistent. I had become a player without a purpose," said Aaron. "For all my adult life, I had been programmed to play baseball and to strive for the next goal. Every year—every day—I had been reaching for something. When I broke Ruth's record, it was like I came unprogrammed. Nothing computed any more. I didn't know where I was going or what I had to do."[60] Aaron did the appropriate thing. He retired from the game.

Sadaharu Oh brought his twenty-two-year career in Japanese baseball to an end when he could no longer kindle the competitive fire. He said that he lost his "fighting spirit." There was nothing left. "I had lost all desire for combat. In my earlier days when I had done badly I came back to the bench in a fury. I was already afire with desire for my next chance." Inexplicably, this all changed when Oh reached the age of forty. He was perplexed and embarrassed. "I did not want to admit," he said, "that my spirit, which had served me so long, had seemingly faded." He tried various approaches. He worked with his lifelong mentor and batting instructor, Hiroshi Arakawa. He then went to his *sensei* (an aikido master) and asked for help. "With all the yearning of my heart I begged him to once more teach me." Nothing worked. Oh finally admitted to himself that it was no use. "I have no anger any more," he reluctantly concluded, "the fire was gone."[61] He hung up his cleats and retired from baseball.

Carl Yastrzemski quit the game when he was no longer willing to play for a losing team. It was midseason 1983. He was forty-three years old and in his twenty-third year with the Boston Red Sox. He had done well during the first half of the season, hitting over .300 at the All-Star break in early July. At the beginning of the season's second half, the Red Sox took a nosedive, lost several games, and dropped out of the pennant race. Yaz became discouraged. He said:

> My intensity left me. I realized that being in a pennant race
> had kept me hitting .300 and drove me. But now, as we continued

to sink, my attention span would wander. When I made an out it didn't eat me up inside anymore. What was wrong with me? I didn't want to kill myself after making an out. I didn't feel like crap when we lost. When the game was over, I'd mentally replay each at-bat, but then I'd be able to walk out of the clubhouse and not worry about them during the car ride home. This went on for a couple of weeks and then I knew it was time. [62]

Yaz decided to talk with the Red Sox manager, Ralph Houk. He said to Houk: "Baseball just doesn't mean that much to me anymore unless we're in a pennant race. I think it's left me. It's just not there." Houk told him that he should trust his feelings. "I've managed and played with some great ones," he said. "Get out at the right time if that's how you feel."[63] Yaz took his advice and quit the game.

Probably as intense and competitive as any player in his prime, Billy Martin evidently lost his competitive spirit as he grew older and moved from one managing job to another, each full of pressure. Lou Piniella had this to say about Martin during his third stint as Yankee manager: "He was older now, and people suggested he was less enthusiastic than he had been. He seemed a little more distracted, a little more tense, a little more angry. He wanted to climb the mountain again, but he had been on top before. He didn't have the same fire, and maybe he didn't have the same burning desire to win. He let too many things bother him. He was a tired man."[64]

Age ultimately catches up with even the best players. At age forty-two, after twenty-six seasons, Ty Cobb decided to hang up his cleats, even though his physical skills were still intact. "Once upon a time," he told a group of admirers, "it would have been irresistible, but now, in a baseball sense, I am too old, too weary of the daily strain. I have lost my ambition. I'm through. I have played my final game." Even though he was far beyond the age when most players retire, Cobb believed that most players stayed around too long. "Ballplayers should retire before they break," he said. "I've known good players who were the idols of fans who finished their careers playing out the string and died broke and broken hearted. My legs are still good, my eyes are as sharp as ever, but the old fire is gone. I still love baseball. I have lived the game, but I know when to stop."[65]

Sometimes teams that have been very successful lose the desire to win, lose their competitive spirit or edge—the thing that was primarily responsible for their success. St. Louis Cardinals manager Whitey Herzog described what happened to the 1986 Cardinals team, the same group of players that the year before had won 101 games and the National League pennant and had gotten to the seventh game of the World Series. The team began losing ball games right from the beginning of the 1986 season. Herzog could not get a handle on what was happening. In an effort to focus more clearly on what needed to be done, he began keeping a diary. His entries give us a bird's-eye view of the decline of a great team.

May 5, 1986. I don't know what is going on here. . . . The ball club is nine and thirteen, four games under .500, but we've lost ten of the last twelve. . . . The thing is we're just not hitting. The team batting average is .204 . . . . We are not playing well in any phase of the game, mentally or physically. . . . We're missing signs, swinging at balls over our heads. . . . And the frustrations are starting to set in. . . . I've held a couple of meetings in the clubhouse, but you really can't rant and rave at the guys. That kind of thing never does any good.

May 24, 1986. I talk and talk with them, but the more I talk, the more meetings I have, the more they just go out and screw it up worse. I really don't know what else to do. It's got me buffaloed. I just can't believe how bad we're playing. I've never seen a club with this much talent play this poorly. It was different when I managed the Texas Rangers. Then we didn't have enough good players to play well. This club, well, I just can't understand it. There's just no intensity on the club. This may be the reason why so few clubs repeat as division winners and pennant winners. All along I thought it had to do with parity in the league and the breaks of the game, but the more I think about this season, the more I think that the intensity evaporates after you've won it. The motivation isn't the same. We have some players who didn't do anything all winter but lie around on their asses. They say they were tired, and that may be true. Hell, they played until the last week of October. But you just can't expect to waltz into spring training, pick up a bat and get it going again. Something has to motivate you. It's just remarkable how the performance levels of so many guys are so far off. Herr is hitting 200 points under what he was hitting a year ago. McGee has gone from .350 to .240, with four lousy stolen bases.

June 10, 1986. We don't have a team any more, just a bunch of individuals who don't have their heads in the game. They anticipate nothing. Mental mistakes happen every night. Their bickering and feuding continues. I can stand losing. But I sure as hell can't stand what's going on around here. My coaches are out there, working their asses off, and nobody seems to give a damn. They just go out there and screw up night after night after night. . . . It's just sickening. People keep talking about last year. Last year, my ass. We are a bad ball club, probably one of the worst in baseball. . . . It's amazing how bad a club we've become.[66]

The team never did turn it around. The 1986 Cardinals lost more games than they won and finished far out of the running in the pennant race.

Steve Garvey, who played on pennant-winners with both the Los Angeles Dodgers and the San Diego Padres, felt that the experience of winning a championship dulled an entire team's competitive spirit, making it difficult to repeat. Writing in the mid-1980s Garvey said:

> While dynasties were once an active part of athletics, repeating even once as champion is almost unheard of today. It seems that there is an energy that can come over a relatively good team for a season and carry them to victory. Once on top, defending that position proves an awesome task. First, there is a complacency in management—nobody wants to make too many changes in a winning combination—while other teams in the same league are scurrying around, trying to improve themselves. With talent so evenly distributed, the balance of power can shift with the moving of a single athlete. A few key injuries can destroy a winning team's chemistry.[67]

"There is also an internal factor that isn't reflected in a team's roster," observed Garvey. "The desire to reach the top is simply greater than the desire to remain there. We all want passionately to prove we're the best—we bring that with us from the sandlots. Once we've done that, a certain hunger often abandons us, and that's all it takes to turn a winner into a loser."[68]

FOUR

Developing Confidence

The Key to Success in the Big Leagues

CONFIDENCE IS HUGE. IT IS THE MAIN INGREDIENT IN A player's success. If you don't have self-confidence, the game is going to bury you. It will suck the energy right out of you. You can do very little without confidence. Unless you trust yourself and believe in yourself, you will be unable to perform. Without confidence, you are very easily intimidated. Several ballplayers that I have been around in the big leagues have lacked self-confidence. They may make it for a while on natural ability, but it eventually catches up with them. As Hall of Fame pitcher Bob Feller put it, "You have to believe you can do it. You can have all the talent, but if you're out there with any question in your mind at all about your ability to win . . . then you are going to be a failure."[1] Dodger pitcher Orel Hershiser stressed the importance of self-confidence when he said, "No human dares to stand on a dirt hill 12 inches high with a 9-inch, 5-ounce sphere in his hand and face giants with clubs 60 feet 6 inches away, unless deep inside he is confident of—even cocky about—his ability."[2] Hall of Famer Mike Schmidt summed it up well when he said, "Some people are born with it, some have to learn it, and some have to foster it through many experiences." Schmidt said that he fell within the latter group.[3] I think very few are born with it. Most learn it the way Schmidt did.

During my years in the big leagues, confidence got me through a lot of things. When my confidence level was high, I was not afraid to make an out. I knew I would ultimately get it done.

Ways to Build Self-Confidence

A lot of mental work is required to build confidence. I don't think you develop self-confidence without putting in the necessary work. A lot has to do with developing proper attitudes. You gain confidence by being positive and optimistic rather than negative and fearful, open to new knowledge and information, willing to accept honest evaluations from coaches, able to honestly evaluate yourself, and willing to change. You also must have a strong interest in and passion for the game, as well as a commitment to getting the job done. My strong passion for playing baseball and my willingness to work at the game started me down the road to developing self-confidence.

Good work habits are an essential ingredient in developing self-confidence. You need to do high-quality work before a game to maintain confidence, and you must begin preparing yourself several hours before the first pitch. You must develop a routine or a plan for your workout, and know exactly what you are going to focus on. Those without a routine or plan get very little accomplished.

Repetition is very important. A hitter needs an offensive routine for batting practice. He needs to hit balls to the opposite field as well as down the line, make sure his feet are solidly under him, and handle each and every pitch he will see during the game. An infielder must take ground balls to his right and his left, and directly at him—as many as he feels he needs to be prepared. He needs to work on double plays as well as throws to first base. Time must not be wasted during practice, and practice must not be monotonous. By the end of the workout he must feel good about what has been accomplished. This builds self-confidence and readies him for the game.

Sometimes it is necessary for a player to put in extra work before the team takes the field for its pregame drills. This is a time when a player may take additional batting or fielding practice, and work on a particular problem or focus on a specific weakness. Work of this kind is essential for developing confidence.

Self-Confidence Gained Through the Support of Coaches and Managers

The input of coaches or mentors plays a big part in enabling a player to develop self-confidence. You don't develop self-confidence all by yourself. Ninety-nine percent of all athletes will tell you the names of at least a couple of coaches who meant a great deal to them, who enabled them to become more confident of their abilities.

In the big leagues the coaches who helped me develop self-confidence were Rocky Colavito, Dave Garcia, and Pat Corrales. When I was a rookie with Cleveland, Colavito was my hitting coach. He was a great hitter with the Indians, a big favorite in Cleveland, a power hitter, and a great right fielder. He was so positive with me. He kept encouraging me and telling me that I was doing great. I trusted him because he had a reputation for telling the truth. Because he believed I had talent and thought I was already a good player his judgment was accepted by a lot of players and coaches on the team. He could find something positive even in things I did wrong. It was great to have that kind of support and to be around someone like Rocky Colavito—especially when you are only twenty years old and in your first year in the big leagues. He was someone I could trust.

Dave Garcia, the base coach and infield coach for Cleveland when I came up to the big leagues, was like a father to me. He was a mentor, probably the most positive person I have ever been around. He made me feel as if I could do no wrong. When I did make a mistake, he had a way of finding something positive in it. He helped me understand how to deal with adversity, how to deal with making outs and errors in the field.

When I played for the Indians early in my career, I always led off or hit second. I had trouble driving in runs. In 1979, when I went to Texas, Pat Corrales, the manager, put me in the four spot in the lineup (the cleanup hitter). I knew he would not have put me there if he didn't think I could do it. As a result, I gained confidence and flourished. My career took off. I was grateful that Corrales had confidence in me and put me in a very responsible position in the lineup.

Rick's manager with Las Vegas in 2002, Brad Mills, did the same thing for him that Pat Corrales did for me. Rick said:

> Confidence is one of the biggest things in baseball. Anytime you struggle with the game, you are struggling with your self-confidence. If you are not playing well, it is tough to have it. Brad Mills, my manager in Las Vegas, kept putting me in the lineup when I was struggling. He had watched me for a while and knew I could play. It is nice when you have a manager who has confidence in you. It gave me a boost, the extra confidence

I needed. I finished the season with a .270 average and hit thirteen home runs.

In an interview with my coauthor, Neal Vahle, Rick said that I helped him with his self-confidence during a critical early period in his career. He said:

When I finished high school and signed with the Dodgers I was really confident. I took a big step backward when I went to Yakima to play rookie ball. I was eighteen playing with guys twenty-one and twenty-two; guys who were better than I was. It was a battle every day facing them, physically and mentally. I lost confidence in myself. I talked to my dad and he told me to keep going out there and play hard. My dad had seen it before. He told me that I was going through something all young players go through, and that I would eventually turn it around. There was nobody I trusted more than him. He helped me realize my career wasn't over at age eighteen. I did what he told me. I got out there, worked hard, and didn't give up.

Manager Tommy Lasorda believed that younger players could improve their self confidence through self-talk. Lasorda, when managing in the minor leagues, had his players saying over and over:

I *believe* I will play in the major leagues because I *believe* in myself. I *know* I have the ability to become a major leaguer; all I have to do is put all of my abilities together. I *will* advance in the Dodger organization because I have the positive attitude and dynamic power within myself. I will always maintain this condition and I will learn all I can because I am *determined* to make the major leagues. I have faith in myself and that, along with the abilities I possess, will propel me toward my ultimate goal.[4]

He also believed that players' self-confidence improved when they took pride in belonging to the Los Angeles Dodger organization. Lasorda said:

The first thing I did when a young man reported to me was to try to instill confidence in him and make him feel he had become part of a new family, the Dodgers. I would meet with each new player and explain, "Son, there are some things that are very important on this team. The most important is believing that you have the ability to play baseball for the greatest team in the world, the Los Angeles Dodgers. Do you believe that?" Invariably, they would solemnly nod their heads and say, "I do." Good. I do too, otherwise you wouldn't be here. Now we have a little tradition on this ball club, that no matter where you are, no matter who you're with, no matter what you're doing, when you hear me yell, "Tell me something!" I want you to respond as loudly as you can, "I believe." And when I should ask, "Who do you love?" I want you to respond, "I love the Dodgers." And when I shout "Where are you going to get your mail?," you respond, "Dodger Stadium." And when I shout, "Who's gonna sign your paycheck?" I want to hear you scream, "Mr. O'Malley."[5]

Lasorda indicated that most of the young players didn't believe he was serious. He said:

They had anticipated meeting a calm professional manager, perhaps someone like their school teachers, and the first person they meet was me, and I was ordering them to scream and shout. What I was trying to do was to build their confidence and their team spirit and enthusiasm. The feeling they gained from this, particularly when people came to watch them, was that they were part of something unique, something special, which reinforced their self-confidence. I never let up on them. From the first time I saw them in the morning till they went home after night games, I was constantly telling them how good they were, how hard they had to work to play in the big leagues, and how fortunate they were to be members of the Dodger organization.[6]

Goose Gossage described how he developed self-confidence through work with pitching coach Johnny Sain. Sain's tutelage was the key for Gossage in gaining the confidence to be a successful closer. He said:

I already had an out-pitch. My fastball consistently registered in the midnineties. It was one of the handful of the hardest in the game and it had plenty of movement. I threw a sinker fastball and a high one with hop. Either could blow hitters away. In 1975 I added a much-improved slider to the mix. All the hours with Johnny Sain spent working on my mechanics began to pay off. I started shutting down batters on a consistent basis. That consistency, in turn, instilled in me a growing confidence that I could do it again and again. Confidence isn't sold over the counter. You can't get it out of a dispenser. Confidence can't be conjured up. The only way to develop confidence is to give yourself a reason to be confident. It's trial by fire.[7]

Willie Stargell of the Pittsburgh Pirates was in a batting slump when Harry Walker, a manager he had difficulty playing for, was replaced by Danny Murtaugh, a man he had known and respected for years. Stargell spoke of the importance of having Murtaugh at the helm:

The sight of Murtaugh was a breath of fresh air for me. I needed Danny's presence to rekindle my confidence. Danny's easygoing, confident style affected me immediately. I diagnosed the cause of the slump almost instantly. I had been holding my hands too high up on the bat handle. I learned to relax more and wait on a pitch.[8]

Joe Morgan remembers how, in his first season in Triple-A ball, he immediately felt the pressure and went into a batting slump. He got no hits in his first twenty at bats. "I was tighter than a drum. The more I failed, the tighter I got. I felt I should be hitting the pitching I was seeing . . . but I just couldn't do anything." Morgan felt he was going to be shipped back to the deep minors, when manager Lou Fitzgerald called him in and gave him a big vote of confidence. Fitzgerald said, "Hey kid, don't worry about anything. You're here for the whole season even if you don't get one hit. So just relax and play."

"It's funny how much that meant to me," recalled Morgan. "Nothing on the field changed, but my thinking did. From then on I had an outstanding season, hitting .323, driving in 90 runs, hitting 12 homers, stealing 47 bases, and being voted the Texas League's MVP that year."[9]

Hall of Famer Frank Robinson attributes his early belief in himself to the faith that his American Legion and high school coach had in him. "In the early fall of 1949," said Robinson, "having just turned fourteen and begun the ninth grade at Westlake Junior High [in Oakland, California], I met George Powles, a man who was to have an immeasurable influence on my life." Powles was the baseball and basketball coach at Mc-Clymonds High School. On the side he also coached four or five other ball clubs every weekend, teams ranking from eight to ten year olds up to his American Legion team. Robinson indicated:

The spring of 1950 George Powles stunned me by inviting me to join his Bill Erwin Post 237 ball club, which had won the American Legion national championships the year before. Fourteen of that team's twenty-five players on the two-year roster ended up playing professional baseball. I was just another player on the Legion team . . . but I remember one game just after my fifteenth birthday that fall. I remember hitting a triple off the 350 mark in right center. . . . George Powles instilled a lot of confidence in me. He was such a thorough and patient teacher that I still draw on the baseball fundamentals he taught to this day. Powles spent hour after hour with us. He was a good person for kids to be around, especially ones like me who didn't have a father. After practice or games we'd go over to his house, sit around and just talk baseball.[10]

Charlie Lau, a successful hitting coach for several teams, also contributed to building Robinson's self-confidence as a hitter, particularly when he was in a slump. About Lau's impact on George Brett and himself, Robinson said:

Charlie Lau is a helluva guy . . . George Brett is gonna hit and I'm gonna hit, but Charlie gets you out of your rut sooner and gives you somebody to talk to and keep your mind right. I need support and confidence, and even the best hitter in baseball— which George Brett is—needs confidence too.[11]

For some players, it's the confidence that their major league managers have in them that really counts. Relief pitcher Sparky Lyle felt that the key to his success was the fact that Yankee manager Billy Martin had enough confidence in him to let him pitch often when the pressure was greatest, usually in critical situations with men on base and the game close. Lyle said that Martin let him do what he did best, and because of that, he became the Cy Young Award winner in 1978. "What I've been saying ever since I came up to the majors in '67," Lyle reiterated, was "if you let me pitch often enough and make me the big guy in the bullpen, I'll do the job for you. I'll come in when it counts and get them out. I can't pitch in games when we're really far behind or ahead. I'm just not into the game. . . . The best time for me to pitch is when we're ahead by a run or the score is tied."[12]

Yogi Berra felt that his work with former Yankee catcher Bill Dickey enabled him to develop self-confidence by reassuring him that he had what it takes to play regularly for the Yankees. Berra said:

> Each day for at least a couple of hours [Bill] Dickey worked with me. He worked me on all the details of catching: how to chase pop-ups, how to spot a batter's weakness, how to move my feet . . . everything. All the while he worked on my confidence. He kept encouraging me, telling me, "Take pride in your position. It's the best job in baseball." He was also motivating by reminding me there weren't many good catchers, and that once I established myself I could have a great career. Dickey helped turn things around for me. Looking back, I realize if I hadn't been tutored by Bill Dickey, I might not have lasted long in baseball.[13]

Willie Mays credits Giants manager Leo Durocher with giving him essential encouragement when it really counted, "at the beginning," said Mays, "at the most important point of my career." Mays was called up to play with the Giants in June 1951 from their farm team in Minneapolis. Mays, who had been hitting a phenomenal .477 in Triple-A ball, immediately went into a deep batting slump. He went 0 for 12, got a hit, and then went 0 for 13. After going 0 for 5 in a doubleheader, he was disconsolate.

"After that game I sat next to my locker and cried." The next thing he knew Durocher was putting his arm around him. "What's the matter, son," he asked.

"Mister Leo," said Mays, "I can't hit up here. . . . The pitching is too fast for me."[14]

Mays said that Durocher wasn't having any of that kind of talk. He pointed to his uniform and said, "Willie, see what's printed across my jersey? It says Giants. As long as I am manager of the Giants, you're my centerfielder. You're here to stay. Stop worrying. With your talent you're going to get plenty of hits." Durocher told Mays that he could do the five things that a ball player had to do to be great—hit, hit with power, run, field, and throw. "Willie," said Durocher, "you could do all five from the first time I ever saw you. You're the greatest ball player I ever saw and ever hope to see." Mays acknowledged that what Durocher told him worked. He broke out of his hitless string by going 9 for 24, and continued to have an excellent year, being voted Rookie of the Year in the National League.[15]

Mays said that with the dismal start he had in 1951 he probably wouldn't have made it under any other manager. "Remember, I was depressed after that start. I wanted to quit. I needed someone to lift my spirits, to give me the confidence I needed at that low point. Leo was that person. He knew what I needed. Any other manager would have sent down a twenty-year-old kid. But Leo made me believe in myself. He forced me to."[16]

Dodger pitcher Orel Hershiser recalled a time when he was a rookie on the Dodger pitching staff, and pitching poorly. After a particularly bad game he was called into Tommy Lasorda's office, expecting to be told that he was being sent back to the minor leagues. Lasorda started the conversation by telling Hershiser that he wanted to talk with him "about your game, the use of your ability, and your mental approach to pitching." He reminded Hershiser how upset he'd gotten with him in recent games when he got behind on the hitters and then gave in to the hitter. "You don't believe in yourself," Lasorda told Hershiser. "You're scared to pitch in the big leagues! Who do you think these hitters are, Babe Ruth? Babe Ruth is dead. You've got good stuff. If you didn't, I wouldn't have brought you up. Quit being so careful! Go after the hitters. Get ahead in the count!" Lasorda reassured Hershiser:

> I've seen guys come and go, son, and you've got it! You gotta go out there and do it on the mound! Take charge! Make 'em hit your best stuff! Be aggressive. Be a bulldog out there. That's gonna be your new name: Bulldog. I want you, starting today, to believe you are the best pitcher in baseball. I want you to look at that hitter and say, "There's no way you can ever hit me." You gotta believe you are superior to the hitter and that you can get anybody out who walks up there. Quit giving the hitter so much credit. You're better than these guys.[17]

Hershiser recalled that something important registered during that little talk. Lasorda believed that he had good stuff. This was important to know. The next time Hershiser was called upon to pitch he strode to the mound "reminding myself what a pleasant surprise it had been to learn that Tommy believed in me, thought I was special, needed me, and thought I would be successful with an adjustment in my approach." Hershiser said that even though his elbow felt tender that day and his arm a little weak, he decided to challenge the hitters:

> I kept the ball low, got ahead in the count on nearly every batter. In three innings, my arm feeling like a rag, I gave up only one run. With my performance I became a believer. I told myself that if I could do that when my arm felt terrible, think what I could do when I felt great. I still didn't like the nickname, and

I was chagrined that anyone thought I needed it. But that day I
became a big league pitcher. My attitude was revolutionized.
I believed I deserved to be there, competing with big leaguers
because I *was* a big leaguer.[18]

Hershiser felt that he owed a lot to Lasorda. "My game had
become focused. And the concentration motivated by the confidence Tommy instilled in me remains a key to my success today." Hershiser recalled the great year he had in 1988 when he
won 23 games and lost only 8, had an ERA of only 2.26, and
won 2 games in the World Series plus pitching a record 59 consecutive scoreless innings. "Do you wonder how a pitcher could
have had the 1988 like I had," he asked. "Do you wonder how
we Dodgers could have been motivated to maintain our intensity all through the season and postseason, in spite of injuries
and setbacks? We owe a lot to Tommy, of course, because he is a
true motivator, encourager, cheerleader."[19]

Lasorda believed that self-confidence was *the* essential ingredient in an athlete's mental makeup. It was the key, he said, in
narrowing the gap between the mediocre player and the very
good ballplayer. "I believed," he said, "the mind controlled the
mechanisms of the body, and if I could make a player believe in
himself, if I could make him really believe he could play in
the big leagues, that player would someday play in the big
leagues."[20]

Lasorda believed that his demonstration of confidence in
shortstop Billy Russell, then a minor leaguer in the Dodger organization, had an impact on Russell's belief in himself, and
made a huge difference in the course of Russell's career. Lasorda
was aware that there were people in the Dodger front office who
did not think Russell had major league ability, and they wanted
Lasorda, who was then his minor league manager, to release him.
Lasorda believed "that with a lot of coaching, a lot of patience,

and a lot of time working on the ball field," Russell would play in the big leagues. Russell, who was aware that some of the Dodger brass did not respect his abilities, felt the pressure, and one day as he and Lasorda sat talking on the bench near the team's right field bullpen Russell said, "I know there's a big cut coming up, and I'm worried about it. I want to know how you feel?" This was Lasorda's response:

> If it will make you feel any better, I'll tell you this much. The only way you'll get released is if I get released as the manager. As long as I'm the manager here, you'll be here, because I believe you have major league ability.[21]

Lasorda saw the impact on Russell:

> You talk about seeing the sun come out on someone's face. He looked as if I had just lifted a building off his shoulders. Relieved of that weight, he began playing the kind of baseball that would eventually make him the shortstop on a world championship ball club.[22]

Self-Confidence Built on Past Success

Derek Jeter described a successful at bat as a Yankee rookie that resulted in his feeling more secure about himself as a major leaguer and boosted his belief in this ability. Jeter had been brought up to the Yankees in September 1995 from their farm club in Columbus, Ohio. He wasn't expected to play, because the Yankees were in a pennant race. His chance came when centerfielder Bernie Williams missed a flight and was late for a game. Randy Velarde, the regular shortstop, was moved to center field, and Jeter was inserted in his place. Jeter got an at bat before Williams arrived. With a runner on first, he hit a double into right center that scored a run, which turned out to be the margin of the Yankee victory. At the time, the Yankees had only five games to play and did not clinch a wild card spot until the final day of the season. Jeter described the importance of that at bat:

> There are times when I reflect on that at bat because I look at it as a defining moment of sorts for me. I think we all have moments or events in our lives where we gained more confidence in ourselves. I was more secure after that game. It was only one at bat, one measly at bat. But I milked that moment for everything I could during the off-season. I ran harder, I lifted more, and I took more batting practice because I was juiced by the feeling that hit gave me. . . . There is nothing wrong with taking those positive moments, remembering they were positive, and letting them work for you.[23]

Jeter acknowledged that he struggled with his confidence during his first two years in the minors. "But even as I struggled," he said, "there was a part of me that believed I could succeed. Sometimes it was a small part of me, but I wouldn't have made it this far if some part of me hadn't felt that way. You've got to find that confidence, even if it's only a sliver of confidence on some days, and cling to it."[24]

Steve Garvey believed that success at the plate early in a crucial game often resulted in a marked rise in a player's confidence level as the game progressed. He illustrated the point by describing a play-off game against the Cubs in 1984 in which he came to bat in the ninth inning with the score tied 5–5. He had already had three chances in crucial situations during the game, and had gotten hits that either tied the game or gained the lead. "As that happens," he said, "your confidence level builds. You actually get better, physically better. Your timing improves, your aggressiveness builds, your strike zone gets better defined. And the crowd senses what's happening, and they get into it."[25]

Babe Ruth's tremendous confidence in his ability to hit as his career progressed was based in part on past successes. In 1927 he started the season atrociously in the batting box. Yet his confidence never wavered. Talking with Leo Durocher, a weak-hitting reserve second baseman who started off the season hot and was leading the league in hitting, Ruth said, "The league is upside down. But don't worry about it, kid. When the season's over I'll be near the top where I belong and you'll be near the bottom, where you belong." Ruth seemed to know he would get his hits no matter who was pitching. One afternoon as fastball pitcher Lefty Grove took his warm-ups, and other Yankee players watched in fear as Grove blazed his pitches into the catcher's mitt, Ruth was heard to say, "Baby is going to hit one today." In his first two times at bat he struck out, but on the third trip to the plate he hit one over the fence. As he trotted back to the dugout he said, "Baby got his today."[26]

Hank Aaron's confidence stemmed from a belief that the batter had a natural advantage over the pitcher. He described it this way:

> In large part my success against a good pitcher was a matter of confidence. Without trying to boast, I can say that never in my big league career did I feel overmatched by a pitcher. I used to tell the writers that I felt I had an advantage at the plate because I had my bat . . . and all the pitcher had was the little ball. They chuckled when I said that, but I meant it. I always thought that if I lost that mental edge, I would lose my special ability as a hitter, and my mental edge was knowing that I could hit a good pitcher's best pitch.[27]

Yankee manager Joe Torre believed that optimism was an essential key. "Without optimism," he said, "that gut-level belief that we can succeed, we are far less likely to realize our dreams. Setbacks and slumps will stop us cold."[28] Torre also believed that ballplayers should set realistic goals and not strive for achievements that were beyond their abilities. He said:

> In order to build faith in ourselves, we must have a realistic sense of our talents, not an inflated one. If a career .250 hitter feels he ought to win the batting title, he's setting himself up for a blow to his confidence. If, however, he strives to hit .300, he's created a realistic goal, and if he adds 10 to 20 points to his average, the effort will have been well worth it.[29]

Willie Mays was known for his belief in himself, even when he was in a slump. One day after a game in which he had again gone hitless, he was interviewed by a reporter who asked him what he was going to do about his slump. "I'll come out of it," he said, "I always do." Then he asked the dumbfounded reporter, "What do you do when you get in a slump?" The reporter told Mays that he never got into slumps. "Bullshit," said Mays. "I read you. I know you get your slumps, same's the rest of us." The reporter saw Mays's point and acknowledged that if he got into a writing slump he'd come out of it too, sooner or later. Mays replied, "Same with me. Quit worrying, I'll get me four hits in a game and be right back up there. Don't worry about nothing."[30] The next day Mays went out and hit four home runs in one game, becoming the seventh man in the history of baseball to do so in a nine-inning game.

Slugger Hank Greenberg of the Detroit Tigers, a Hall of Famer who enjoyed a long career in the majors in the thirties and forties and became one of the all-time leading home-run hitters, increased his self-confidence by talking himself into believing that pitchers were inferior athletes and not worthy of his respect. He learned, he said, "to despise the pitchers. I never even thought they were athletes. I just thought they were kids who had good arms. Basically I had determined in my mind that pitchers were not intelligent and were inferior. That was part of what I had to convince myself of so that I could hit them. I don't know if every other hitter felt the same way, but I know that's how I felt. I tried to put them down in my mind to enable me to have a little confidence."[31]

Some ballplayers, through their own ability and self-confidence, raise the level of their team's belief in itself when they are in the lineup. Yankee pitcher Whitey Ford had this impact on the team. His manager, Ralph Houk, said:

> He gave the club stability, a sense of confidence built on the knowledge that "Whitey's pitching tomorrow," and that Whitey would probably win. The confidence such a great pitcher generates cannot be measured, but in the case of the 1961 Yankees it was an extraordinary help in keeping the team from collapsing altogether in the depressing early weeks of the season, as well as raising it to its sustained, pennant-winning accomplishment later on.[32]

Ron Guidry, who pitched for the Yankees in the late seventies and early eighties, had the same impact. Sparky Lyle, who played with him, said that manager Billy Martin believed the team's confidence rose when Guidry was on the mound. Quoting Martin, Lyle said, "Our hitters feel less pressure and hit better than they do for other pitchers. They know he's only going to allow a run or two, so they relax at the plate and hit better."[33]

Steve Garvey's presence in the San Diego Padres lineup helped raise the confidence level of the team. In 1983, after thirteen seasons with the Dodgers, which included several National League pennants and one World Series championship, Garvey signed with the San Diego Padres, a recent expansion team that had never won a pennant. In 1984, his second year with the team, the Padres finished first for the first time in its history. Garvey played a central role, having one of his best seasons at the plate and in the field. Timothy Earl Flannery, a utility player for the Padres and a senior team member, said that Garvey's presence had made the difference:

> Steve filled a vacuum on the team, a power vacuum. And I don't mean hitting home runs. He seemed to remember everything— how this pitcher pitches, and how to play that batter. But it was more than the things he told us. Just having a guy like him in the lineup gives you confidence. You see the way he does the little things that are so big—moving runners from first to second, getting the sacrifice fly in the last inning. And when it comes down to the game situation with the winning run on second and two outs, the guy you want up is Steve. Everybody has a role on this club—that's his.[34]

Members of teams that have won in the past have a much greater belief in themselves as a team than those without winning traditions. The confidence level of the Cincinnati Reds in the 1970s, teams that became known as the Big Red Machine, seemed to build as their wins multiplied. As Joe Morgan described it:

> There is an attitude that a powerhouse team gets [and we usually had it] that can be mistaken for cockiness. It is not that. When we walked out on the field we *expected* to win. Most teams go out *hoping* to win. There is a difference. There were many times, we won *before* the first pitch was ever thrown because other teams were intimidated.[35]

The 1955 Brooklyn Dodgers exuded this same type of self-confidence as a team. Pitcher Sandy Koufax, then a rookie, saw what he believed was "an extraordinary team in every way." It was packed with great ballplayers. "The infield was Hodges, Gilliam, Reese, and Robinson. The outfield was Snider, Furillo, and Amoros. The catcher was Campanella. Not only could they all hit the ball out of the park, they could all field their positions with anyone." Koufax saw it as a confident team:

> Not cocky, not complacent, just absolutely sure of itself. It was a team that had been winning pennants (or just barely losing) for so many years that there was a settled air about the locker room, a lack of tension—meaning job security—that I later learned was very rare in a big league club. There was not quite as much exultation after winning a game (unless it had been a particularly dramatic win) and not quite so much gloom after a losing game (unless it had been a particularly galling loss). When the Dodgers won, they expected it; when they lost, they expected to win the next day.[36]

The confident attitude of New York Mets manager Davey Johnson during the 1986 season apparently rubbed off on the team; the Mets won both the National League pennant and the World Series that year. Catcher Gary Carter said that Johnson predicted the team would win from the first day of spring training. "We're not only going to win," Johnson told the team, "we're going to win *BIG*. We're going to blow the rest of the division away." Carter said Johnson repeated that prediction to anyone who would listen. "His confidence, his certainty," recalled Carter, "was infectious. We believed it." The Mets had finished second two years in a row and had won ninety-eight games the year before, and they were a young team. As the season got underway, Johnson kept telling the team, "We're going to win *BIG.*" Carter saw the impact on the team. "Pretty soon we all swallowed the conviction whole."[37]

By the end of May the Mets were ahead of the pack by six games. "We were comfortable," recalled Carter.

> We were like a long-distance runner who gets out ahead of the pack early, and who looks, at times, as if he can be caught, but who knows he won't because today is his day. His lead may not be enormous, but it is comfortable because he is equal to anyone trying to catch him. When this happens, self-confidence takes over and lifts and carries you like a wave.[38]

Ballpark Size and Its Impact on the Confidence of Hitters and Pitchers

Small ballparks, like the one in Houston, have a psychological effect on both hitters and pitchers. Veteran pitcher David Cone described the impact on the confidence of both when he said.

> It is nice to have an offensive park. It's nice to have your hitters feel confident. The problem is, it takes its toll on the pitching. If you're a team that only has two or three high-quality starters, those guys get kind of put to the grindstone. It is going to hurt you more than it helps you. It wears on a pitchers' psyche. It makes them throw more pitches; they pitch a little differently. It certainly takes its toll. It can be very wearing mentally, emotionally and physically.[39]

Ed Wade, general manager of the Philadelphia Phillies, noted the effect of small ballparks on the Phillies' pitching staff. He said:

> Houston is scary. That wall seems scary; it sits there and you know its there. When you go in there, you hope your pitchers

don't adjust to what they're doing. It's human nature. Guys are going to peek and they're going to see what they want to see.

Wade noted the adverse impact of large ballparks on hitters' confidence. He said, "Any time a team walks into a ballpark where it looks like it's going to take a rocket to get the ball out of there, it can affect the hitter. . . . It has a psychological effect."[40]

Actions of Coaches and Managers That Inhibit a Player's Self-Confidence

Many managers and coaches do not know how to help players develop self-confidence. Many forget what it was like when they were young players. Those who are able to manage veteran teams, where most of the players have developed self-confidence, often have difficulty with younger, less experienced teams. Many simply cannot manage a younger player who is working on developing self-confidence. This is something we as coaches need to get better at in our game. The average service time of a major league ballplayer is only three to four years. I think the short tenure is in part due to their inability to develop the confidence needed to play in the big leagues.

Evidently, Casey Stengel, who did a great job with veteran players, did not have the patience to deal with the problems of rookies, and in some cases behaved in ways that destroyed their self-confidence. Second baseman Jerry Lumpe, who came up as a rookie to the Yankees during the Stengel era, said:

He sure wasn't patient with us younger players. I can tell you that. Stengel was constantly on my case. Casey liked his veterans. I'd hit up in the lineup, but if I went bad for a few games, he'd drop me to eighth. Then he'd drop you out of sight. But he'd let veterans work their way out of slumps. I can understand that, because they've proven themselves with past performances. But it's not very good when you're a young player getting passed over. It can damage your confidence. . . . He'd criticize a young player in the press to motivate him, but that doesn't work with everyone.

Stengel once said of Lumpe to a reporter, "He's the greatest player in the world until you stick him in the lineup."[41]

Overconfidence

The biggest sin, when it comes to overconfidence, is not respecting your opponent. You begin to think the game is too easy, you get too nonchalant, your level of commitment drops, and you allow your body to relax too much. You think you have the game figured out. Disaster is sure to follow if you allow yourself to get into this mind-set.

When I was managing the Colorado Rockies in 2002, we got a scouting report that probably resulted in the team becoming too complacent. The season had just started. We had beaten the Cardinals in the final game of a three-game series and were leaving St. Louis for Los Angeles. The Dodgers had lost the first three games of the 2002 season. A report from an advance scout said, "The Dodgers are playing without any effort, like they don't care." I told the team not to listen to that part of the scouting report. I knew the Dodgers were a good team, and I knew that to avoid overconfidence, we needed to respect them as a worthy opponent. Evidently the scouting report and not my message got through to the players; we lost three in a row.

Examples abound showing how overconfidence has caused players to lose focus and drop their level of play. Goose Gossage described how overconfidence cost him an important save in a World Series game between the San Diego Padres and the

Detroit Tigers. It was game five and Detroit was ahead 3–1. Gossage, who was in the Padres bullpen, was asked by Tim Lollar, a fellow pitcher, how he fared against Detroit's power hitter Kirk Gibson when they were both in the American League. Gossage crowed, "I think he has one hit off me lifetime. He's lucky to have that one. It was a broken bat single. I own the guy." Gossage was pitching in the eight inning when Gibson came to bat with two runners aboard and Detroit leading 5–4. Gossage needed to get Gibson out if the Padres were to get out of the inning and stage a comeback in the ninth. Gossage reported the sequence of events:

> First base was open, and Dick Williams [the Padres manager] signaled from the dugout that he wanted me to walk Gibson intentionally. [Gibson had already hit a two-run home run.] I didn't like the idea at all. I yelled to Dick that I didn't agree with his strategy. I had a great record of success against this guy. Williams came out to the mound to pursue the point. "Let me pitch to this guy," I pleaded. "I can get him out. I know I can." Dick mulled the situation over a few seconds. "All right, go after him," he said. On the second pitch—WHAM—Gibson made a liar out of me. Seems I didn't own him, after all. Gibson's tremendous blast into the upper deck put the Tigers ahead, 8–4, and put the game out of reach.[42]

Reflecting on his conversation with Lollar in the bullpen earlier in the game, Gossage admitted that he had committed a "cardinal sin." He said, "I jinxed myself by bragging to Tim Lollar about how well I had handled Gibson in the past. That kind of talk can backfire on a player big-time, which is why it's always a good idea for a ballplayer to keep his mouth shut and his focus on the moment."[43]

FIVE

Intuition, Instinct, Hunches, and Gut Feelings

WEBSTER DEFINES INTUITION AS THE POWER OF ATTAINING direct knowledge without rational thought. Information gained intuitively is directly apprehended and often takes the form of a hunch or gut feeling. Many ballplayers and managers, myself included, often use the word "instinct" when referring to intuition. For example, I believe that ballplayers must let their instincts guide them. Sometimes we let our brains get in the way of our instincts. We break things down too much and get too analytical. At some point we need to stop taking in information and rely on our natural talents, which is another way of saying that we need to let our instinctual feel for the game take over. When the ball is in play you have to trust your instincts. For me, playing third base, I had to have a feel for my body, a feel for the pitcher, and a feel for the hitter.

In the batting cage, I used gut feeling to let me know when I had sufficient batting practice to get ready to hit in a game. As a hitter I was concerned about the location of my feet and my hands. I took batting practice until I sensed that they were positioned correctly. Sometimes that happened rather quickly. Other times it did not. I didn't try to hit the ball hard, like a lot of players. I was focused on my feet and hands. As soon as I felt good about where they were located, I could get out of the batter's box. It was the key to my hitting.

Over the course of a baseball season I often had hunches about what was going to happen on the field. On several occasions, as the pitcher completed his delivery, I knew the ball was going to be hit to me at third base. I would find myself, on occasion, knowing that the hitter was going to get a hit or make an out before the event happened. At bat I would get the feeling that I was going to hit the ball hard some place, and then I would do it.

David has had similar experiences and believes that everyone in the game has some level of intuitive knowing. He said:

> I can be watching a game or playing a game, and suddenly it hits me: This guy is going to hit a home run on this pitch, and it happens. It is a scary feeling to be standing on third base and you know the guy at bat is going to hit a home run and there is nothing you can do about it. And you don't know how in the world you knew. Somehow you just saw it coming. Almost every time a player on your team hits a home run some guy in the dugout will come up to you and say, "I just called that." Many times when I am playing third base a manager will want me to play close to the line, and I have the feeling that the batter is going to hit the ball in the hole between third and short. It takes everything I have to go over to the line because I believe the batter is going to hit the other way. Often my hunch has been right. I believe as a player you need to get to the point where you are open to acting on a hunch, because it may enable you to make a great play.

I believe your instincts work better in game situations when you have prepared yourself mentally to play, are aware of everything that is happening on the field, have your mind focused on the present moment, and the game has, so to speak, slowed down for you. David is of the same opinion. He put it this way:

> I think intuition is a big part of baseball, and I think it is based on a lot of things. It develops through experience, paying attention, seeing everything, taking in as much information as you can, and knowledge of the game. In short, intuition is based on your preparation, how much work you have put in. Then it becomes a reaction. It becomes something you don't have to think about consciously. You don't make a decision. You just react.

Ballplayers whose game is based on sound fundamentals play on instinct. As David pointed out, they just react. They don't need to think about what they are doing. Instincts are developed through practice. By the time a ballplayer reaches the big leagues, the basics of throwing, catching, and hitting have become instinctive because players have been doing it for so many years. Many, however, have not committed to instinct many of the fundamentals of baseball—such as bunting; moving the runner from second to third; executing cutoffs and relays, pickoffs, rundowns; and executing double plays. Every position has different fundamentals that must be learned. Ballplayers' instincts become better in game situations if they continue to work on these fundamentals. Many major leaguers do not want to work on fundamentals because they believe they learned them in the minor leagues. They do not realize that to play on instinct they must continually work throughout their careers on these fundamentals.

Players who have not developed sound fundamentals are prone to making mental mistakes.

Mark Belanger, the former Orioles shortstop, is an example of a player who recognized the importance of developing sound fundamentals. In a practice session he would handle as many as one hundred ground balls, committing every conceivable play to memory. He believed his instincts as an infielder needed to be "honed through repetition until they were second nature." Later, as a coach, Belanger emphasized to aspiring infielders the importance of repetition. "If you take enough ground balls in enough situations," he told them, "you'll eventually get to a point where it's like you're remembering plays rather than waiting for them to happen."[1]

Former Dodger manager Tommy Lasorda was right on when he said:

> Practice, young man, practice. That's the way my players made it to Dodger Stadium, through endless hours of practice, practice and more practice. And through those hours of practice they learned to do things instinctively. I had to teach Tom Paciorek to hit the ball to right field. I told him, "You've got to have your hands out in front of the bat in order to hit the ball over there. You have to drag the bat around. But when the ball is coming at you ninety miles an hour, you can't stop to think, I've got to have my hands out in front of the barrel, because the ball will be by you. . . . You have to practice it over and over and over so when the time comes you'll be able to do it.[2]

Most ballplayers I know rely on intuition or instinct or gut feelings in game situations. Ricky Henderson, the best leadoff hitter of all time, who I believe should be a first-round-ballot Hall of Famer, said he plays much better when he doesn't fill his mind with data on opponents. In the batter's box he wants his mind clear of intruding thoughts. "I don't want to know about opposing pitchers," he said. "I don't want to be in a position where I'm concentrating too hard on the opposing pitcher's stuff. I don't want to get up to the plate and start trying to guess what the guy's going to throw." Henderson thinks that hurts more than it helps. He said, "Baseball is a reactive sport. Sometimes it is not as important to think as it is to react. It's like being a kid again. When you're a kid nobody tells you what to do on a baseball field. You just react on your own, let your instincts take over. If you start thinking too much you've got a problem."[3]

Baseball legend Ty Cobb credited himself with having incredibly fine intuition. He had great speed on the base paths and led the National League in stolen bases for several seasons. "I could tell to the second," recalled Cobb, "what my opponents would do on almost every pitch." His biographer, Charles Alexander, confirmed Cobb's self-assessment. "No one who ever saw him sail around the bases, breaking every law of nature, obviously anticipating the behavior of infielders in tenths of a second, his body a blur as he flashed by, would doubt it."[4]

Pete Rose apparently had the ability to see things on the field before they happened, and as a result had great anticipation during a game. Reds manager Sparky Anderson, a guy whom I would have loved to play for, described Rose's ability as "a gift of great vision" or "instinct." Anderson believed that only the very best athletes possess this "vision of the whole field," only a handful in each sport. "All these people who are truly great," said Anderson, "Magic Johnson, Joe Montana, Wayne Gretzky, they cannot do it without that vision. They make the play, the pass, whatever, because they see everything and they know what's going to happen. You can't teach that. It's vision, instinct. They see it happen before it happens. That was Rose."[5]

Tim McCarver, who had a successful career as a catcher for

the St. Louis Cardinals, believed that many players "think too much." McCarver had great admiration for pitchers Bob Gibson of his own club and Orel Hershiser of the Los Angeles Dodgers. They had, said McCarver, "a sort of paradoxical intelligence, one that allowed them not to do anything to hinder themselves. It's a sort of intelligence you use almost paranormally. It allows people to do phenomenal things."[6]

McCarver also believed that the best catchers selected pitches intuitively. He reported:

> The appropriate thing for a smart, conscientious catcher to do is make rapid decisions. Bob Gibson made perfect sense when he said, "The first sign you think of, put it down." The catcher should fire down the first thing he thinks of. It's like a multiple-choice quiz in school, where your first guess is usually the right choice. If you go back and rehash all the possibilities, you'll get confused and take yourself into the wrong answer. You might make mistakes with quick choices, but over the long haul, it's the right approach. If you put down tentative signs you're going to get tentative pitches.[7]

When playing left field for the Boston Red Sox, baseball legend Ted Williams used intuition in positioning himself to play opposing hitters. Lacking great foot speed, he felt he needed to anticipate where the ball would be hit. "Knowing I was no speed demon," he recalled, "I developed an instinct for situations that came up, being alert to what was going on and having it register intuitively." He recalled a specific occasion at Yankee stadium when catcher Yogi Berra was at bat. Berra was a left-handed pull hitter, which meant that he almost always hit the ball to right field, the opposite field from which Williams was playing. When Berra was batting Williams normally positioned himself toward the centerfielder, creating a wide gap between himself and the left field foul line.

On this particular at bat Williams noticed himself moving toward the left field line, a place where Berra almost never hit the ball. "Sure enough," Williams recalled, "Berra hit a long fly ball down the left field line." Williams easily made the catch, and as he turned to throw the ball back into the infield he noticed Berra running hard into second base, still sure he had gotten a hit. A look of chagrin came across Berra's face when he saw that he was out. The next inning, as Williams approached the batter's box, Berra took off his catcher's mask and said, "How the hell can you play me over there. I don't hit the ball over there." Pleased with himself, Williams did not let Berra know that he had defied reason and relied on an instinct to make the play.[8]

Berra himself recognized the importance of using intuition as a hitter. Admitting that he was always thinking when he played, he acknowledged that "you can't think and hit at the same time." He said, "You don't have time to think when a pitch is being thrown at ninety miles an hour." Other faculties are involved. "To succeed at anything," he said, "you need good intuition and observation."[9] Pitcher Jim Bouton, who was a teammate of Berra when both played for the Yankees, remembered that Berra did not rely on reasoning in the batter's box. "I remember Yogi standing around the batting cage trying to explain hitting to some of the guys," Bouton recalled, "and he started to talk about his hands and his legs and he couldn't make himself clear. Then he said, 'Aw, just watch me do it.' "[10] Mark McGwire's approach to hitting was similar Berra's. While batting McGwire eliminated thought and let the game come to him. He reported:

I just go out and play baseball and don't think about the technical part of it. When you start thinking about it you start

screwing yourself up. I just go out there and let my ability take
care of it.[11]

Bouton, who pitched for several major league ball clubs in addition to the Yankees and wrote *Ball Four,* a best-selling baseball
book, discovered that he was most effective on the mound when
he eliminated all thought and acted on gut feeling. "If you have
to think about it," he observed "you tend to do things mechani-
cally rather than naturally." Bouton came to recognize that "by
feeling rather than by thinking, my body chose the proper pitch,
speed and location." Bouton said that when he warmed up to
pitch before a game, he tried to create in his mind "an abstract
feeling" of what it was like when he was pitching well. "It can't
be explained," he said. "It's a *feeling,* and the feeling you get when
you're doing something right, a sort of muscular memory. I find
the best way to arrive at this feeling is to eliminate all other
thoughts and let my mind go blank."[12]

Bouton often defied reason to rely on intuition, as he did
when pitching to Bill White, a St. Louis Cardinal hitter with
good power. Bouton usually threw left-handers a lot of slower
pitches (change-ups), and White knew it, but in White's first
three times at bat that day, Bouton didn't throw any. The fourth
time White came to the plate Bouton struck him out on a
change-up. The next day White was quoted in the newspapers
saying, "I waited all day for that change and he never threw it.
Then I gave up looking for the damn thing and started looking
for the fastball, and here it came." Bouton said that if he had
stuck to the pregame plan from the coaches, which called for
lots of change-ups, White probably would have clobbered one
of them. By relying on gut feeling, Bouton said he threw the
pitch at exactly the right time.[13]

Bouton said that his team's most successful pitcher, Mike

Marshall, believed it hurt his game if he planned in advance how to pitch to an opposing team's batters. "I have to wait until I get out on the mound," Marshall told Bouton. The way he would pitch to a batter depended on how he felt in the moment. Bouton believed that baseball superstars Willie Mays and Mickey Mantle did everything intuitively. Bouton never found either of them to be particularly good at articulating what they were doing. Nevertheless, he said, "they just knew what to do and did it."[14]

Dwight "Doc" Gooden, one of the premier pitchers in the National League when I was playing, was a mainstay on the pitching staff of the New York Mets. He got people out because he had such great stuff. Unlike many pitchers, whose skills are confined to the pitching mound, Gooden possessed, according to Met teammate Keith Hernandez, an extraordinary "genius for the game." Hernandez recalled a game early in Gooden's career when he demonstrated this unusual feel for the needs of the moment on the diamond. Pitching against the Cardinals, Gooden was guarding a 3–2 lead with two out and a runner on first in the bottom of the ninth. A ball was hit, not hard, directly at Hernandez, who was playing first base and holding the runner to the bag. From the stands it appeared to be an easy out because Hernandez was just a few steps off first base when the ball arrived. Hernandez reported what happened:

Billy Hatcher, a right-handed hitter, cues one toward me at first. The ball behaves erratically; it's a sidewinder. With a sidewinding grounder, I want to get in front of the ball and block it, nothing else. I succeed in getting my mitt on this one, but the ball bounces off to my right. Only five feet from the bag when I handle it initially. I have to dive away to pick it up now. I can't get back in time. Hatcher is fast. Here's Dwight's genius.

He's covering first. I shovel the ball to him for the final out. There aren't five pitchers in baseball who would have recognized the danger on that play and run to cover the bag. All would break instinctively, but almost all would then slow up, seeing that I'm practically on the bag as I wait for the ball, and of course, Hernandez couldn't misplay it if he tried to. Dwight knows better. His *instinct* made the play.[15]

Keith Hernandez was a mentally astute first baseman who prided himself on his knowledge of the intricacies of the game and liked to play hunches. During his career with the New York Mets he enjoyed playing for manager Davey Johnson, who was also willing on occasion to rely on intuition. Hernandez recalled a game situation that demonstrated how he and Johnson gauged their actions by using a sixth sense. It was the fourth inning of a game against the St. Louis Cardinals on July 31, 1984. There were runners on first and second and a good-hitting pitcher, Dan Schatzeder, was at bat. It's a bunt situation, and the first baseman would normally play in on the grass, but Hernandez felt he should stay back. He said:

I signal to Davey that I want to play back a little—even with the bag—for just one pitch. . . . I have a hunch that he may swing away on the first strike. Davey signals okay. And damned if Schatzeder doesn't rifle a grounder to my right. I dive for the stop, get the runner at second, and Lynch [the pitcher] covers first for the double play to end the inning. Big cheer from the crowd for my stop and the ensuing double play, but the point easily missed is why I was in position to make the play in the first place. If I'm in on the grass, playing for the bunt, I don't have a chance on that ball. RBI single, big inning brewing. I play a hunch. Davey goes along. Despite his reputation for working with computer records, Davey is more of a "hunch"

manager than any I've played for or seen. Davey loves to roll the
bones, seven come eleven. Take chances. I like it.[16]

Sandy Koufax and his Dodger catcher, John Roseboro, developed this same rapport. They seemed to operate together intuitively as one person. Koufax described how this mind-to-mind
communication took place:

> John Roseboro and I have been together for so long and can
> fall into such a complete rapport that we can go batter after bat-
> ter, inning after inning, as if there were only one man, one mind
> involved. I will get the ball back and think, now I want to hit the
> outside corner, low with a fast ball—and I'll look down and see
> the sign for a fast ball, low on the outside corner.[17]

Koufax described a situation in a World Series game against
the Yankees in which the Dodgers were leading by one run going into the last of the ninth inning. Mickey Mantle was coming up third in the order, and it was Koufax's hope that, because
Mantle was such a power hitter, he would get the first two batters out and pitch to Mantle with nobody on base. The first batter got a single, and when Mantle came up there was one on and
one out. Koufax described what went on in his mind and what
then took place:

> Mantle had to be pitched to and this was no time to make an-
> other mistake with him. Roseboro called for a fast ball, high and
> inside. Good. That's what we've been doing with him basically
> in both games, crowding him. Mantle fouled it off. We came
> right back with another fastball, high and inside, crowding him
> even more, and Mickey swung and missed. And then came the
> most vivid memory of the entire Series. As I got the ball back
> and began to look for the sign, I thought to myself, I'd like to

take something off my curveball. Now, why does a thought like that come to you? A change-up curve is exactly what you don't throw to Mantle, particularly in a tight spot where it can cost you a ball game. Change-up curves are what Mantle hits out of ballparks. I hadn't thrown a change-up in the entire game, as far as I could remember. And at the same moment that the thought came into my mind, there flickered the answering thought. But how will I explain that I threw it if he hits it out of here? I know it isn't brave, noble, or professional to worry about being second-guessed. It's just human.

And while the thought was still half formed in my mind, I was looking down toward the plate, and John Roseboro was putting down two fingers, the sign for a curve. He was putting them down hesitantly, though, so hesitantly that I had the feeling there was something more he wanted to tell me, something that couldn't be communicated by a sign. Normally he'd pull the fingers right back. This time he left the fingers there for a couple of seconds and then, slowly, still hesitantly, he began to wiggle them, the sign to take something off it.

As soon as I saw the fingers wiggle, I began to nod my head emphatically. I could see John begin to smile behind the mask, and then the fingers began to wiggle faster, as if he were saying to me, "Sandy, baby, you don't know how glad I am that you see it this way too."

As for Mantle, Lord only know what he was thinking when he saw my head bobbing up and down so vigorously. The one thing he should have been thinking was: They're not going to give me anything to pull—which would mean that the last thing in the world he'd be expecting would be a change-up curve. . . . As it was I copped out just a little. I did take something off my normal curve, but I didn't throw it real slow. It was a good pitch, though. It broke right down in there for a called strike three.

As soon as we hit the clubhouse, I grabbed Roseboro. "What

was the matter, John?" I said. "You seemed a little hesitant about wiggling the fingers on Mantle." And he grinned back and said, "I wanted to call it, but I was thinking: How are we ever going to explain a change-curve if he hits it out?"

That's how close the rapport between us can get. Not only did we have the same idea at the same moment, we even had the same thought about what could happen back in the clubhouse.[18]

The rapport Koufax and Roseboro had, the kind that activates gut feelings—a rapport that is not based on reasoning—is common among ballplayers. Graig Nettles reported a similar kind of rapport with Bucky Dent, who he played with as a Yankee. Nettles, who did not have the same experiences with other shortstops, said:

> Bucky was as good a shortstop as I've ever played with. We had a great rapport. It was though we could sense where the other was going to be. Sometimes the ball would go into the hole, and in an instant I knew I could get it if I dived, but I would know that Bucky was going to be there, so I didn't dive for it.[19]

As I indicated above, many ballplayers, including David and me, get so tuned in to what is happening in a game that they know what is going to transpire on the field before the event actually occurs. Nettles described one such circumstance in an American League playoff game between the Yankees and Kansas City. It was during the fifth and final game, and the score was tied going into the bottom of the ninth. Nettles came into the dugout as the Yankees came up to bat. He knew that a home run would decide it, and decide it soon. He reported:

> It was funny. We came into the dugout in the bottom of the ninth and I told Carlos May, "Get ready to pick up all the gloves

from the dugout. When someone hits a home run this inning, all the fans are going to come streaming in." No sooner had I said this than Chris Chambliss hit the home run. Even before he hit home plate, fans were flying onto the field.[20]

Babe Ruth himself often remarked about his ability to know beforehand what was going to take place on the diamond. Ruth was on a home-run binge in 1921. On September 21 he hit his fifty-fourth of the year, tying his own previous record. Six days later, in the Polo Grounds in New York, he hit his fifty-fifth home run, a new world's record, against St. Louis pitcher Bill Bayne. Ruth said after the game, "The minute Baynes let go of the ball I said to myself, 'Here comes number 55. It was the funniest feeling I ever experienced! My arms and legs seemed to sense what was going to happen!"[21] Hitting against Cubs pitcher Charlie Rush in a World Series game, Ruth seemed to know beforehand that he would hit a home run. After taking two called strikes, Ruth stepped out of the batter's box, pointed with his bat toward the centerfield bleachers, stepped back in, and blasted the next pitch over the centerfield scoreboard.

Teammates of Ruth often spoke about his extraordinary intuitive powers. Leo Durocher, who was a utility infielder on the 1928 Yankee team, spoke in superlatives about Ruth, saying that "Babe Ruth was the greatest instinctive baseball player who ever lived." He was a great hitter and he had been a great pitcher. "The only thing he could not do was run, but when he went from first to third, or stole a base for you—he invariably made it because instinctively he did the right thing."[22]

Orel Hershiser pitched his best baseball when he relied on intuition. He calls it "going unconscious" or being creative. "I love to be creative on the mound," he said. "I love to get into a rhythm with my catcher, to get to the place where we both know which pitch should be next, to be able to get him to change without even shaking him off. I get a rush from being in sync, from knowing my stuff is good and is working, from knowing my mechanics are not only right but also unconscious. That's when it's the most fun. Rock and fire. Change speeds, change locations, trick 'em, fool 'em, work 'em. Go for the strikeout only when you need it. Otherwise, get out of there with as few pitches as possible."[23]

Yankee manager Casey Stengel once observed that Willie Mays had more of this sixth sense than any other modern-day player. Mays was a multigifted, natural athlete who made difficult plays look easy. His famous over-the-head catch in deep center field off a drive by Vic Wertz in the Polo Grounds in New York City, in a World Series game against Cleveland, has often been attributed to his great instincts as a outfielder. Looking back at his career Mays described a catch that seemed to him to be even better, and more instinctive, than the Wertz catch. This came on a drive off the bat of Ed Bouchee of the Cubs at Candlestick Park in 1960. Mays remembered it as a ball "I never hoped to catch." Bouchee had hit a sharp liner with good depth to right center. Mays ran to cut it off, knowing that if he missed it the right fielder would play it off the fence. The ball "was past me," recalled Mays, "not only past me, but bending ever farther away from me into the wind. At the last minute, I literally stuck out the glove and snatched it out of the air when it was past me. My whole body had cooperated." Charles Polherty, the *San Francisco Examiner* photographer, has a picture of the catch, and "it shows me coming down on my left foot at the moment of the catch, which going to my own left gives me up to a yard's extra reach." Mays gave no rational explanation for how he made the catch. He did it, he said, on "what they call instinct."[24]

Mays acknowledged that he used intuition particularly when it most counted. "I developed a special intuition in the clutch, a sense that I was meant to win the game. I wound up hitting more home runs in extra innings than anyone else who ever played—twenty-two to be exact. That is six more than Babe Ruth hit after the ninth inning, and seven more than another clutch player, Frank Robinson, hit during his career."[25] Mays believed that everybody used their instincts to play the game. He saw nothing unusual about it. "I have it," he said. "You do too. Remember when you were a kid and tried the running broad jump. You *instinctively* hit the push-off board with your favorite foot, no matter how far away you started from, no matter how fast you ran, no matter which foot you started on. It's nothing special. More people have it than realize it."[26]

Many baseball observers believed that Mays was much more tuned in than other major league players. Baseball writer Charles Einstein, who wrote a biography of Mays, observed the quick starts that Mays got on balls hit to center field were the result of a highly developed intuitive sense. Einstein called it "a sixth sense that puts some fielders in motion *before* the hitter makes contact. There is no teaching this; some have it, some don't."[27]

On occasion Mays even seemed to have known what was going on in an opponent's mind and adjusted his play accordingly. In a game the Giants played against the Atlanta Braves, Hank Aaron was on first base when a ball was hit to deep right center field. Mays turned his back to the infield, and after a long run toward the fence, made an over-the-head catch. Meanwhile, Aaron, who thought the ball was in for extra bases, had rounded second and was on his way to third when he saw that the ball had been caught. He raced back toward first base, not bothering to retrace his steps and touch second base. Not knowing where Aaron was after he caught the ball Mays wheeled and threw, not to first base where Aaron would have had to return had he been running on the hit, but to second base.

Upon catching the ball, the second baseman was puzzled as to why Mays had thrown the ball to him. Aaron had already re-treated to first base and there was no longer time for a play on him. Looking out at center field, he saw Mays jab his forefinger straight down. With this cue the second baseman stepped on the bag and then looked at the umpire, who called Aaron out for not touching second on his return to first base. The question in everyone's mind after the game was, according to Charles Ein-stein, "How did Mays *know* Aaron had missed second on his way back? He himself was turned away from the action at the time." When asked by reporters, Mays said, "I know the way he runs." Mays in fact was intimating that his intuition told him Aaron had failed to touch second base and that a throw to the base would result in a putout. Looking back on his career, Mays con-firmed the fact that intuition rather than rationality guided him. "It may seem that everything I did on the field was natural," he commented, "because in so many of the throws I made, or balls I caught, I followed my instincts."[28]

Despite Mays's great speed and wide coverage in the outfield, a talent that can often lead speedy centerfielders to collide with other outfielders or crash into fences, there were few times, ac-cording to Einstein, that Mays ran into another player or smashed into a fence. Einstein attributes this to Mays's well-developed sixth sense. "Sometimes he literally seemed to wrap himself around other bodies without touching them," said Einstein, "like the dancing laser-beam ghost in the Haunted Mansion ride at Disneyland. He once did this to Bobby Bonds in a network telecast game at Candlestick [in San Francisco], running simulta-neously against Bonds and the fence without appearing to touch either."[29]

In 1974 in his twenty-first year as a major league ball player, Hank Aaron was closing in on Babe Ruth's all-time career home run record. But he was one short of tying the record, which stood at 714 homers, when the season ended. At the beginning of the 1975 season, the media and the fans focused on when Aaron would break the record. Aaron had hoped to break it in front of a home crowd in Atlanta, but the Braves first had to play a three-game series with the Reds in Cincinnati. Braves outfielder Darrell Evans was the on-deck hitter in Cincinnati when Aaron tied the record. Aaron apparently sensed he was going to hit one out. When he came out of the dugout he told Evans, "I'm gonna do it right now."[30]

After tying the record Aaron made no predictions about breaking it until the team returned to Atlanta, going homerless for the rest of the Reds series. In the first home game of the season in Atlanta, just before his second at bat, Aaron again said to Evans, "I'm gonna get it over right now." And he did, hitting the record-breaking home run in that at bat. Evans later said, "He [Aaron] didn't say it the first time he batted that night, when he walked. But he said it before he went up there and hit number 715."[31]

Restaurateur and celebrity-hobnobber Toots Shor once asked Joe DiMaggio what made him great. DiMaggio told him it was his ability to anticipate—to know where the ball was going before it got there. "That's what did it," said Shor, "figuring out the play before it happens." It helped DiMaggio both at the plate and in center field. Shor said, "That's why he was in front of so many balls when others were diving for them. That's why he was such a good curve ball hitter. He knew when the pitcher was going to throw a curve ball."[32]

His first Yankee manager, Joe McCarthy, also observed DiMaggio's great instincts. "He did everything so easily. . . . You never saw him make a great catch. You never saw him fall down or go diving for a ball. He didn't have to. He just knew where the ball was hit and he went and got it."[33] Late in his career, when he was slowed by a heel injury and couldn't cover as much ground in the outfield, he still was the best outfielder in baseball, according to left fielder Gene Woodling, who played beside him in the final years. "Pure running speed," said Woodling, "doesn't mean much if you don't know how to use it. Nobody used running speed the way DiMaggio did, on the bases or in the field. He just had this incredible knack, that timing, that second sense that separates the great players from the average players."[34]

The timing, the second sense—and the know-how and smarts—that go into making a great ballplayer seemed to come together in a great catch against the Cleveland Indians. Pitching for the Yankees that day was Eddie Lopat, who was famous for his three pitches—slow, slower, and slowest. Lopat was master of the off-speed pitch and because of his great control pitched successfully for the Yankees. As the game against Cleveland progressed Lopat began having uncharacteristic trouble finding the plate. Shortstop Lou Boudreau, who always hit Lopat hard, was at bat. Lopat recalled:

> There were a couple of guys on and I turned around to rub up the ball and check the outfield. DiMaggio was playing straight away. That's the way I expected it. But I throw two pitches and I'm off the plate and I'm behind two and nothing. The next pitch has to be a strike. I throw the fastball over the middle of the plate and Boudreau socks it. It was a line drive over Rizzuto's head at shortstop, and I figured it would go through the gap for a double or a triple and I would be gone. All of a sudden I turn and look up. The ball is hanging up and DiMaggio is catching it in left center field. I couldn't believe it. When the inning is over I ask him about the play. "When you went 2 and 0," he said, "I moved about seventy or eighty feet into left center. I knew you wouldn't let him pull the ball when you started working on him, so I played straight away. When the count went 2 and 0, I figured you had to come in with a pitch so that's when I moved.[35]

How did DiMaggio know where to move? From ballplayer reports about how he played center field, he knew intuitively where to go without figuring it out beforehand. Dario Lodigiani, a third baseman for the Chicago White Sox who played with DiMaggio in junior high school in San Francisco, remembered that the future Yankee Clipper played the outfield using his intuition, even as a teenager. Lodigiani recalled:

> In center field what made him better than anyone else was his instincts. He would move almost before the crack of the bat. If the ball was going to be pulled, he'd be leaning to his right. If it was going to be hit to his left, he was breaking that way as the pitch came to the plate. Amazing. And he didn't play you the same way on each at bat.[36]

Both as player and manager, Dick Williams followed where his heart led him rather than what his head told him. "That's the way I played, and that's the way I decided to manage," he acknowledged. Though he did not ignore statistics and gave them proper consideration in his managerial decisions, he said that whenever there was a question, "the heart was going to win every time."[37] Williams, a friend of my dad's who could be nice to you one minute and call you every name in the book the next, described a World Series game in which his Oakland A's were playing the Cincinnati Reds, and Reds slugger Johnny Bench came to bat in the eighth inning. Bench represented the go-ahead run. Williams ordered the pitcher to walk Bench and pitch to the dangerous clutch hitter Tony Perez. By so doing he knew he was breaking "all the unwritten Series rules." You simply *never* put the go-ahead run on base.

Williams decided before the Series began that, no matter what happened, he was not going to let the future Hall of Famer

Johnny Bench beat him. "I couldn't live with myself if he did. Even if it did mean going against percentages." Perez managed only a fly ball that scored a run, which took the A's into the ninth with a one-run lead, enough to win the game. "Like most moves of the heart," Williams recalled, "it paid off."[38]

Leo Durocher, who played for the Yankees in the 1920s and managed the Dodgers and the Giants in the forties and fifties, succeeded in part because he relied on hunches. Dodger pitcher Kirby Higbe recalled that "more times than not they worked out for him." Giants outfielder Monte Irvin, who played for Durocher during the 1951 season when the team won the National League pennant by one game, said:

> Durocher was making fantastic moves, taking the pitchers out at just the right moment, putting in the right pinch-hitter, moving men around the field as if he just *knew* where the ball was going to be hit. He was uncanny.[39]

Irwin believes that Durocher won six or seven games that year for the Giants by relying on hunches.

Joe Torre, a smart manager who is not afraid to delegate and who uses his players well, believes strongly that a manager can not rely on hard facts alone in making tactical decisions during a game. He said:

> You combine hard information with your hunches to make the best possible call. . . . I've learned that winning decisions in baseball are a mix of carefully strategy, close observation, playing the odds and pure intuition. . . . A baseball manager must also trust his instincts, drawn upon experience, about when to pull a starter from the game; his intuition about whether a hitter's bat is coming alive or going cold. Many baseball decisions are based

on a mixture of smarts and instinct. . . . If you favor facts over instincts, and things keep turning out badly, you've got to start listening to your gut.[40]

Torre also believes that his Yankee players need to rely on their instincts on the diamond. He said, "I don't overload my players with information, because I don't want them to lose their instincts on the mound or at the plate."[41]

Red Schoendienst approached managing in the same way, believing that it was a mistake to depend too much on rational analysis based on available information. He said:

> When I managed, we didn't have all the computer printouts and charts and data that are available to managers today. I think some of the guys rely too much on all that stuff, going strictly by the numbers and "by the book" and never taking a chance or a gamble on gut feeling. If baseball was meant to be played strictly by the numbers and "by the book" you could let a computer tell you what moves to make and you wouldn't need a manager. Baseball is still a people game, and managers have to remember that.[42]

When I managed the Tigers and the Rockies we had the computer printouts, described by Schoendienst, that provided a wide variety of statistical data. All the relevant information on the opposing team's hitters was available. In addition to their batting averages and their record against our team's pitcher, you could find out whether this guy was a good fastball hitter or liked the breaking ball, whether he hits in the hole or goes to the opposite field. Reliance on the statistics often led to a choice that conflicted with what my instincts told me to do. In those cases it took courage to trust a hunch or an intuition since it went against what the fans, some team members, and the press might think was the right thing to do. If the decision did not produce the intended result, the press would hammer you. I agree with Red Schoendienst and believe data of this sort should be used as a guide but not as a crutch. Like him, I trusted my intuition in making decisions on the field because I felt it was more reliable than the numbers or some else's observations.

SIX

Mental Imagery

Seeing with the Mind's Eye

BASEBALL'S BEST BALLPLAYERS USE MENTAL IMAGERY TO improve their game. They use imagery to visualize what they are going to do at bat or in the field. They do it every day, and as a result they can slow the game down. Nothing goes too fast for them because they visualize so clearly.

The ability to use mental imagery is not God-given. You are not born with a great imagination. You cannot imagine something if you have never done it before. The imaging comes last, after the work has been done. It is an ability that comes after you have played the game for a while. A coach cannot tell a young player to visualize this or that. It is not that simple. You cannot use imagery effectively unless you have worked at using it and experienced it over and over again. The game's best players are noted for their mental competence, imaging capability, work ethic, and self-discipline. Their greatness is based in part on their ability to imagine themselves always doing something positive.

I used visualization to hit curveballs. I was able to see in my mind the arc of the ball and its location over the plate before it was pitched. When I knew where a pitch came from and where it was going, I was ready. I could use imagery. I could now slow the game down, and be prepared to hit. Imaging requires self-confidence. You have to be confident before you can imagine anything. My use of visualization improved as my career proceeded.

Imagery did not always work. Against certain pitchers I could not use it. When facing a new pitcher—one whose deliveries I had never seen before—it was necessary to bat against him at least once, and in some cases several times, before I could visualize myself doing something positive. Visualizing the pitches of a knuckleballer was difficult because of the ball's unpredictable flight. Because great pitchers like Jim Palmer, Ferguson Jenkins, Steve Carlton, Gaylord Perry, and Catfish Hunter changed speeds so well, threw an assortment of curveballs, and mixed their pitches, visualization was next to impossible.

How Professionals Use Imagery

While effective use of visualization takes experience, there is nothing wrong in encouraging young players to begin using it. When Tommy Lasorda was coaching in the minor leagues he taught visualization techniques to young ballplayers. He indicated that developing self-confidence was a part of the process. He taught those training under him how to make mental pictures. He urged them to give themselves verbal commands, even during the hours they spent away from the playing field. "Start your day," he told them, "with a positive mental picture. I want you to see yourself, picture yourself, in your mind, wearing a Dodger uniform, playing in beautiful Dodger stadium. Picture yourself, you are completely poised and perfectly self-controlled. This image you see in your mind of yourself—the way you will be—will give you the self-confidence and power to achieve

your goal." The verbal commands were also important. "Say
to yourself," he urged, "I *believe* in myself. I *believe* I have the
confidence to play to the best of my ability. . . . Remember
self-confidence, self-control, concentration, controlled relaxation, and determination, those are the keys. . . . You *can* do it.
You *must* do it. You *will* do it. All you have to do is believe in
yourselves."[1]

David said that he uses imagery during the day of a game. He
uses it in much the same way that I did. He said:

> Running through my head throughout the day will be images
> of the pitcher I am going to face. I will be asking myself, "What
> does his slider look like, what does his sinker look like?" I don't
> have a formal routine, but I will do it to some extent before
> every game. It is a part of my preparation—probably something
> I should do more of because it is really effective—the last piece
> of the puzzle to get myself ready to play.

Mike said that he used images of me playing that have
helped him:

> A video highlighting my dad's career has been very helpful. If
> I struggle defensively, I picture him throwing a ball across the
> field, and it seems to click for me. That's imagery I have used
> throughout my career. If I can picture my dad making a great
> play, my body tries to emulate him. It's funny. People in baseball
> who know us say I do everything the same way he did.

From the time he was a youngster learning to play the game,
Hall of Famer Ted Williams, one of the game's greatest hitters,
used imagery to improve his batting. Williams's technique, it appears, was not too different from mine. He described it as "hitting at an imaginary pitch and visualizing what I would do with

it." His biographer, Ed Linn, said that Williams used imagery regularly, both on and off the field, to improve his performance at the plate. During a game he could be seen in the outfield in between batters swinging his glove as if it were a baseball bat. Linn said it was either because "he had just seen a new pitcher and was putting him into his computer, or he had been fooled by a veteran who had gone to something new."[2]

Williams described how he dealt with difficult circumstances:

As I got older and more familiar with the pitchers, they were getting more familiar with you and when, surprisingly, somebody would do something a little different, especially in a tough spot, Jesus, they'd get you out going the other way, you know. I'd want to deal with that immediately.

Linn said Williams would handle it in the outfield. "So when you saw Ted out in the field the next inning, shadow swinging, he wasn't feeling exuberant as was generally supposed. He was doing some instant visualization on how he was going to handle this new way of pitching to him." Williams acknowledged that Linn was correct: "The same way I was doing it in the backyard when I was a kid," Williams recalled. "Absolutely. I did that all my life."[3]

Roberto Clemente of the Pittsburgh Pirates occasionally used imagery rather than eyesight, when the situation demanded, to make a throw from the outfield. On one particular occasion when he used imagery, he was observed by Nellie King, a relief pitcher who was in the Pirates bullpen in right field at Forbes Field in Pittsburgh. Clemente was playing right field when a ball was hit down the right field line. King said the ball was a "kind of blooper that spun into the Pirates bullpen, which was adjacent to some of the field seats. The seats near the right field bullpen were almost on the line, and he [Clemente] ran behind the seats. He could not see home plate." The seats, filled with spectators, blocked the bullpen's view of the catcher. "I was in direct line with Roberto as he threw the ball. And I couldn't see home plate, but he could somehow tell where home plate was . . . and he threw it right into home plate—right on home plate," preventing the runner from scoring. "When he got behind the box seats, he couldn't see home plate. He had to throw over the [the top of them] but the son of a gun threw it right on target."

After the game King asked Clemente how he knew where to throw the ball. Clemente said:

> Nellie, when the ball was hit to the outfield and I turned my back on the infield, it's like a camera is going on in my mind, and I can see everything behind me. I'm going to the wall, I visualize every base, and I know where every runner is when I catch the ball and make the throw to the base where I should.[4]

Playing third base, I had experiences similar to that of Clemente. Balls were often hit hard down the third base line, making it necessary to dive and come up facing away from first base. I can still feel myself diving down the third base line and catching a ground ball behind me. The ball was out of my hand and in the air before I picked up first base. Even though it was awkward and difficult throwing from that position, most of the time my throw was on the money. I made the throw because I could see first base in my mind's eye, and I was confident in my ability. It was a great feeling to know where everything was located on the field.

Clemente evidently used imagery before every game to prepare himself to play. He would lie on the training table, apparently asleep. Teammates would go by him, said his biographer, Phil Musick, and snicker, because he seemed so out of it. In

reality, Clemente's mind was very active. He was mentally re-
hearsing his battles against the pitcher. Clemente described his
process this way:

> What I like to do is lie there and think about the game we
> will play that night. Say Tom Seaver is going to pitch. I think
> about him; how he likes to pitch to me. I see myself at the plate.
> First time up he throws me a fastball inside for a ball, then go
> slider away and I hit it on the line to right for a single. Next, fast-
> ball away, curve in, and I see the hole between short and third,
> and I pull the ball through it. Next time low slider, and I hit it
> hard back up the middle. The fourth time he go fastball away
> again, then change-up, and I see it coming and wait and then I
> hit it down the right field line. In my mind I have seen all the
> pitches Seaver has; I have hit against him four times. Then I get
> up and go out there and get four hits because I have seen all of
> his pitches. Some nights you get four pitches you can hit, and
> you get four hits. Some nights you only get one pitch you can
> hit, and I hit it because I have already seen the pitch in my
> mind.[5]

Third baseman Graig Nettles had an extraordinary ability to
field balls hit very hard, both far to his left and far to his right.
His Yankee manager, Ralph Houk, considered him to be one of
the greatest third basemen who ever played the game. "Nettles
could play the hitters better than any third baseman I ever had,"
said Houk. "He'd play off the base and get a ball you couldn't
believe, and the next time the same guy came up he'd hit one
down the line and Nettles would be there. I don't know how he
did it."[6]

Nettles described the mental imagery that gave him great anticipation. "I envisioned it in my mind before every pitch. I picture the ball being hit both ten feet to the left and ten feet to the

right. I never expect the ball to be hit right at me. As the pitcher winds up, I see the batter hitting the ball over the bag or into the hole and me diving for it. I'm ready to go either way. I've already rehearsed it in my mind so it doesn't surprise me when it happens." Nettles indicated that some third basemen visualize only those balls coming directly at them. "I know that some players envision the ball hit at them, and they are ready for that, but they don't envision it hit ten feet to either side. As a result, they don't get a good jump on it."[7]

Early in my career with Cleveland I played with Nettles, who was a mentor to me. I took over third base for the Indians in 1973 when Nettles was traded to the Yankees. Whenever we saw each other we continued to talk baseball, and specifically how to play third base, since as a rookie I played the outfield when I came up to the Indians from the minor leagues. Nettles gave me the structure for becoming a good third baseman, which included having a routine or plan of action. He convinced me that my move from the outfield to third base would be successful. Like Nettles, I used visualizations early in my career to catch routine ground balls. As I result, I did not worry about balls hit directly at me. This freed me up, enabling me to visualize a wider range of ground balls, hit both to my left and right.

Orel Hershiser said his use of imagery developed as a result of watching video replays of games in which he pitched. "I watched these videos, replaying them so I could form what they revealed. I watched with my coaches, and I watched them alone." He explained the effect this ultimately had on his mind:

After years of the detailed examination, something interesting began to happen. I realized that in my mind's eye I could see myself without coaches and without video tapes. I had felt and visualized my mechanics in such detail that I could actually "watch" what I was doing as if I were someone else watching me do it. When a coach suggested a change, I could make the adjustment, execute the pitch, then "watch" to see if I had done the right things.[8]

Sandy Koufax described a somewhat similar imaging process that he used while on the pitcher's mound:

Five or six times a year you have really good stuff and perfect control and it lasts over the full nine innings . . . the ball seems light, and your rhythm is so perfect that the baseball almost seems like an extension of your body. Not only can you feel yourself at work, you seem to be able to observe yourself at work. . . . When I am having a really good day . . . I have a mental picture of myself in action. Even while I am winding up, I have a picture of exactly what the ball is going to do, and exactly where the catcher is going to catch it.[9]

Mike Stanton, who has had a successful career as a relief pitcher for the Yankees, among others, described how he used imagery while pitching, and said he had used it for several years: "I don't picture a particular hitter, or visualize whether or not he swings. Instead, I see myself making a particularly [high] quality pitch, then I step up and perform."[10]

Barry Bonds said that he uses visualization to prepare himself to face certain pitchers. In a remarkable interview with ESPN's Rick Sutcliffe, Bonds explained how he treated an at bat against a pitcher who throws in the high nineties. He imagines himself playing catch with the pitcher, casually absorbing the heat with his glove. Then he mentally replaces his glove with his bat. This process takes away any sense of urgency or the fear that he might strike out if he doesn't speed up his swing.[11]

Hall of Famer Mike Schmidt was confident that it was possible to create in the batter's box what he visualized in his mind. It was not that difficult. He advised players to eliminate thoughts "that detract from the ability to make happen what you have seen in your mind." Visualizations worked, he said. "If you visualize getting a hit, and believe it, you can make it happen."[12]

Sometimes images come automatically, seemingly without any effort, and enable a ballplayer to make an extraordinary play. In the eleventh inning of the sixth game of the 1975 World Series between the Red Sox and the Cincinnati Reds, ultimately won by the Red Sox in the twelfth on a home run by Carlton Fisk, Joe Morgan came to bat with a runner on first. He hit a ball solidly to right field, which Morgan thought was going out of the park. As he watched, he noticed that right fielder Dwight Evans was not giving up on the ball, racing back to the fence. Evans leaped and made a diving catch of the ball as it was about to go into the stands, a game-saving catch for the Red Sox. "I couldn't believe it," said Morgan, and neither apparently did others watching the game.[13]

The use of imagery apparently enabled Evans to make the phenomenal catch. As Morgan was at bat, Evans began going over in his mind what he would do if the ball went into the stands. A mental image then went through his mind. "I saw the ball going in and myself diving after it, and then it really happened."[14] Morgan was incredulous when he later learned that just before he hit the ball, Evans had a picture pop into his mind where he saw himself in the stands taking a home run away from him. He called it the "spooky side" of that play. "That's hard to believe," he said, "but in this particular game anything was possible."[15]

As a young boy growing up playing sandlot baseball in Alabama, Willie Mays listened to the radio and idolized Joe DiMaggio. He saw himself as the legendary Yankee center fielder who did things so easily and well. "All the hours I spent catching a ball or throwing it or hitting it—in my mind, it wasn't me, it was the great DiMaggio." Mays's mental imagery went so far that he saw himself, even as a boy, as DiMaggio's successor. "Funny," he recalled, "as a kid I always thought I'd be the one to replace DiMaggio." While Mays never became a New York Yankee center fielder, he became the idol of Gotham as the New York Giants center fielder.[16]

One of baseball's all-time best base stealers, Maury Wills used imagery to help him gain an advantage on the base paths. An admirer of Jackie Robinson, who was always a base-stealing threat, Wills sought to emulate Robinson's ability to round second on a single, make a wide turn, and then hesitate just long enough to convince an outfielder, particularly a strong-armed one, that he could nail him going back into second. As soon as the throw was made, Robinson would break for third and make it easily.

Wills said he "visualized that happening all the time." He described an All-Star game in which he "took off from first on a hit [a single to left field], went around second wide, then feinted as if I were going back." Rocky Colavito, noted for his rocket arm, fielded the ball and threw to second. "A lesser player," said Wills, "would have followed the book and thrown the ball to third. He wasn't a lesser player. He fired into second and I threw it into high gear and continued to third base." Wills later scored, giving the National League an insurance run in a 3–1 victory.[17] (Rocky Colavito has a slightly different version of what happened. He said that "he had Wills picked off and should have been out by ten feet, but Bobby Richardson [the second baseman] made a throw that sailed and was off target, allowing Wills to get to third base.")

In the final twenty-seven games of 1967, a season that ended with the Red Sox clinching the pennant on the last day, Red Sox outfielder Carl Yastrzemski had 96 at bats and got 40 hits for a .417 average. In the process he drove in 26 runs and scored 24. His phenomenal play was in part due to his use of both intuition and mental imagery. He recalled that during the last weeks of the close 1967 pennant race, "Every fiber in my body was tingling and my awareness of everything going on the field was so high I felt as if I had ESP." During that stretch of games he experienced "a lifetime of thrills. I knew it was my time and I grabbed it."[18] He described how imagery helped him perform at critical moments during these games:

> I was on a roll. It was getting to the stage where I honestly believed that there was nothing that could come up that was beyond me. It got to the point where my confidence level was so high I'd go to bed at night and think of different situations when I could come up and win the game in the last inning. The thing was, something always *did* seem to come up. And then I'd imagine a new situation the next day, and I just knew I'd be there, be the guy who had to do it or we'd lose. It almost got to be psychic.[19]

Yaz knew that something extraordinary was happening, something that he had not experienced before in his career. "It was almost as if I was setting up the situations, not the team, that I was beyond what my surroundings dictated. You start thinking that way, that it's up to you and sure enough it is. After the game I'd always think, 'How can I help the Red Sox win the game tomorrow.' I wanted to be put on the line every time."[20]

Yaz described a critical game, the final one of the season against the Minnesota Twins. The Red Sox were tied for the league lead, and a victory would give them the pennant. "I continued to image that I would be the key man again," he said. "It was a conviction I couldn't shake, didn't want to lose." He came up to bat in the sixth inning with the bases loaded and the Sox behind 2–0. As he walked to the plate he said to himself, "Keep it under control. This is the situation you've wanted time and time again." He had imagined himself as "the ultimate hero" in just this situation. He had to put out of his mind all thought of hitting a home run because the Twins pitcher, Dean Chance, threw hard sinker balls that were almost impossible to hit for home runs. "As I put dirt on my hands, I started a litany: Base hit, base hit, base hit, up the middle. Don't try to pull the ball."[21]

Chance threw a sinker that started to tail away. Yaz knew just what to do with it. "I knew just where it was headed. I drilled it to center for a single that scored two runs, that ultimately led to a five-run inning, enough to win the game." Yaz believed it was his mental preparation and the rituals that he put himself through that made the difference, that got him into the zone. "Maybe wishing had made it so," he recalled. "Those dreams I had of putting myself in the clutch, where it was up to me and where I would come through."[22]

Imagery in Dreams

Some players get mental pictures in their dreams. Pitcher Billy Pierce, who made a major contribution to the pennant-winning 1962 Giants team, had a rich dream life. A recurring dream gave him confidence that the Giants would be successful in their drive for the National League pennant. Willie Mays remembered Pierce coming into the locker room and telling everybody a dream he had had in which he saw the Giants winning the pennant. Mays said that the guys laughed Pierce off, telling him to go dream some more and report back. A few days later Pierce came into the locker room and said, "I had the same dream again."

One of the players yelled out, "I don't want to hear it. Every time you dream like that we lose." Pierce was upset, telling the team that he didn't have control over what he dreamed. Again he was asked to have another dream. Mays said that the next day Pierce came into the clubhouse, shook his head, and said, "Same dream." Nobody really believed him, but his dream turned out to be accurate; the Giants won the pennant in the last days of the race.[23]

Negative Imagery

Negative images and negative thoughts have much in common. Both are rooted in fear of failure, which is big in baseball. Ballplayers who are mentally tough have learned, when negative mental images cross their minds, to shift attention to the positive. They have disciplined their minds to the extent that negative images, like negative thoughts, are noticed and quickly blocked out or eliminated.

As described in chapter 2, Mike employs particularly useful methods for dealing with negative thoughts and images. Self-talk and affirmations have helped him shift attention, calm down and relax, and focus on the positive.

SEVEN

Exercising Leadership

The Way Ballplayers Lead

I USED TO HATE IT WHEN GUYS WOULD COME INTO THE clubhouse after losing and say, "We need somebody who can lead." Leadership is very tricky and very important. A team is in trouble if it has only one guy who can lead. You need five or ten guys who can lead. In fact, the more leaders you have, the better chance you have of winning. The more you win, the more leaders you have. So they work hand in hand.

Leadership is exercised in different ways, and no one guy on a team can do all the things that good leadership requires. Let me list the ways players on a team can lead:

- Has a passion for the game and the success of his teammates. He wants to be involved.
- Is a good teammate, and shows compassion for guys who are struggling.
- Has the utmost confidence in his ability to play the game. (Pete Rose epitomized this quality of leadership.)

- Is willing to go out on a limb, get into people's faces, to hammer somebody if that's what's needed.
- Keeps his eyes and ears open.
- Gets everybody's energy going in the clubhouse before the game. (Outfielder Tom Goodwin was particularly good at that when I managed the Rockies.)
- Leads by example on the field talentwise and by being productive. Teammates play better because he is there.
- Has a good sense of humor.
- Plays in pain and with injuries.
- Commands the respect of teammates.
- Is not concerned about his reputation.
- Is vocal in the dugout, gets on the other team and his teammates.

As you can see, it is highly unlikely that any one player on a team will possess all of these qualities. That is why a team needs many leaders. Not everybody is able to lead. Some guys are phony about it. Whenever it suits them they will do it for themselves. I call those guys convenient leaders.

David has views on leadership that are somewhat similar to mine. He said:

I think leadership is misunderstood by a lot of people. Every team wants a leader, every manager, every front-office guy wants someone to step up and be a leader. You have got to be able to do a lot of things to be a leader. You need to be able to communicate, play hard, lead by example on the field, be competitive, and play the game the right way. All these things make up leadership. The more leaders you have on a team, the better the team. Take, for example, the players for the New York Yankees over the last several years. Most of those guys are leaders. Take the Mariners, who I played for a couple of years ago. Edgar Martinez, Brett Boone, and John Olerud, to name just a few, were all great leaders.

Ballplayers I Have Known Who Could Lead

When I think of players I knew who excelled as leaders I think of Pete Rose, Jim Sundberg, and Ray Fosse. Rose, more so as a player than a manager, was relentless in his passion for the game. There was no doubt in anyone's mind that he wanted to see the game played the right way. He gave the game the energy it deserved and was not intimidated by anybody. Jim Sundberg caught for the Rangers and was a great leader. As I mentioned before, he had an operation for hemorrhoids and played the same night even though the temperature was higher than 100 degrees. His tenacity was contagious. He played because the team needed him, regardless of how he felt. Fosse, a great catcher, exercised leadership in the locker room and behind the scenes. He dealt with things in the corner, not out front.

Barry Bonds leads by example and by being productive. Marquis Grissom credited Bonds with helping him stay consistent during the 2003 season. Grissom is in the twilight of his career. He became the Giants everyday center fielder after being platooned by the Dodgers in 2002. Batting third in the lineup, he has kept his batting average around .300. Grissom indicated that it wasn't anything Bonds told him. He was helped by watching Bonds at the plate. Grissom said, "He's done so much for me this year it isn't funny. It is the mental part of the game, not giving away at bats. He's been a big part of my success. It's good to see a specimen like that every day. It gives you a lift and some motivation."[1]

Giants manager Felipe Alou indicated that the team played better when Bonds was in the lineup. "Maybe he doesn't get enough credit," said Alou. "Without Barry there's a sense of insecurity here. Even if they walk him every time, we know he's here. And we anticipate every time he comes up to hit."[2] The Giants' record with and without Bonds in the lineup supports Alou's assessment. By September 1, 2003, with Bonds in the lineup the team had won 82 and lost 53. Without Bonds the Giants were below .500, having won 13 and lost 15. The Giants went on to win the National League's Western Division and gain home field advantage in the play-offs.

Hall of Famers Who Were Great Leaders

Major league baseball has produced many players who have strong leadership abilities. In fact, some guys are so good at leading that they can take on a leadership role on teams where the manager's skills are lacking. Described below are six ballplayers who possessed an extraordinary capacity to lead. They exhibited, as Leo Durocher stated, "a personal magnetism that infects everybody around them with the feeling that this is the man who will lead them to victory."[3] They are Joe DiMaggio, Jackie Robinson, Willie Mays, Mickey Mantle, Whitey Ford, and Roberto Clemente.

JOE DIMAGGIO

When Joe DiMaggio came to the Yankees as a twenty-one-year-old in 1936, the Yankees had gone three years without a pennant. DiMaggio was looked upon as the man who would get the team back into the pennant hunt. He had hit .398 for the Triple-A San Francisco Seals, and looked like a sure-fire big-leaguer. He did not disappoint. In the thirteen seasons he played with them, the Yankees won ten American League pennants and nine world championships.

DiMaggio had an immediate effect on the team; leading it in hitting, and making it a pennant winner in his first year in the majors. Yankee second baseman Frankie Crosetti recalled his impact:

> DiMaggio made the Yankees a new club in those days. He just made everything look easy. . . . He did things instinctively. When he started playing [in 1936] you could see we started making plays we had never made before. He would never throw to the wrong base. He just did everything he was supposed to do. . . . He was the big guy we were looking for, the home run guy, and we started winning regularly after he joined the club.[4]

Yankee manager Joe McCarthy felt that it was DiMaggio's clutch hitting that made the difference. McCarthy said:

> He could hit great pitching. Some of them can get two, three hits off the bushers, and not much off good pitching. He got them off everybody. He didn't care who was pitching, Feller, Grove, any of them, he just hit them. He hit the ball, not the pitcher. And he could do it in the eighth and ninth inning when the game was on the line, and a lot of them can't hit very good then. . . . When Joe was here a year or two we started depending on him more and more. He's the man who made our club go.[5]

Jim Hegan, who caught for the Cleveland Indians and later coached, was among the many opponents who tried to find flaws in DiMaggio's play and couldn't. "Joe didn't have any weakness in the game," Hegan said. "He did every thing well. . . . DiMaggio was special all over, at Yankee stadium or on the road. He could catch the ball anywhere; hit any pitch, do whatever had to be done to help the Yankees win a ball game. He was just a complete player. I've been in the game more than thirty years now. I've never seen anybody do as many things well as Joe could. He was by himself."[6]

Sports writer David Falkner saw the same qualities in DiMaggio's play. "The hallmark of DiMaggio's style," said Falkner, "was ease—ease in everything, from his long fluid swing, launched from a spread, seemingly immobile position, to the way he pursued fly balls. . . . With DiMaggio, center field had added to it one last dimension—majesty. Strength up the middle, with DiMaggio in center, came to mean royalty at the top."[7]

His teammates loved to play with him because he was team oriented and a winner. Pitcher Vic Raschi, who played with DiMaggio in the years following World War II, was expansive in his praise. "He was the greatest all-around player I ever saw," said Raschi. "He was a quiet leader on a ball club. Never said much, never argued. But at the same time he evoked tremendous respect and inspiration."[8]

Pitcher Charles "Red" Ruffing appreciated having "the Yankee Clipper," as DiMaggio came to be called, out in center field. "It was just kind of nice to turn around and watch him standing out there and you knew you had a pretty good chance to win the ball game." Ralph Houk, who was the bullpen catcher for the Yankees during the DiMaggio years, and later the Yankee manager, noted that DiMaggio gave "words of encouragement all along the line." Houk continued:

He never complained about anything. Even in 1949 [when DiMaggio was in the waning years of his career] when he had the heel injury and couldn't play, he never moaned. He just worked hard every day to get ready. When he did, that was the greatest show I ever saw. Here's a guy coming out of an operation, no spring training, goes in against the best pitching in baseball and tears the cover off the ball. That's some exhibition of guts. See, the thing that made Joe tick was winning. That's all he

cared about. He was a winner. He didn't care what he did personally as long as the team won. When we lost and he had four
hits, he was really down. He was just a great team player. The
only thing you can really say about Joe now is the same as we all
said then: He has just a hell of a lot of greatness in him. I never
saw him do anything wrong. I never heard a bad story about
him, not one, in all the years I played with him. That's almost
unbelievable for a guy who was in baseball as long as Joe. . . .
Without doubt he was one of the greatest leaders in the history
of baseball.[9]

DiMaggio led by what he did and the way he acted. He
didn't rant and rave at his teammates, but no one wanted to get
on his bad side. Hank Bauer, who played left field for the Yankees during DiMaggio's last years, commented on how he kept
players in line. "Once in a while a guy didn't hustle," Bauer
said. "DiMaggio never said anything to anybody about not hus-
tling. He'd just look at you. That was enough. Nobody wanted
to risk DiMaggio's displeasure. If Joe looked at a guy like he was
unhappy about something, that guy would really bust his ass after that."[10]
Yankee second baseman Jerry Coleman shed further light on
DiMaggio's ability to lead by doing:

What always impressed me about DiMaggio was his style. He
knew instinctively what to do. Once we were playing the Indians when somebody hit a single and tried to get to second on a
ground ball I had fielded. I got it to Rizzuto [the shortstop] just
as the guy arrived, and he smashed into Phil and drove him into
left field. It was a clean hard slide. Nothing was said. The next
inning Joe singles and is stretching it into a double. Joe Gordon,
his old teammate, was playing second base. Here comes the
throw and here comes DiMaggio. He hit Gordon so hard you

could hear his bones creak all over the park. He was safe and that was the end of it. Nobody had to spell it out. We were even. That's what I mean by leadership.[11]

Coleman gave DiMaggio one of the greatest compliments a player could ever get when he said, "He was a winner in every sense of the word. He was simply the greatest ballplayer I ever saw, and it's not easy for a man to carry that burden. Joe carried it with class and dignity." DiMaggio was so highly respected by his teammates that they asked him to be the arbiter in doling out World Series money. Teammate Phil Rizzuto reported that "DiMaggio was the leader. Everybody looked to him when we had our meetings for splitting up World Series shares. DiMaggio would decide who would get a full share and who wouldn't."[12]

Billy Martin, who played second base for the Yankees in the last years of DiMaggio's career, and who also later became a Yankee manager, commented specifically on DiMaggio's presence when he said, "When Joe walked into the Yankee clubhouse it was like a senator or the president of the United States walking into a room. All eyes would turn to him."[13] Pitcher Lefty Gomez, a fellow San Franciscan and a Yankee veteran who became DiMaggio's first close friend in the major leagues, shed further light on DiMaggio's greatness when he said, "I guess Joe is different than a lot of the rest of us. We are known as baseball players and that's about it. Joe always seemed more than just a baseball player. He seemed like a figure, a hero, that the whole country could root for."[14]

Jerry Coleman probably best summed up DiMaggio's leadership ability and impact on the Yankee team in maintaining a winning tradition when he observed:

DiMaggio never talked about it . . . but he exuded Yankee tradition, he had this tremendous class, aloofness, his presence on the field and in the locker room was just unbelievable. When he walked into a room it was like he was all by himself. I remember once being at a Graziano-Zale fight in Newark. . . . Here you have Frank Sinatra and Walter Winchell and then DiMaggio comes in and they all start screaming. They didn't care about any of the others. When Joe came in, he stopped traffic. In the spring of 1950, we stopped in Los Angeles, Fort Worth, New Orleans, and finally Tampa-St. Pete, and every place we stopped he walked out—and this was before television—and people just went crazy. The way that rubbed off on the rest of the players was interesting. You see, as a Yankee player you're carrying the banner for them. You always say, "I'm gonna do my part." And when you get nine guys on the field who are thinking that way, you're never going to lose. If you go out there and say, "I'm gonna get five hits today," that's the wrong approach. The approach was always, "I don't want it to be me if this thing goes sour." Every player had a stake in the Yankee tradition, and Joe was the guy who carried that banner highest of all."[15]

JACKIE ROBINSON

"There was an aura around Jackie Robinson," said baseball executive Peter Bavasi. "He was an exceptional man, a presence." The first black man to play major league baseball, Robinson, age twenty-eight when he joined the Dodgers, made an immediate impact where it most counted—on the diamond. His hitting, fielding, and base running earned him the National League's Rookie of the Year award. It was necessary for him to excel if he was to do what no member of his race had been allowed to do— make it in the big leagues where only whites had been allowed to play. The testimony of his teammates and opponents alike indicates that his contribution went far beyond his game statistics, which during his ten-year career were always impressive.[16]

Joe Garagiola of the St. Louis Cardinals remembered Robinson as "a tremendous clutch player. In a big game, in a big spot,
he seemed to be able to do whatever had to be done." Garagiola
commented on the pressure Robinson was under when he was
the only black player in baseball. "Jackie took an awful lot of
heat in those early years. I don't know of another player who
could have handled that and not exploded. I mean they called
him every name you could imagine, and threw at him and cut
him and did everything to run him out of the league. There
should be a special place in baseball recognizing Jackie for more
than just his baseball ability. He was a very special man. . . .
Jackie Robinson was very tough with or without a bat in his
hand."[17]

Robinson had the uncanny ability to make things happen on
the diamond when they counted most. Hall of Famer Ralph
Kiner remembered him as "the only player I ever saw who
could completely turn a game around by himself." Kiner credited Robinson with having an unequaled ability "to run the
bases, to intimidate pitchers, to take the extra base, to hang in
there under the worst kind of pressure . . . [and to] antagonize
the opposition."[18]

Teammate Roy Campanella saw that same ability to come
through when it was needed most. "He could get the base hit
when you needed it," said Campanella. "He could steal a base
when you needed it. He could make the fielding play when you
needed it. Jackie could beat you every way there was to beat
you. I have never had a teammate who could do all the things
that Jackie Robinson could do. . . . I have never seen a ballplayer
that could do all the things that Jackie Robinson did."[19]

As his career progressed, he was much admired by his teammates. Pitcher Clem Labine said, "He was the most exciting
player I ever saw, and he gave me goose bumps almost every
game I played with him." Pitcher Carl Erskine felt that playing

with Robinson improved his game. "Jackie plays so hard, with such intensity," said Erskine, "that he made you try that much harder. You simply couldn't let up if you were on the same ball club as Jackie Robinson. I know that I became a better pitcher, a tougher competitior, because I played with Jackie."[20]

Pitcher Ed Roebuck, who came up to the Dodgers when Robinson was in the latter years of his ten-year major league career, found himself in awe of him. Robinson "*was* the Brooklyn Dodgers" as far as Roebuck was concerned. Robinson helped smooth the way for Roebuck. "He made me feel at home. He'd come out to the mound. He knew how I felt. 'C'mon Ed,' he would say. 'You can do it. You can pitch up here. We all know you can.'"[21]

Biographer Maury Allen observed that Robinson was a charismatic leader both on and off the field. He was an accomplished ballplayer and an intelligent, articulate, and forceful presence both in the clubhouse and with the press. "He would debate anybody," recalled Allen. "He had become a spokesman, a national hero, a figure of history . . . a man other men wanted to emulate. Blacks across America were inspired by his success."[22] The Reverend Jesse Jackson, who was an athlete in school and interested in sports when Robinson was playing for the Dodgers, probably best summed up Jackie Robinson's contribution when he said:

> Jackie Robinson was our champion, our hero. . . . Jackie Robinson rose above segregation, rose above discrimination; he was a man of dignity and honor. When he came into baseball and assumed that pioneering role, he knew he was responsible for people, for all the people, he knew he had to be good and force people to respect and honor him. . . . [He was] this proud knight in baseball armor, and he was not inferior. He showed that it was talent and intelligence and skills that could lead a man out of the poverty and persecution of his surroundings. He was

a marvelous player, dynamic, exciting, a true Renaissance man, with a variety of abilities. It destroyed so many racist concepts about the shiftless, lazy black man. He literally lifted black people out of depression by his success. He was a therapist for the masses by succeeding, by doing it with such style and flair and drama. He helped level baseball off, to make it truly a game for black and white, with excellence the only test of success.[23]

In the mid-1980s a former Dodger teammate of Robinson, pitcher Joe Black, was appalled when he read a comment by a young St. Louis Cardinal rookie, Vince Coleman. Coleman told a newspaper reporter that he had never heard anything about anyone named Jackie Robinson. Black took it upon himself to write to Coleman. "Vince," he said, "Jackie Robinson was more than an athlete. He was a man. Jackie Robinson stood alone as he challenged and integrated modern-day major league baseball. His task was not easy or quick. He suffered many mental and physical hurts. He accepted and overcame the slings, slams, and insults so that black youths like you could dream of playing major league baseball."

Black lamented the fact that Robinson was being forgotten—even by his own people. "Unfortunately we tend to forget about people who stick their necks out for all of us," said Black. "They get chopped off but we get the benefits. That's the way it was with Jackie. I think all black players should understand today what they owe Jackie. I think all of baseball should know that. Jackie Robinson changed the game and changed America for the better."[24]

WILLIE MAYS

When Willie Mays came up to the majors at the age of twenty, his manager, Leo Durocher, saw in him all the earmarks of a superstar. When Mays joined the New York Giants early in the 1951 season after hitting .477 with the Giant's Triple-A farm team in Minneapolis, Durocher told his teammates, "There's something about Willie Mays. I don't know whether you see it. But I see it. He's a young boy. He's a baby. But he's got more talent in five minutes than the rest of us will ever have in our lifetimes."[25]

The Giants were in a slump at the time, mired in the second division. Management hoped that Mays, who had sparkled in Minneapolis, would get the team going. In his first appearance against the Phillies, Mays was 0 for 5 at the plate, but the Giants won the game. The next day they won again. Mays was 0 for 3. The day after that they won a third time, to sweep the Philadelphia series. Mays was 0 for 4. Despite his rough start, Durocher saw that with Mays in the lineup, his team came to life. "This boy can take us all the way," Durocher told columnist Tom Meany as the team boarded the train from Philadelphia to New York. "Some day he may even get a hit," responded Meany. Despite Mays's failure in the batter's box, Meany found himself weirdly in agreement with Durocher.[26]

The team was more relaxed and confident with Mays around. Charles Einstein reported on the mood of the team during its train ride back to New York. "From somewhere in the noisy car came that high sudden peal of laughter. The Giants, sullen at worst, uncommunicative at best, had through some alchemy become a relaxed band of merry men. Willing fingers shot out to goose trainer Bowman as he threaded his way down the aisle. There was a chorus of 'It's Howdy Doody Time.' "[27]

Einstein noted that several sports writers who were following the Giants agreed that a euphoria had set in the moment Willie joined the team. "He's a Rousseau's Natural Man," wrote Gilbert Millstein in the New York Times. Rival manager Charlie Grimm said, "He can help a team just by riding on a bus with them."

Einstein observed that there was "an ebullience there that no one could or would want to touch."[28]

Mays's first major league hit came in the next game against the Boston Braves ace Warren Spahn. It was no bloop single but a home run that went not only over the fence but over the stands and out of the ball park. It was a signature blast, the first of six hundred home runs that he was to hit in his twenty-three-year career. The hit caught everybody's attention. Einstein reported that the ball "immediately disappeared into the night over the left-field roof at the Polo Grounds. At last word it was still traveling." After the game, Leo Durocher was flabbergasted. "I never saw a fucking ball get out of a fucking park so fucking fast in my life. He swings, and bang it's clearing the fucking roof and still going up." Radio commentator Russ Hodges said afterward, "If that's the only home run he ever hits, they'll still talk about it."[29]

The Giants, with Mays's inspirational play providing a catalyst, went on to win the National League pennant in 1951 for the first time in over a decade. During that first season the quality of Mays's play caught the attention of several astute observers of the game. Baseball scout Charlie Metro spoke about the first time he saw Mays playing center field for the Giants. A longtime observer of young players, Metro was not one to get excited about every new talent. In Mays he saw something he had never seen before. After fixing his eyes momentarily on Mays, he found himself riveted:

> That's all I did for the rest of the game. I watched Willie. Watched him standing there, because he wasn't standing there. He was always moving. With all my experience, I never knew there was a dimension to the game like that. He had me like a bird transfixed by a snake.[30]

William Goldman, an award-winning novelist and screen-writer, and Giants baseball fan, described his experience of Mays the first time he saw him play in the Polo Grounds:

> I fell in love with him that afternoon. And watching him then, I realized unconsciously that it was about time he arrived on my horizon, because during all those years of being bored by baseball, of sitting in bleacher seats for pitcher's battles, or dying with the heat while the manager brought in some slow reliever, I'd been waiting for Willie. He was what it was all about. He was the rea-son. In my head, there was a notion of the way things ought to happen, but never quite do. Not until Willie came along. And then I could finally sit there and say to myself, "Oh sure, *that's it*."[31]

Durocher described the qualities that made Mays a superstar and more. He could "hit, hit with power, run, and throw." He also had "the other magic ingredient that turns a superstar into a super-superstar. 'Charisma.' He lit up the room when he came in. . . . My definition of Willie Mays walking into a room is the chandeliers shaking."[32] Giant teammate Monte Irvin, who played the outfield with Mays for several years, commented on what it was like to be on the same team as Mays. "Playing alongside Willie every day was exciting," Irvin said. "He kept pulling one miracle after another and as many times as you watched him you still never quite got used to it."[33]

Mays himself, when asked to comment on his unique talents and ability to inspire his teammates, stressed the fact that natural ability alone was not enough. Hard work was involved. "I had to learn on and off the field. If you have the right attitude, the younger players will follow your lead. It's not easy to get to this point. It takes a long time, I found out, but it's not really how old you are, it is the kind of ballplayer and person you are."[34]

MICKEY MANTLE

When Mickey Mantle came to New York as a nineteen-year-old in 1950, he was heralded as the next Yankee superstar, the ballplayer who would follow in the footsteps of Ruth, Gehrig, and DiMaggio and lead the Yankees to world championships. Tom Greenwade, the Yankee scout who discovered and signed Mantle, told a sportswriter:

> I don't quite know how to put it, but what I'm trying to tell you is that the first time I saw Mantle I knew what Paul Drichell felt when he first saw Lou Gehrig. He knew that as a scout he'd never have another moment like it. I feel the same way about Mantle.[35]

Mantle had extraordinary talents. As biographer Robert Creamer noted:

> He was a switch-hitter who hit with breathtaking power from both sides of the plate, he had a powerful arm, and he ran with a speed that was almost unbelievable. In practice sprints among the players, he not only won all the time, he ran away from everyone else.[36]

"My God," his manager, Casey Stengel, said, "the boy runs faster than Cobb."[37] Stengel wanted to produce "a great player who was his boy." As Creamer said:

> Now he had him—a youngster with Cobb's speed and Ruth's power, raw material with the potential to be the greatest player of all time, waiting to be a taught by Stengel. Casey said to a friend, "Can you imagine what McGraw would say if he saw this kid?"[38]

Stengel was frustrated with Mantle because he did not, in Stengel's view, become the dominant player he had imagined. Nevertheless, he helped the Yankess reached the World Series several years, hit for average and for power, won the triple crown one year, and put up Hall of Fame numbers. Stengel was still disappointed because he hadn't become the greatest player ever. Columnist Milton Gross wrote in 1954:

> Casey wanted his own name written in the records books as manager, but he also wanted a creation that was completely his own on the field every day, doing things no other player ever did, rewriting all the records.[39]

By 1960 Mantle had matured as a ballplayer and was living up to the billing he had gotten as a rookie. Ralph Houk, the Yankee manager in the early 1960s, saw him as the team leader, the guy whose mere presence on the field made a difference. Houk said, "There was nobody like him when it came to playing ball. I was always a Mantle man. Who wouldn't be." After Houk got the job as Yankee manager, he went to Mantle and said:

> "You're the leader of this ball club." I did it because of his talent and his competitiveness. He wanted to win so bad. I told Mickey, "I'm going to the press and telling them you're the guy." Mickey said, "Well, Ralph, I just don't know." I said, "Mickey, this is what I'm going to do." Mickey said, "What do I do?" I said, "Just be yourself. The guys get fired up just watching you go all out." I never saw him more determined than he was in 1961. It seemed like he always gets the big hits. I thought it was going to be his greatest year, and he did have a great year, but it could have been so much more if he hadn't got hurt.[40]

Mantle hit fifty-four home runs that year—the same year Maris broke Ruth's record with sixty-one. Had Mantle not been out of the lineup for several weeks late in the season, it is likely he would have broken Ruth's record that year also.

Yankee teammate Johnny Blanchard described how Mantle's style of play inspired the team:

> Just playing every day and never complaining, he was the leader. You never had to tell him to hustle or go all out, and everybody knew that and tried to emulate him, tried to give that little extra simply because they knew what he was doing. We knew he was hurting and tired, and he would never ask out of the lineup. If you saw that over and over again, day after day, season after season, you'd know what an inspiration he really was.[41]

Pitcher Luis Arroyo, who was the Yankee closer in 1962, credited Mantle with providing the kind of support he needed most. Arroyo said:

> I'll never forget this. We're in this real close ball game, a tie game, I'm supposed to go out and pitch the next inning. We need the game real bad, I know. Mickey comes over to me and says, "How you feeling?" I say to him, "I'm a little tired." He says, "Don't worry about it, I'm the next batter, this game's over." And just like that he goes out to the plate and hits one out. We won the game. We beat Detroit, the team that was right on us. So we go home. And he did that.[42]

As a veteran player, Mantle showed his leadership by extending himself in ways that were very helpful to younger players. Joe Pepitone, who many in baseball thought would become the next great Yankee after Mantle retired, said that during his rookie season, Mantle invited him to move in with him at the St. Moritz in New York City. Mantle offered his support when he learned that Pepitone was in the middle of a divorce. Pepitone reported:

> I stayed with him for a month. We'd go out to dinner, just have a great time together. He came to me and said, "I heard about what's going on with you, come and live with me, don't worry about it." He taught me a lot about a lot of things—feelings, the way I handled myself. See he had been taught by guys like Hank Bauer when he came up, so he told me about all the things I'd have to deal with, the fans, the media, the other players, how to stay straight, make sure I didn't go out and get a beer gut right in the beginning. He told me it took a special person to be a super-star ballplayer. He has to be able to do everything.[43]

Ralph Houk saw Mantle as a leader because of his attitude, skills as a player, and ability to inspire the team. Houk said:

> He was the biggest help to me. I think the fact that he knew I was depending on him to keep things going made him take on more responsibility. . . . The other players thought so much of him. Like the way he'd come back after an injury. He'd be hurt and not able to play, and then he'd come back and—*wham!*—first time up he'd hit one. He was amazing. Just amazing. All the players liked him, and they all respected him. When you have a player that's good who plays as hard as Mantle did, it just sort of makes the other guys play harder too. Mickey had great natural ability. Oh, he could run. He could flat-out motor. . . . He could hit from both sides, and he had a great arm. There wasn't any-thing he couldn't do. You have to have someone who is the leader, the one the others look to, and you have to let him know

you consider him the leader. I told Mickey that, and I told the press. . . . He became the leader and he was ideal. A leader has to be a good ballplayer to start with, because how can you lead a club if you're not one of the stars? Mickey was a great ballplayer, but it was his attitude toward winning, going all out, trying all the time, that made him such a good leader.[44]

WHITEY FORD

Pitchers are not often thought to be team leaders because they play, at most, only every fourth day. Yet Yankee pitcher Whitey Ford, "the Chairman of the Board," as catcher Elston Howard called him, was seen by his teammates and by his manager as the guy who inspired the ball club when they needed it most. His career spanned fifteen years and his won-lost record was one of the best in Yankee history. He pitched in eleven World Series and his record in the postseason games was better than that of any other Yankee pitcher. He was elected to the Hall of Fame in 1974. This is what those who played with him had to say about him.

Tony Kubek: "Whitey Ford was the greatest pitcher in the history of the Yankees. On the mound he was so sure of himself, so cocky. But in other ways he was almost shockingly humble. . . . He could be quiet, introspective, and very aware of the feelings of others. That is why guys on the team so admired him. On the field he was a forceful leader. In the clubhouse he was even more of a presence. He made a point to spend time not just with the stars or the guys who were having a tough time. He wanted everyone to feel a part of the Yankees, and it meant an awful lot to a young player when Whitey Ford spent some time just making small talk. On the mound he was just amazing. He was so confident out there, and that rubbed off on the rest of us. Whitey was in control of every pitch and every situation. I always considered him the consummate pro.[45]

Johnny Blanchard: "The best thing [about catching him] was that you never had to think about that much because Whitey was calling the game. You didn't have to worry about going to the mound to settle him down, because it seemed he never got upset. There was one time in 1961 when I remember Whitey calling me to the mound. Right away, I started thinking that something was wrong, he must be hurt. Then I was thinking about how much trouble we would be in without Whitey. So I asked, 'Whitey, what's wrong?' Whitey said, 'Nothing.' I said, 'Then why bring me out here?' Whitey said, 'I figured you could use a break.' Name another pitcher who ever said something like that to a catcher."[46]

Ryne Duren: "Whitey's personality had a bearing on his success. Everyone liked him. On a professional level the other teams almost overrated him; when Whitey Ford was pitching they figured they would lose because Whitey had won so often. Because Whitey never showed up the other team, the opposition wasn't as angry or determined to beat him as they were to beat other pitchers."[47]

Moose Skowron: "I loved playing behind Whitey because he never got on me if I made an error. . . . With some guys, you boot one ball behind them, and they'd throw their glove into the air. Not Whitey. He'd always remember the big hits you got for him. And after you made an error, he seemed to bear down more to get out of the jam. It was like he wanted to take the pressure off you."[48]

Mickey Mantle: "Whitey was going for his twentieth win on the last day of the 1956 season. He got beat 1–0 when I dropped a fly ball in center field. Then I ended the game with Whitey on third. I popped up to the second baseman. I didn't want to go into the clubhouse. Whitey was my best friend, and he could have finally won twenty games, and I blew the whole damn thing. If there was a trap door on the field I would have used it.

I finally went into the clubhouse, and Whitey saw how bad I felt. He came up to me and said, 'Ah Mick, the heck with it. We'll get 'em.' And Whitey meant it; that's why the players loved him. They always used to say that 'as Mantle goes, so go the Yankees.' I guess I thought I was an inspirational leader and all that crap, but we all knew that the real leader of the Yankees was Whitey. Line up all the pitchers in the world in front of me, and give me first choice, I'd pick Whitey."[49]

ROBERTO CLEMENTE

Many times during his long career with the Pittsburgh Pirates, Roberto Clemente demonstrated the qualities of leadership and presence that made him a great ballplayer. He boasted a lifetime average of .317, won twelve Golden Glove awards, a World Series, and a National League MVP award, and was instrumental in the Pittsburgh Pirates winning two world championships. His biographer, Phil Musick, said, "He seemed without flaw, and played, always, with an enthusiasm so contagious that you went home from the games and immediately began rummaging in the closet for your own baseball glove."[50] Clemente's personal presence and leadership ability were never more evident than in the Pirates' 1971 pennant-winning season. Past the age of thirty-five at the time, he was still in his prime. His teammates found inspiration in the way he played.

Outfielder Gene Clines said, "You watch Roberto and you can't help getting all psyched. There's this old man out there busting his ass off on every play of every game. Look, I'm twenty-five. If he can play like that, shouldn't I?"[51]

Pitcher Steve Blass said, "No matter what the situation is, we're always aware of what he can do. If the other team's got a rally going, he'll make some unreal catch to kill it. He's the only guy who turns the other players on. Seeing him come dashing in and sliding across the wet turf on his knees to make a catch with the spray coming up all around him . . . well, that's excitement." After Clemente had made a great catch and hit a two-run homer to win the game for the Pirates in the last weeks of the pennant race, Blass said, "That's what he does for us . . . he keeps us in games. With him around you're never out of it." Blass also commented on Clemente's effect on his teammates in the clubhouse before a game: "Everything in the clubhouse would center on Roberto the last ten or fifteen minutes before a game. Only the club would be in there then, and you're there with people you really trust, twenty-five men going through the pressure cooker of a pennant race. That was Roberto's time. . . . He helped keep us together."[52]

Teammate Dave Giusti said, "We lost a few on the coast and then we dropped one in Montreal and we were going horse-shit." Clemente offered the advice that got the team back on track. Guisti recalled that Clemente would say, " 'Hey we're not doing this,' or 'Hey, we're not doing that.' He didn't do it often, mostly when we were down. Other guys tried to do that. But hell, who were you going to listen to? He'd get on us and then suddenly we'd be on our way."[53]

Clemente was particularly good at bolstering players whose play was not helping the team. After pitcher Jim "Mudcat" Grant blew a critical game in the ninth inning with poor pitching, Clemente went over to his locker and said, "Forget this game; it is gone. You can't change it. You helped this ball club last year and you will again. I know you can still pitch." Grant had been disconsolate about losing. He'd given up a three-run home run in the ninth, giving the Dodgers a victory. "It was a dumb pitch," he recalled. "I felt terrible. Everyone got dressed quickly—I guess they wanted to leave me with my misery. But

Clemente came over and talked to me. All he did was spend twenty minutes holding my hand because he knew I was suffering. He's a guy who has been in baseball so long, and he had three hits that night, and he came over to help. It's the warmest thing anyone's ever done for me in baseball."[54]

Clemente also helped bolster rookie shortstop Jackie Hernandez. The Pirates' regular shortstop, Gene Alley, was injured late in the season and the Pirates brought up the youngster to replace him at a critical point. Steve Blass remembered how Clemente helped. "After Alley got hurt you could see Roberto walking in the clubhouse after games and spending time with Jackie. He bolstered Jackie's confidence. Day after day he made Jackie feel a part of the club. He was just sensitive to the fact that he could help Jackie contribute."[55]

Clemente himself downplayed the importance of what he said to his teammates, feeling that what really counted were his actions on the field. He said, "For me, I have to produce to be a leader. You can't be a leader with your mouth. I just say some things in the clubhouse after we lose . . . I tell everybody not to worry, that we'll be all right when we go to Pittsburgh. When the fellows have their heads down, you have to pep them up. If I put my head down they say, 'Why try?' A man they trust, if he quits everyone quits."[56]

Dodger shortstop Maury Wills admired Clemente because, through his skills and his ability to lead, he made the Pirates a much better team. Wills said, "I've been asked if I ever saw anyone better than Willie Mays. The answer is yes. Roberto Clemente was *much* better than Willie Mays. It wasn't just his arm. He could do everything better. . . . We hated Clemente's guts because he was so good. He had a style about him of arrogance, cockiness, and defiance."[57]

Roy McHugh of the *Pittsburgh Press* said that after Groat and Houk left the Pirates, Clemente took over as the team leader.

"New players looked up to him and the whole atmosphere changed."[58] Baseball commissioner Bowie Kuhn put in a few well-chosen words about why Roberto Clemente was the superstar he was. "He was indeed the perfect and classic ballplayer," said Kuhn. "He made the word 'superstar' seem inadequate. He had about him the touch of royalty. Somehow, somewhere, for me he should have been a king."[59]

The Leadership Role Played by a Team Manager

I believe a manager's job is to make it possible for guys on the team to lead. A manager does not need to be the center of attention. The less said about the manager, the better. The focus should be on the players. The best managers are the ones who step back and let the players play. If the team is successful, the manager will get appropriate credit. There are a lot of good managers in the game, and I can name several. Nevertheless, I have observed more mismanagement than good management in baseball. You have guys who understand the game, but they don't know how to handle people.

A good manager really cares about his players. He knows how to help players develop confidence, and he helps them to feel good about themselves. If a player needs improvement in a specific area, a manager must let him know about it. A good manager cannot let a player slide.

Of the managers in the game today, Bobby Cox of the Atlanta Braves sets the standard. His players trust him because they know he cares about them. He demands respect and gets respect because he respects his players. He doesn't have to show people how tough he is, but he is one tough SOB. Joe Torre deserves a lot of credit for the way he has handled the Yankees. Joe has credibility and presence. He is intense and smart. He has been able to step back and give the players their due. He's not the type of manager who sticks his chest out and says, "These guys could not have done it without me." While Torre is highly capable, I believe the Yankees would have won even if they had a lousy manager because of the leadership talent on the team. They have a group of players who have established themselves as winners, so they probably would have won even without a guy like Torre. They wouldn't have won as big, but they would have been winners.

EIGHT

Having Fun

I HAD A LOT OF FUN PLAYING BASEBALL. WE WHO HAVE made a career of major league baseball do it because it is fun. If we didn't enjoy it, we would choose another profession. There were times in certain games when I was so thrilled to be a part of the competition that I wished the game would never end. For me, the more intense the game was, the more competitive it was, the more fun it was. Winning, of course, was the most fun. Everyone is happy and having a good time. Like many other ballplayers, I believe that playing well and having fun go hand in hand. The most successful teams are the ones that have the most fun.

David has had a lot of fun playing the game and has talked about what having fun has meant to him:

Having fun is really important. It helps you play better. In fact, the more fun you have the better player you are going to be. We all grew up playing the game for fun. A lot of times the game may not be going well for you, and if you say to yourself,

"I'm going to go out there and have fun," it brings the game back to where you were when you were young and the game was simpler for you. If you are not having fun, it will catch up with you. You are not going to have much success.

Graig Nettles, whom I admired as a player and mentor and who had a great career in the seventies and eighties, talked a lot about the need to have fun. For him, having fun was a big part of the game and the major reason he played. He said:

What I love about the game of baseball is that whether you win or lose, it's still so much fun. You go out on the field, and you're using your body to do something that you love to do. You learn it when you're four or five, and you're able to do it until you're in your forties, and every day is different and exciting and something to look forward to. There are peaks and valleys, and even when you're mired in one of the valleys, it's still fun.[1]

Nettles thought Yankee owner George Steinbrenner did not understand that having fun and winning went hand in hand, and that his attempts to put pressure on his players to win and his rah-rah speeches backfired. "George has taken an awful lot of the fun out of the sport," said Nettles. "I'm sure George is a Vince Lombardi fan from way back. 'Winning is everything,' but that's a bunch of bullshit. There are different ways of going about winning, and in my opinion there is only one way to win: by having fun. The only reason anybody plays baseball in the first place is that it is fun. So why should you get all serious about it just because you're getting paid to play?"[2]

Nettles insisted that having fun had nothing to do with the money you made, and I agree with him on that. He said:

The fans don't understand this, but the amount of money you're making has nothing to do with whether the game is fun or not. The money and the game are separate. The fun has to do with how well the team is playing. If I was making a million a year and we were out of it, it would not be fun. I'm not saying the money isn't important. I am saying that the fun is still more important than the money. The fun part of the day is being in the locker room with the twenty-five guys or being out on the field.[3]

Nettles is right on when he refers to the value of having fun in the clubhouse with your teammates. For me, the clubhouse is a sacred space. The camaraderie you have in a team environment is not available anywhere else. You can share personal things. It is great having a bunch of teammates rooting for you, and caring about you, whether you get a hit or strikeout. You can have so much fun talking about baseball, hammering each other, getting on each other, talking about the great game a guy just had. Guys really enjoy being around each other in the clubhouse. The fun you have there translates into better performance on the diamond.

Some guys are particularly good at creating good team chemistry in the clubhouse and making the game fun for other players. When I was managing Colorado, Tom Goodwin and Brian Hunter gave their teammates an energy transfusion before each game. Guys couldn't wait to get to the clubhouse to see what those two would do next. The energy the team had on the field was a by-product of what they did. By making it fun to be in the clubhouse, they made a major contribution to the success of the team.

Catcher Gary Carter played for the New York Mets in the mid-1980s when the team enjoyed great success. It appears that the Mets had players like Goodwin and Hunter, who could, through their antics on the field and in the clubhouse, put energy into the team. Carter said that the more fun the team had, the better it played.

> The '86 Mets were happy and loose, and when a team is that way the funny guys start acting up and the funniness spreads. . . . There were the "rally hats" when we started building a big inning—the bill of the hat turned up and cradling a baseball, for good luck. A towel over the head was supposed to be lucky. When the Mets were hitting it sometimes looked like a convention of sheiks out in our dugout.[4]

Joe DiMaggio also believed that success on the field was enhanced when there was good team chemistry and players cared about each other and were having fun. He recalled that the world champion Yankee team of 1937 played good baseball because the game was a lot of fun. "Their long distance hitting," he said, "reminded writers of the famed 'Murder's Row' of other years. What nobody outside our tight-knit circle could know [was that] we worked so hard because we were happy about playing ball together. Everybody was interested in the welfare of everybody else. And ballplayers do their best under those conditions."[5]

In his long career, Hall of Famer Dave Winfield played for several major league teams. He described the joy of being with other players, doing things well on the field, and succeeding:

> Professional, or not, there has to be some joy in it, if only to relieve the pressure that builds over a 162-game season. A team doing well can have a lot of fun, talk some outrageous trash in the locker room, on the bus or on the plane. There's fun to be had on the field, too. Hitting back-to-back home runs. Stealing

bases, sliding, scoring. Throwing the other guy out at the plate. You can have a *great* time.[6]

I can identify with Winfield's comments about the fun of playing on a major league diamond. Part of the thrill for me was waiting in the dugout ready to run out on the field, having the confidence to know that I was going to play a good game. One of the most gratifying things for me during a game was to hit the ball hard or make a great play at third base that resulted in a big out that gave the team a better chance of winning.

Pete Rose believed that the game had to be fun or it wasn't worth playing. "You should always be trying to have some fun," he said, "and if you're not having fun, do something else."[7] Baseball would be a much better game if guys could play with the intensity that Pete played with and also have the same amount of fun. Pete played with the incredible mix of fun and intensity that all ballplayers are searching for. He saw himself as an entertainer with the fans coming out to watch him. It made the game much more fun for him. Sportswriters often commented on Rose's ability to make the game fun for the fans.

Teammate Tommy Helms commented on how Rose's ability to have fun contributed to his endurance over the course of the season. Helms said: "Everybody gets tired by the end of the season, but Petey didn't, and I think the reason was that the game was so much fun for him. He played the second game of double-headers and got that big finish every September because he was mentally fresh. And that was because he was still having fun."[8]

The late sports columnist Red Smith reported, "He played happy." He played with "a lascivious enthusiasm. If someone bought a ticket just to see Pete Rose it was for a simple reason. It felt good watching him."[9] Sportswriter Roger Kahn once observed that Rose "had a great feeling for the fans. He knew how to sell the game. He knew how to make it fun for people who came to the ballpark." A teammate, Merv Rettenmund, saw the same quality in Rose, saying that Rose wanted "the fans to feel good when they leave the ballpark."[10] Not many players had that "foremost in their minds," believed Rettenmund, but Rose did. "He saw the game as entertainment. If everybody thought like he did," Rettenmund said, "the game would be a lot more exciting."[11]

Hall of Famer Mike Schmidt pointed out that ballplayers who viewed the game as a job or as a good way to make a living were not as successful as those who played for the fun of it. Schmidt said:

> The players who think baseball is just work and do it for the money or the fame or as an ego trip, just don't do as well. It's guys who love to play the game, and have a good time doing it, who will do the best and be rewarded in the end.[12]

I see it the same way. There is no team chemistry when the guys are more interested in their stats than in the outcome of the game, or focused on how much they are going to make next year. Nobody on that kind of a team is having much fun. Teams like that don't win.

Schmidt said that there were periods in his career when he couldn't think of anything he'd rather be doing than playing baseball, because it was so much fun. "The idea that someone is paying me to do this," he said, "seems absurd."

Tommy Lasorda made a good point when he said that ballplayers who have fun playing the game are mentally fresh and ready to play good baseball:

> I have always believed that one of the most important sounds in any clubhouse is laughter, because a team that is laughing is

happy, a happy team is a relaxed team, a relaxed team is a confident team, and a confident team is a winning team. Laughter is
food for the soul, and I wanted any team I was with to be as well
fed as I was."[13]

After becoming manager of the Los Angeles Dodgers in
1977, Lasorda changed the atmosphere of the Dodger clubhouse
by making his office accessible to his players:

> I wanted that office to be a place that my players felt comfort-
> able walking in and out of, where they could sit down and have
> something to eat, watch television, even use my telephone—for
> local calls. I wanted to create a relaxed, enjoyable atmosphere.[14]

While a member of the winning Cincinnati Reds teams of
the 1970s, Joe Morgan learned that there was a big difference
between playing loose and playing uptight. It had to do with
having fun. After moving to a new team, the Houston Astros, a
ball club that had tightened up in the clutch the year before,
Morgan tried to help the younger players come to see the importance of making the game fun for themselves. "I knew that
laughter and having a good time could count just as much as
swinging the bat or catching the balls."[15]

Rickey Henderson thought that it helped his game to have fun
on the field, to engage not only with his teammates but even with
the fans. "I laugh and talk with the fans throughout the game,"
said Henderson. He says he will smile and ask the fans in left field
how they are doing. Henderson said he does that because "it
loosens me up. The last thing I want to be is tense. Talking and
laughing make me relax. Other people try to relax in different
ways. They'll meditate or even smoke a cigarette or chew to-
bacco. I talk. . . . It's become nature for me, almost a habit, to
combine work with pleasure. I've been doing it so long."[16]

Babe Ruth made a career out of having fun. Heywood Broun, a sportswriter who followed the Yankees, once said that Ruth was "a liberator who endeavored by personal example to show that no fun could ever hurt you." In the locker room he loved to yell, play practical jokes, and wrestle around with the younger players, and he could violate every training rule in the book and yet perform superbly.[17]

His manager, Miller Huggins, tried to get him to tone down his lifestyle. "You've got this country goofy, Babe," he said, "but all this success may spoil you, ruin your career." He told Ruth that he should go to bed earlier and be careful about what he ate and drank. He felt that with proper rest, Ruth could take off twenty-five pounds. Huggins promised, "You'll hit even *more* home runs."[18]

Ruth gave it a try and went to bed at nine that night. The next day he went hitless. He did it for three nights in a row and each day he failed to get a hit. Ruth decided to have no more of this and the next night went out and played cards all night, relaxing and enjoying himself. "In between," said a reporter who was with him, "the Babe ate probably fourteen sirloin and hamburger sandwiches with some odds and ends thrown in." The next day, after only two hours' sleep, he hit two homers, one of them over the center field scoreboard.[19]

It has been my experience that you can play for a losing team and still have fun. When I was a rookie with the Cleveland Indians in 1972, the team was not a good one. We lost a lot of games. When the Yankees came to town we would have over fifty thousand people in the stands. With other teams the attendance was under five thousand. It was special for us to play the Yankees because they were the best. We played better against them than against other teams. When we played them, my heart pumped up, and I had more energy. The Yankees gave you something to shoot for, and when we beat them, which we did occasionally, it was a lot of fun. Part of the fun of going to the ballpark for a game is knowing you have a chance to win. Without a chance of winning, a lot of the fun is taken out of the game.

NINE

On Winning and Losing

WE ALL WANT TO WIN. IN BASEBALL, THAT'S ULTIMATELY where we find the pleasure and the enjoyment. Winning is fun. After a victory everybody on the team is happy and having a good time. Nevertheless, I would much rather be with a group of guys who lay it all out on the line both on the field and in the clubhouse—and lose—than win with a bunch of guys who care only about themselves. I do not aspire to be around guys who don't care about me or aren't concerned about whether I care about them. I think Mike has put his finger on the problem, particularly in the minor leagues, when guys care more about their individual stats than winning. He said:

> In the minor leagues, guys tend to make baseball an individual sport because they are trying to make it to the big leagues. It is hard to play when you are all wrapped up in yourself and your numbers. Everybody plays better when they pull together to win and make winning the number-one goal. It works better when you think about driving a guy in or moving the runner

over from second to third. Just thinking the right way—playing the game to win makes a big difference. I don't know how many times you get a base hit when you are simply trying to move a guy over. It helps the team and helps your numbers if you think about putting your team in a position to win. It has been my experience that most guys who are on winning teams have good years.

Winning Isn't Everything . . . It Is the Only Thing

For many in major league baseball—and I don't include myself among them—nothing else matters but winning. It is the only thing that many coaches and players focus on. Sandy Koufax expressed a point of view shared by many ballplayers when he said:

> Belonging to a baseball club is like being a member of a social club such as the Rotary Club or the Knights of Columbus. Only more so . . . There is among us all a far closer relationship than the purely social one of a fraternal organization because we are bound together not only by a single interest [playing baseball] but a common goal: to win! Nothing else matters and nothing else will do. A winning clubhouse after the game is one of the rare places where you will find thirty people smiling happily.[1]

Cal Ripken Jr., whose father played and managed in the major leagues, said that from a young age his total focus was on winning:

> I was raised in a family where everything was competition. If you didn't win, it wasn't fun. . . . Winning is still the purpose of

playing. The fun is to win. It brings everyone together as a team. . . . There is nothing better than playing on a team that's winning.[2]

Joe DiMaggio epitomized the Yankee attitude toward winning. "The thing that made Joe tick was winning," said his manager, Ralph Houk. That's all he cared about,"[3] Yogi Berra expressed an attitude toward winning that he felt was special to playing for the New York Yankees:

> You did feel like a family being part of the Yankees, like we were brothers. . . . We really were a true team and were confident we'd win—that was the Yankee culture we grew up in. Winning was always the bottom line.[4]

As a young player Lou Piniella had been more focused on personal performance than on winning. Playing for manager Earl Weaver in the minors shifted his attitude. Winning became all important. Piniella said:

> I learned a lot of baseball from him. Mostly I had learned the importance of winning. Until then I had been concerned with my individual records and performances, and my own development as a player. Weaver taught me that, on a professional level, there was nothing more important than winning, no matter who contributed. He instilled in me his own burning desire. I am indebted to him for that.[5]

Red Schoendienst played for the St. Louis Cardinals for ten years before being traded, ultimately, to the Milwaukee Braves, where he was instrumental in helping the team win the National League pennant in 1957. He stressed the importance of winning when facing his former teammate and close friend Stan Musial. Friendship made no difference when they were on opposing sides. Schoendienst said:

> The strange part was when I got to first base and stood there next to Musial, my roommate for ten years. . . . Not many guys talked to players on the other teams back then. You really didn't even want the guys on the other team standing around watching while you were taking batting practice. It was really a more competitive game, almost like war. You had to find a way to win somehow; that was the only thing that mattered.[6]

Losing Is Like Death

For those who see winning as all-important, losing can be a bitter pill to swallow. Tommy Lasorda described the trauma of losing when he said:

> Every loss, every season, is tough, and experience has not made me a better loser. I've been the losing manager in some very painful ball games. Losing that one game play-off to Houston in 1980 made me sick. Losing the pennant on the last day of the 1982 season when Joe Morgan hit a home run killed me. Losing the World Series to the Yankees in 1977 and 1978 buried me. There have been many times in my career when we've been four yards off shore and drowned. Is one loss tougher than another? They're all tough. Trying to pick out the most painful loss in a career is like trying to decide if I'd rather die from poison or in the electric chair.[7]

Billy Martin, who played and managed for the New York Yankees as well as several other teams, had a more difficult time than most in dealing with losing. Lou Piniella described how

Martin reacted to losing the World Series in 1981 after winning the pennant with the Oakland A's:

> He sat there alone behind his desk, tears in his eyes, his green and white Oakland uniform soaked in sweat. His feet were up on his desk and he was staring straight ahead. I knew how hard this man took losing. No manager I ever played for suffered more when he lost. He was often inconsolable after a defeat. His whole life revolved around winning.[8]

Don Baylor observed that same life-and-death attitude in Martin. Baylor said:

> Billy could not take losing. That applied to individual games as well as the entire season. . . . Mere losses took a phenomenal toll on him emotionally and physically. . . . He starts the season in the best of health . . . tanned and rested. . . . Halfway through, he looks like death. The stress and his lifestyle leaved him haggard.[9]

Sandy Koufax recalled the difficulty he had in dealing with being the losing pitcher. "When you win," he said, "there is a big W before your name. When you lose, there is that big black L, and not all the perfume in the world can wash it away. Of all the sad words of tongue or pen, the saddest to me are these: *Losing Pitcher, Koufax*." Koufax noted that every major league ballplayer was aware of the consequences of losing. "No publicity man," he said, "can add one point to your batting average, and no friendly critic can take away one loss from your pitching record. We have an absolute democracy—or maybe it's an aristocracy—of ability. You either make your contribution to the overall effort, or you can go home."[10]

Koufax recognized that it was necessary to deal with the reality of loss and to recognize that losing was a part of the game. "No matter how successful any individual player may be at any moment," he said "we all know there are days of grief for him ahead. We all know that if you play this game long enough, it—just *it*— is going to humble you."[11]

Pitcher Jim Bouton, who achieved fame with his book *Ball Four,* described the lengths some managers go to stress the importance of winning:

> After a loss the clubhouse has to be completely quiet, as though losing strikes a baseball player dumb. The radio was blaring when we came into the clubhouse and Joe Schultz [the team's minor league manager] strode the length of the room, switched it off and went back to his office. After that you could cut the silence with a bologna sandwich. The rule is that you're not supposed to say anything even if it's a meaningless springtime training loss. Feeling remorse has nothing to do with it. Those who did poorly in the game and those who did well, even those who didn't play, all are supposed to behave as if at a funeral. The important thing is to let the manager and coaches know you feel bad about losing. I'm sure they believe that if you look like you feel bad about losing then you're the type who wants to win.[12]

When Winning Is No Longer an Obsession

For many years during his career as a player and manager, Sparky Anderson held to the Vince Lombardi dictum, "Winning isn't everything . . . it's the only thing." Anderson described himself as "a winaholic." He said:

> I took winning to limits nobody could have imagined. I don't think there has ever been a person who took losses harder and

kept them inside longer than I did. I crossed all boundaries of reality. . . . I actually believed Sparky Anderson was put on this earth solely to win. . . . When we lost, I believed there was not time for any nonsense like eating. Everybody was supposed to put their head down in dead stone silence and think about what had just gone wrong. A piece of everybody's body was supposed to die after a loss. It was a time to bleed. . . . Every loss sliced a little piece of my innards. It felt like a four-sided razor blade inside my body. It started to twist and turn from the top of my throat and work its way slowly down to the pit of my stomach. I bled. I cried. But I kept it all inside so no one could see. After each loss I sat quietly with the writers. I answered all their questions. I never raised my voice.[13]

Anderson took losing personally. It affected his self-image, his sense of who he was. He said:

I always looked at losing as a personal failure. Losing, to me, was an embarrassment. I always felt like I had let people down. I felt like I was less of a man. There was dishonor in losing. And I felt like it was all my fault.[14]

It is not surprising that while managing the Detroit Tigers in May 1989, he collapsed from exhaustion and left the team for two months. His illness taught him a lesson. He changed his attitude toward winning and losing. "For the first time in my life I finally understood what baseball really is," he reported. "It is a game you must play hard, but it's still a game."[15] He continued:

I accept losses in a different way now. I am no longer embarrassed by them. I no longer feel insulted or that I let anyone down. Not as long as I've prepared my team to perform at its highest level. Once I've done that, there's nothing else I can do. . . . Winning now is a wish for me. It's no longer an obsession. Losing is not a tragedy. . . . It's taken a long time to wake up.[16]

Joe Torre, who had a long and successful career as a catcher for the Cardinals, Mets, and Braves before he became a manager, distinguishes between being successful and winning. His attitude toward winning is much the same as mine. He acknowledged that "winning is a valid goal. It is the pot at the end of the journey." Nevertheless, as he sees it, "success and winning are not always one and the same." As a player, if you focus on playing "to the best of your ability" and concentrate on "being the best you can be—as an individual and team member," then you have your "priorities straight." You are not "living and dying by your latest win-loss record," or concerned only about whether "you've made it to the top of the heap that year."[17] Torre continued:

> I hold a point of view that's not too popular these days: Being great at your profession doesn't mean you're going to be a winner. This one's even less popular: Giving 100 percent doesn't guarantee a victory, either. You don't control all the conditions that make it possible for you to be a winner. . . . Getting the most out of your ability is all you can do. . . . Even being super-talented and committed is not a guarantee of victory. The breaks are not always going to go your way.[18]

Orel Hershiser expressed a point of view on winning and losing that makes a great deal of sense, a point of view I agree with. He saw himself as a competitor who always wanted to win, yet he believed that a higher principle was involved. He called it "selling out to the process." The principle, he said, was not "sell out to the results" or "sell out to winning." Selling out to the process meant "complete commitment, surrender—just doing it." What concerned him most was the level of his performance, not whether he won or lost. If he performed well and lost, he was not downhearted. If he performed poorly and still won, he would be dejected after the game. "My dejection after a win," he said, "could have come from my knowing that the win had come *in spite* of my performance. He explained:

> During a crucial moment in the game, I had laid a fastball over the middle of the plate, right in the hitter's wheelhouse. Instead of blasting it 350 feet, like he should have, he popped it up to the shortstop. I knew the hitter well enough to know that if I did that again, he'd hit it out. Regardless of the result— which in this case had been good for me—I knew success had not come from my good work, but from the hitter's failure to deliver.... And there were times when I had my best stuff. My regimen before the outing was satisfactory. My mechanics, my rhythm, the velocity and movement of the ball during the game were everything I had prepared for.... In spite of all I was do- ing, batters hit my best stuff and I took the loss. This did not upset me.... If I lost, even though I was performing at a reason- able level, I knew that the "law of baseball probabilities" would turn my way and I would eventually win . . . and win more of- ten than lose.[19]

Throughout his long career, Pete Rose took a balanced ap- proach toward winning and losing. His biographer, Michael Sokolove, commented on attitudes that helped Rose play at a high level for many years:

> Over the whole century-long history of baseball, of all the thousands of players who have populated major-league rosters,

it's possible that no player was more mentally suited for the game than Pete Rose. And one reason is that he was such a surprisingly good loser. A personal failure never put him into a funk. He didn't bash water coolers, turn over clubhouse food trays, pick fights with teammates or writers. He didn't take the game home with him and he didn't sulk. Whether he got four hits or went hitless, he was the same person after the game.[20]

Hall of Famer Mike Schmidt also took a broad, balanced view of winning and losing, focusing more on performance than on the win-loss column. Like me, Schmidt placed primary importance on effort. He said:

At the end of a game, if I can come back to the locker room and look in the mirror and say I gave as much of myself as I could, I can feel like and call myself a winner. I'm a winner on that particular day, whatever the scoreboard says about my team's individual performance. I think that the desire to be this type of winner, along with the personal pride and gamesmanship—the desire to excel—is enough motivation for an athlete at any level. Whether you're a highest-paid athlete in the majors or on the grade school basketball team, an inner desire to perform well and to contribute to your team will make you a winner.[21]

Early in his pitching career, Jim Bouton, who came up to the majors with the Yankees, had a chance to pitch in a World Series game against the Dodgers and one of their best all-time pitchers, Don Drysdale. Before the game, sitting in the dugout next to Ralph Houk, the Yankee manager, Bouton was experiencing how much fun it was just to be there. His feelings in that moment did not depend on whether he did well in the game or whether the Yankees were victorious. He recalled that he said to Houk, "You know something, Ralph? Whether I win today or lose, this is a helluva lot of fun, isn't it." Houk responded, "It sure is. I know just what you mean." Bouton respected Houk for not saying, "Whaddaya mean, lose? We're gonna win," a remark he believed a lot of other managers would have made.[22]

Seeing Losing in the Proper Light

If you have a passion for the game, you want to win, so losing is never easy. It seems to me that Mike has put losing in proper perspective. He said:

> Losing is definitely not fun. Unfortunately, when you lose, guys just want to get out of the clubhouse—they do not want to be there. You can't take losing that way. If you let losing really bother you, it can be a long season and the game is going to beat you down. When you lose, you should look back at why you lost and see what you could have done to help your team win. Then it has got to be over with. I have seen managers who lose four or five games in a row and they come into the clubhouse saying, "I hate to lose. I don't know about you guys but I hate to lose." It is such a big joke. If you have to say you hate to lose, you've got a problem. If you go home thinking, "we lost four in a row and we better win tomorrow," that is like saying, "I hope I get a hit." It is negative energy. If you have too many guys hoping to win, then you have no chance. You have to make it happen. You have to go out and do some things to win the game.

Steve Garvey spoke about the need to come to grips with losing—to see it in the proper light. "Disheartening as losing is," he said, "it is part of the game. While I had never gotten comfortable with losing, in the fifteen years of major league service, I have learned to live with it. Experience does that."[23]

Lou Piniella, who had winning teams when he managed the

Yankees and the Mariners, had to come to grips with losing when in 2003 he became the manager of the Tampa Bay Devil Rays. Even though the Devil Rays were a low-budget team with few established players, Piniella thought he could still win. In June 2003 he spoke with Pat Jordan of *The New York Times* and said:

> Look, I'm here to win games. No matter how much growing a team does, you don't want to lose every night. You gotta win. That's a manager's fun. I feel I can win anywhere. I'm gonna have success in Tampa Bay or I'll take off my uniform.[24]

In July, after the team lost 17 of 21 games, Piniella recognized that he needed to revise his thinking on winning and losing. He told Jordan:

> Losing beats you down. It's not an easy transition for me. I'm win-oriented. I came to the realization a few days ago that I can't be concerned with losses. I should evaluate and develop talent for next year. But that's easy to say. My ego told me I would win in any situation.

Piniella laughed and added, "Now I've been humbled."[25]

Yogi Berra acknowledged that players would not learn the game if they won all the time. Knowledge and insights about how to play the game are deepened through losses. He said:

> I am a very competitive person. I don't like to lose at anything. . . . But I learned a long time ago that losing is a learning experience. It teaches you humility. It teaches you to work harder. It also is a powerful motivator. I've always said, somebody's got to win, somebody's got to lose. Accept losses and learn from them.[26]

After suffering a second loss in the 1992 World Series to the Atlanta Braves, Minnesota Twins pitcher Jack Morris was asked by reporters to explain why, in the space of a few days, he had lost not just once but twice. Was something wrong with him? His World Series career record had been outstanding. Coming into the series against Atlanta he had never lost. He had recorded four victories and no defeats, and the year before, he had pitched the crucial seventh game of the 1991 Series, shutting out the Braves 1–0. The reporters wanted to know whether he had lost his touch. Was he suddenly too old to handle World Series competition?

Morris told the reporters that he had given it everything he had. He said:

> I threw the pitch I wanted. I live and die with the fastball. It wasn't good enough, but it was my best. If you want me to lie down and cry, I'm not going to do that. . . . You just have to admit that you weren't the best you could be. I tried and I wasn't. Once you admit that everything comes back to reality.[27]

Morris acknowledged that to be a winner, he had to learn how to deal with defeat. "Early in my career," he said, "I refused to believe I could lose. What I learned is that losing is a part of the game. It's a part of the game I never really appreciated, but there is a way to appreciate it, because it makes winning more fun. Without it, winning would be boring, and I would probably retire and choose another profession." Morris went on to talk about the sport of baseball and what it taught him about life:

> I think what really gets me is how fantastic this game is. How humbling it is. They hit two balls right inside the lines tonight [doubles by Nixon and Pendleton]. So many times those breaks

went my way. Tonight they blew up in my face. This is one helluva game.[28]

Morris's attitude toward winning and losing is like my own.
His response to reporters after losing a key game in the World
Series provides a perfect example of how I view winning and
losing. In baseball you cannot win all of the time. If you do
everything you possibly can to win, then you can live with the
results. To me the effort and the understanding you must have to
play the game right are the most important things. As a manager, I was okay when we lost if we played the game right. Winning is not the most important thing to me. Playing the game
the right way is. I want to deserve to win.

As a player I always thought, after a loss, that I could have
done something a little better that would have given us a chance
to win. "I should have been looking for the breaking ball that
struck me out," or "If I'd played the hitter a little closer to the
line the ball wouldn't have gotten through." The game doesn't
mean much unless you give it all that you have got. You lay it on
the line, accept the outcome, and then you move on.

If winning becomes an obsession, the process becomes secondary. You often hear guys on a team saying, "We gotta win,
we gotta win. I am not going to stay here because they don't want
to win. We need more guys here who know how to win.
What's wrong with the front office?" Guys like that don't
know what they are talking about. They don't recognize their
own responsibilities. Winning is the result of the whole organization doing the right thing. You keep plugging away, playing
the game hard, accepting your responsibilities, and trying to
bring in guys who can play. It does not take 120 million dollars
a year in salaries to do it. The success of the Oakland A's and the
Minnesota Twins has proved that. Mismanagement at all levels is
more of a problem than lack of spending.

I had a good career, but there were things I missed that I wished I had been a part of. I missed out on some of the fun because I didn't have the opportunity. During my eighteen-year career in the big leagues I did not play for a team that got into the play-offs or made it to the World Series. I didn't get a chance to celebrate those successes or share the joy of them with anybody. I can live with that now because I recognize it just wasn't meant to be.

David has had the chance that I didn't get, both with the Seattle Mariners in the American League play-offs and the San Francisco Giants in the World Series. He had to deal with defeat with both teams. This is what he said about it:

> It is a terrible feeling when you lose in the play-offs or the World Series. However, it didn't take as long to get over it as I thought it would. You gave it all you had. The other team played better and deserved to win. With the Mariners we had all that success—winning 115 games during the season. Then we lost to the Yankees in the play-offs. It came down to a couple of games and it didn't happen. It makes it a lot easier to live with yourself if you know that you did all that you could. More times than not, you are going to get another opportunity, and maybe next time it will be your chance. That's what makes the game fun, what makes it interesting, and makes you want to keep playing. Much as I would have liked to win in the World Series, getting close to it was a great experience. It makes you want to win even more.

TEN

Summary

The Mental Game

THE MENTAL PART OF THE GAME IS SO IMPORTANT AND SO demanding. My success in the big leagues depended to a large extent on how I prepared myself mentally. Before each game, the mental preparation that enabled me to perform at a high level both in the field and at bat involved a lot of hard work. During the game, each pitch created a new situation, with several factors to be considered. A high level of awareness was required to avoid making mental mistakes. I don't ever remember being mentally fresh after a game. In fact, when we went off the field my mind was more drained than my body.

Developing Savvy, Know-How, and Smarts

Becoming a smart baseball player takes effort and no small degree of intelligence. It took me several years to develop the savvy and know-how needed to excel in the game. It is true, I did have an advantage. I grew up in a baseball family. My father, Gus Bell, had a successful fourteen-year career with the Pittsburgh Pirates, the Cincinnati Reds, the Milwaukee Braves, and the New York Mets. I was born while he was playing in Pittsburgh.

The game was easy for me as a youngster playing Little League baseball in Cincinnati. I simply went out and played and relied on my natural talent. When I was fourteen years old, things changed. I began playing with guys a few years older than I was. The game became hard, and I realized I had to do something about it. I had a passion for the game and already knew that I wanted to be a major leaguer. I began talking with my father—who, by the way, never pushed me into baseball—and my coaches. I sought their advice because I was aware that I had to become smarter about the game. I spent more time going to baseball games and watching the Reds on TV. But now I watched differently. I paid attention to how players positioned themselves on the field, and observed the different deliveries of the pitchers and styles of pitching. In short, I became a student of the game. I learned by looking, listening, and asking questions.

I worked hard to get to the point where nothing surprised me, where no situation on the diamond was unfamiliar. I got to know the pitchers and what I could expect from them, and I found out how to play the hitters. I came to grips with my own abilities—what I could and could not do. I did not lie to myself. I knew that those who succeeded at this game were smart base-ball players. I knew that you could not show up at four P.M. the night of a game, put on a uniform, and go out and play winning baseball without a plan of action or a thought in your head.

The Importance of Good Coaching

I learned the finer points of the game from my father, and from a few very special coaches. My dad was the best coach I ever had. He stressed the mental part of the game rather than the physical. He always waited for me to come to him, and I went to him a lot because I knew he would be honest with me. He would not mince words and gave good, sound advice. He knew me better than anybody else, knew what I needed. I had some great coaches, but he was the all-time greatest. From working with my father I realized that I learned the most when I sought advice. I believe other players do also. They learn more when they seek out a coach for help rather than waiting for a coach to come to them.

Learning from Each Other

This may sound surprising to those unfamiliar with baseball, but in the big leagues, players learn more from each other than from their coaches. Their relationships with each other are much closer than their relationships with coaches. Ballplayers are more comfortable with each other than with their coaches and spend time with each other away from the ballpark in social settings. Veteran ballplayers in the major leagues know a lot about the game and can be of great help to younger ones coming up. Graig Nettles was the third baseman for the Cleveland Indians during my rookie season when I was the centerfielder. I had the good fortune to watch him play, and he was the guy I learned a lot from.

It wasn't any one thing he said but a combination of things. He helped me get ready for each at bat and learn from it. He taught me a lot about how to play third base. He preached about the need to know the strengths of the hitter, the kind of stuff the pitcher had going for him and the pitch selection, as well as the importance of being aware of the situation on the field. He helped me get my priorities straight, helped me know how to position myself before each pitch and impressed on me the need to be aggressive to the ball. He said nothing about the physical or mechanical part of the game. It was all mental. He helped me see that faulty mental preparation was often the cause of a physical error on the field. You simply were not ready to make the play.

Self-Evaluation as a Tool for Improving Performance

I think a key element in any player's mental makeup is his ability to make a correct evaluation of his own performance. I believe that self-evaluation after a game is extremely important. If you have had a subpar performance, you need to figure out what happened. A lot of players get caught up in themselves and don't take the time after a game to reflect. They want to go home and forget about it. They are afraid to face what went wrong. They don't think about how they could have improved their play. These players don't last long in the big leagues.

Effective self-evaluation does not turn into self-criticism. Self-evaluation is objective and positive; self-criticism is negative and destructive. Those who criticize themselves beat themselves up, get down on themselves, think that nothing they can do is good enough. They deplete their energy and in the end wear themselves out. I have observed many ballplayers who are too self-critical. Too few ballplayers at the major league level have learned to evaluate their performances objectively.

We can learn so much from our experiences, particularly our failures—striking out, making an error, a base-running mistake, being out of position, not communicating with a teammate. The best players analyze what went wrong after a less than satisfactory performance. For me, self-evaluation became a key to better performance on the field.

Focusing on the Present Moment

The ability to concentrate, to stay focused on the here and now, is probably the most important ingredient in a ballplayer's mental makeup. Hitting a baseball that travels at upwards of ninety miles per hour is a daunting task. It is equally difficult to pitch a baseball with velocity and movement to a precise location sixty feet away. High levels of concentration are required to do both.

When I began playing baseball growing up in Cincinnati, my father gave valuable advice about how to concentrate. It was advice that stuck with me all through my baseball career. He said, "Never look past the ball." If you come up to bat thinking about hitting a home run or getting an RBI or raising your batting average, he said, you are not focused on the only thing that is important—the baseball. You will never be successful if you allow anything other than the baseball to enter your mind. If you get distracted, you might make contact, but it won't be solid contact. When he explained that to me, my concentration as a hitter improved. Hitting the baseball became my sole focus. There was nothing else.

The Mobilizing Force of Anger

Some people can use anger to their advantage and others can't. I learned to use anger to improve my focus early in my career. When I was a young player I had trouble driving in runners in scoring position. I wanted to do it so badly that I would lose focus. I was trying to relax at the plate, because I thought it was the right thing to do. My hitting coaches had told me that I would hit better if I was relaxed. It wasn't working for me. I told my dad and he said: "Does relaxing in the batter's box feel natural? Does that feel normal? Is that the way you want to be?" I told him that I felt squeamish when I tried to relax. My body felt like it was in different pieces. I didn't feel at one with my body. He told me to use my natural aggressiveness to my advantage. He said, "Just be angry. Get mad at the ball. Don't back off.

Be really aggressive." He said that being angry and aggressive would focus me on what I was doing in the batter's box. I took his advice and became a much better hitter. Thereafter I used anger to my benefit. Being angry was by design. I felt better when I was angry, when my teeth were clenched. I could see the ball better when I was angry. It made me more competitive. When I was angry I moved faster, had more energy, wasn't worried about things and played better.

Anger doesn't work for everybody. In fact, anger hurts a lot of guys. Their minds become unclear and they lose concentration. They get too wired and the game speeds up too much for them. They lose touch with what is important. Most guys whose anger is out of control don't last long in the big leagues. Anger worked for me because I kept it within bounds. I chose to get angry because it was consistent with my personality. I was simply being myself. Before I let myself get angry I was trying to be cool. It didn't work for me. Some guys think that it is good to get angry and they try to fake it. When something goes wrong on the field, they come back to the dugout acting like they are pissed off. You can tell when guys aren't really comfortable with anger. They are lying to themselves, and somehow think they can fool people.

Slumps and How to Handle Them

While everyone in baseball is prone to slumps, hitters and pitchers seem to be the ones most affected by them. Slumps for hitters seem to follow a predictable course. It happens this way. You make an out and then you try to make up for it in the next at bat. You are going to try to do better, even hit a home run. Then the last at bat creeps into your mind, and the trouble begins. You screw up the next at bat, and the next and the next because you are trying to make up for your previous failures. You make two, four, or eight outs in succession, and then you become obsessed. You lose concentration because too many things creep into your mind—your batting average is falling, you're not helping the team, you can think of nothing positive. You are distracted, become mentally soft, don't want anyone to know that you are not mentally tough. You begin thinking that the problem lies in your physical ability. You can't do it anymore and your career is over. You are unwilling to allow for the fact that it might have to do with your mental state. You are in a slump.

The worst slump I ever had occurred in 1985 during my last year with the Texas Rangers. I had been in the big leagues for thirteen years, was thirty-four years old, and until then had been a pretty consistent player. I had gone through slumps before and handled them pretty well, never getting to the point where I doubted my ability to play. The slump began in August when the team fired the manager and decided to stress youth and cut down on salary. I was told they were going to trade me. It took six weeks before they could work out a trade. During that time I went into a funk. I was a zombie. I felt like I was a player without a team. I couldn't concentrate, or do what I needed to do to prepare myself to play. My batting average dropped to something like .219.

When a trade went through to Cincinnati, my hometown, I was happy. I was finally coming home to play. But the slump deepened. I seemed unable to focus. I had been a good player, an All-Star, and now I was a bad player. I was tight and tormented. I went to my dad and told him I was embarrassed, afraid to make an out. I was thinking of retiring because I couldn't hit anymore. My dad didn't accept my excuses. While he was compassionate, he was not kind to me. He knew what I was going through because he had been through it himself. He told me something that alleviated the fear. He said, "Since you are already trying to make an out, go out and hit the ball to the shortstop. It will help you stay down on the ball and it will keep you from overswinging." In a crazy way it made sense to me. I instantly came out of the slump, drove in 25 runs in September, hit home runs, and batted over .300.

Dealing with the Fear of Failure

Fear of failure is big in baseball. It is so easy to lapse into negative thinking, and be afraid to make a mistake or make an out. So many bad things happen if you make an out. Ballplayers must learn how to shift attention from the negative to the positive. That's what mental toughness is all about. Those who are mentally tough have disciplined their minds to the point where they do not allow negative thoughts to creep in. They block out all the fear, all the anxiety. In the face of adversity they are able to keep the minds focused on the positive.

Getting into the Zone

Baseball becomes a lot of fun when you get into a groove, into the flow of the game where everything clicks, and the game slows down. The good players in the majors are all proficient at hitting, throwing, and catching. What separates the best players from the good players is the ability to slow the game down. To slow the game down you need to be able to eliminate distractions. You need to think fast to slow the game down. As your mind slows down and your concentration deepens, you get locked in, get into the zone. You are no longer conscious of the crowd. You don't hear anything. It is like being in a soundproof room. You are so focused that it is like being on the diamond all by yourself. I got in the zone more often as my career went on. It was the result of my experience. I was smarter. It became easier to push the distractions out of my mind.

Competitive Drive

Many major league ballplayers think that their natural ability alone will get them to the promised land. They fail to realize that talent gets you only so far. You will not succeed in the big leagues without strong desire, determination, intensity, a sense of urgency, a willingness to work hard and to push yourself to the limit. Many ballplayers have just enough competitive drive to get themselves on a major league roster. They don't have the desire or determination, however, to be really successful. Competition for me comes down to this: Who is willing to take the extra time to plan a workout? Who is willing to organize their time so that they can be better prepared? Who is willing to take batting practice until their hands bleed, if that's what it takes to figure it out? Who is willing to do what it takes to win?

I had a strong desire to compete. I think I may have been born with it, although my father did a lot to bring it out in me. So did my high school basketball coach, Jerry Doerger, at Moeller High in Cincinnati. Doerger was a "get after it" kind of guy. He would never let us feel like we were doing enough. There was no such thing as being satisfied with our performance. He never wanted us to feel giddy, or too thrilled with our success. He just kept pushing and pushing. He made you feel like you were never inferior, that you couldn't be beaten. He kept me on edge, instilled in me a sense of urgency. If it hadn't been for him and the competitiveness that rubbed off on me, and the energy I got from it, I would not have achieved as much as I did in baseball.

Developing Self-Confidence

Confidence is huge. If you don't have self-confidence the game is going to bury you. It will suck the energy right out of you.

You can do very little without confidence. Unless you trust yourself and believe in yourself, you will be unable to perform. Without confidence, you are very easily intimidated.

A lot of mental work is required to build confidence. I don't think you develop self-confidence without putting in the necessary work. A lot has to do with developing proper attitudes. You gain confidence by being positive and optimistic rather than negative and fearful, open to new knowledge and information, willing to accept honest evaluations from coaches, able to honestly self-evaluate, and willing to change.

Good work habits are an essential ingredient in developing self-confidence. You need to do high-quality work before a game to maintain confidence, and you must begin preparing yourself several hours before the first pitch. You must develop a routine or a plan for your workout, and know exactly what you are going to focus on. Those without a routine or plan get very little accomplished.

Many managers and coaches do not know how to help players develop self-confidence. They forget what it was like when they were young players. Those who are able to manage veteran teams, where most of the players have developed self-confidence, often have difficulty with younger, less experienced teams. Many simply cannot manage a younger player who is working on developing self-confidence. This is something we as coaches need to get better at in our game. The average service time of a major league ballplayer is only three to four years. I think the short tenure is in part due to their inability to develop self-confidence.

Relying on Intuition, Hunches, and Gut Feeling

Many ballplayers and managers, myself included, often use the word "instinct" when referring to intuition. For example,

I believe that ballplayers must let their instincts guide them. Sometimes we let our brains get in the way of our instincts. We break things down too much and get too analytical. At some point we need to stop taking in information and rely on our natural talents, which is another way of saying that we need to let our instinctual feel for the game take over. When the ball is in play you have to trust your instincts. For me, playing third base, I had to have a feel for my body, a feel for the pitcher, and a feel for the hitter.

In the batting cage, I used gut feeling to let me know when I had sufficient batting practice to get ready to hit in a game. As a hitter I was concerned about the location of my feet and my hands. I took batting practice until I sensed that they were positioned correctly. Sometimes that happened rather quickly. Other times it did not. I didn't try to hit the ball hard, like a lot of players. I was focused on my feet and hands. As soon as I felt good about where they were located, I could get out of the batter's box. It was the key to my hitting.

Ballplayers whose game is based on sound fundamentals play on instinct. They just react. They don't need to think about what they are doing. Instincts are developed through practice. By the time a ballplayer reaches the big leagues, the basics of throwing, catching, and hitting have become instinctive because players have been doing it for so many years. Many, however, have not committed to instinct many of the fundamentals of baseball—such as bunting; moving the runner from second to third; executing cutoffs and relays, pickoffs, rundowns; and executing double plays. Every position has different fundamentals that must be learned. Ballplayers' instincts become better in game situations if they continue to work on these fundamentals. Many major leaguers do not want to work on fundamentals because they believe they learned them in the minor leagues. They do not realize that to play on instinct they must continually work throughout their careers on these fundamentals. Players who have not developed sound fundamentals are prone to making mental mistakes.

Over the course of a baseball season I often had hunches about what was going to happen on the field. On several occasions, as the pitcher completed his delivery, I knew the ball was going to be hit to me at third base. I would find myself, on occasion, knowing that the hitter was going to get a hit or make an out before the event happened. At bat I would get the feeling that I was going to hit the ball hard someplace, and then I would do it.

Using Mental Imagery

Baseball's best players use mental imagery to improve their game. They visualize what they are going to do both at bat as well as in the field. It helps them slow the game down so that nothing goes too fast for them. Imaging is an ability that requires self-confidence and comes after you had experience playing the game. You must work at it to use it effectively. I used imagery to hit curveballs. I was able to see in my mind the arc of the ball and its location over the plate before it was pitched. It is important to note that imagery does not always work. Most hitters find it impossible to use it when up against great pitchers who change speeds on their pitches, throw an assortment of curveballs, and mix their pitches.

Exercising Leadership

I used to hate it when guys would come into the clubhouse after losing and say, "We need somebody who can lead." Leadership is very tricky, and very important. A team is in trouble if it has only one guy who can lead. You need five or ten guys who can lead. In fact, the more leaders you have, the better chance you have of winning. The more you win, the more leaders you have. So they work hand in hand.

Leadership is exercised in different ways, and no one guy on a team can do all the things that good leadership requires. A ballplayer can lead by:

1. Having a passion for the game and the success of his teammates.
2. Being a good teammate, and showing compassion for guys who are struggling.
3. Having the utmost confidence in his ability to play the game.
4. Being willing to go out on a limb, get into people's faces, to hammer somebody if that's what's needed.
5. Keeping his eyes and ears open.
6. Getting everybody's energy going in the clubhouse before the game.
7. Leading by example on the field talentwise and by being productive.
8. Having a good sense of humor.
9. Playing in pain and with injuries.
10. Commanding the respect of his teammates.
11. Not being concerned about his reputation.
12. Being vocal in the dugout.

As you can see, it is highly unlikely that any one player on a team will possess all of these qualities. That is why a team needs many leaders. Not everybody is able to lead. Some guys are phony about it. Whenever it suits them they will do it for themselves. I call those guys convenient leaders.

The Leadership Role Played by a Team Manager

I believe a manager's job is to make it possible for guys on the team to lead. A manager does not need to be the center of attention. The less said about the manager, the better. The focus should be on the players. The best managers are the ones who step back and let the players play. If the team is successful, the manager will get appropriate credit. There are a lot of good managers in the game, and I can name several. Nevertheless, I have observed more mismanagement than good management in baseball. You have managers who understand the game, but they don't know how to handle people.

A good manager really cares about his players. He knows how to help players develop confidence, and he helps them to feel good about themselves. If a player needs improvement in a specific area, a manager must let him know about it. A good manager cannot let a player slide.

Having Fun

I had a lot of fun playing baseball. We who have made a career of major league baseball do it because it is fun. If we didn't enjoy it, we would choose another profession. There were times in certain games that I was so thrilled to be a part of the competition that I wished the game would never end. For me, the more intense the game was, the more competitive it was, the more fun it was. Winning, of course, was the most fun. Everyone is happy and having a good time. I believe, as do many other ballplayers, that playing well and having fun go hand in hand. The teams that are most successful are the ones that have the most fun.

Part of the fun of going to the ballpark for a game is knowing you have a chance to win. When you play for a team that has no chance of winning, you will eventually get worn down. Without a chance of winning, a lot of the fun is taken out of the game. In baseball, the bottom line is winning.

On Winning and Losing

We all want to win. In baseball, that's ultimately where we find the pleasure and the enjoyment. After a victory everybody on the team is happy and having a good time. Nevertheless, I would much rather be with a group of guys who lay it all out on the line both on the field and in the clubhouse—and lose—than win with a bunch of guys who care only about themselves. I do not aspire to be around guys who don't care about me or aren't concerned about whether I care about them. For many in major league baseball—and I don't include myself among them—nothing else matters but winning. It is the only thing that many coaches and players focus on. For those who see winning as all-important, losing can be a bitter pill to swallow. In a more balanced approach toward winning and losing, the focus is on performance and level of effort rather than on the win-loss column.

Losing needs to be seen in its proper light. If you have a passion for the game, you want to win, so losing is never easy. Nevertheless, to be a winner, you have to learn how to deal with defeat. Losing is part of the game. In baseball you cannot win all of the time. If you do everything you possibly can to win, then you can live with the results. To me the effort and the understanding you must have to play the game right are the most important things. As a manager, I was okay when we lost if we played the game right. Winning is not the most important thing to me. Playing the game the right way is. I want to deserve to win.

If winning becomes an obsession, the process becomes secondary. You often hear guys on a team saying, "We gotta win, we gotta win. I am not going to stay here because they don't want to win. We need more guys here who know how to win. What's wrong with the front office?" Guys like that don't know what they are talking about. They don't recognize their own responsibilities. Winning is the result of the whole organization doing the right thing.

As a player I always thought, after a loss, that I could have done something a little better which would have given us a chance to win. "I should have been looking for the breaking ball that struck me out," or "If I'd played the hitter a little closer to the line the ball wouldn't have gotten through." The game doesn't mean much unless you give it all that you have got. You lay it on the line, accept the outcome, and then you move on.

Notes

INTRODUCTION

1. Falkner, David. *Nine Sides of the Diamond: Baseball's Greatest Glove Men on the Fine Art of Defense*. New York: Times Books, 1990, p. 17.
2. Rains, Rob. *Mark McGwire, Home Run Hero*. New York: St. Martin's Press, 1998, p. 166.
3. Berra, Yogi, with David Kaplan. *When You Come to the Fork in the Road, Take It*. New York: Hyperion, 2001, p. 59.
4. Stargell, Willie, and Tom Bird. *Willie Stargell: An Autobiography*. New York: Harper & Row, 1984, p. 163.

CHAPTER ONE: SAVVY, KNOW-HOW, SMARTS

1. Houk, Ralph, and Robert Creamer. *Season of Glory: The Amazing Saga of the 1961 New York Yankees*. New York: G. P. Putnam's Sons, 1988, p. 51.
2. Hershiser, Orel with Jerry B. Jenkins. *Out of the Blue*. Brentwood, Tennessee: A.W. Wolgemuth & Hyatt, 1989, p. 20.
3. Hershiser, Orel, with Robert Wolgemuth, *Between the Lines: Nine Principles to Live By*. New York: Warner Books, 2001, pp. 56–57.
4. Glavine, Tom, with Nick Cafardo. *None But the Braves*. New York: HarperCollins Publishers, 1996, p. xii.
5. Curry, Jack. "The Art and Science of a Master Pitcher." *The New York Times*, March 30, 2003, Preview '03, p. 7.
6. Koufax, Sandy, and Ed Linn. *Koufax*. New York: Viking Press, 1966, p. 10.
7. *USA Today*, May 17, 2002, p. 2C.

8. Ford, Whitey, and Phil Pepe. *Slick: My Life In and Around Baseball.* New York: William Morrow and Co., 1987, p. 56.

9. Ibid.

10. Ibid., p. 46.

11. Houk, Ralph, and Robert Creamer. *Season of Glory: the Amazing Saga of the 1961 New York Yankees.* New York: G. P. Putnam's Sons, 1988, p. 181.

12. Lally, Richard. *Bombers: An Oral History of the Yankees.* New York: Crown Publishing Group, 2002, p. 52.

13. Berra, Yogi, with Tom Horton. *It Ain't Over.* New York: McGraw Hill, 1989, pp. 1–2.

14. Ibid., p. 57.

15. Aaron, Hank, with Lonnie Wheeler. *I Had a Hammer: The Hank Aaron Story.* New York: HarperCollins Publishers, 1991, pp. 269–271.

16. Ibid., p. 219.

17. *San Francisco Chronicle,* April 11, 1994, p. D2.

18. Ripken Jr., Cal, and Mike Bryan. *The Only Way I Know.* New York: Penguin Putnam, 1997.

19. Alexander, Charles. *Ty Cobb.* New York: Oxford University Press, 1984, p. 90.

20. Ibid., p. 121.

21. Ibid.

22. Oh, Sadaharu, and David Falkner. *Sadaharu Oh: A Zen Way of Baseball.* New York: Times Books, 1984, p. 56.

23. Sokolove, Michael Y. *Hustle: The Myth, Life, and Lies of Pete Rose.* New York: Simon and Schuster, 1990, p. 12.

24. Ibid., p. 13.

25. Ibid., p. 89.

26. Linn, Ed. *Hitter: The Life and Turmoil of Ted Williams.* New York: Harcourt Brace & Co., 1993, pp. 193–196.

27. Ibid.

28. Ibid.

29. Ibid.

30. Ibid. pp. 196–198.

31. Ibid.

32. Allen, Maury. *Where Have You Gone Joe DiMaggio?: The Story of America's Last Hero.* New York: E. P. Dutton, 1975, p. 134.

33. DiMaggio, Joe. *Baseball for Everyone.* New York: McGraw Hill, 2002, p. xiii.

34. Stargell, Willie, and Tom Bird. *Willie Stargell.* New York: HarperCollins Publishers, 1984, p. 214.

35. Mays, Willie, and Lou Sahadi. *Say Hey: The Autobiography of William Mays.* New York: Simon and Schuster, 1988, p. 42.

36. Ibid., p. 189.

37. Ibid.

38. Rains, Rob. *Mark McGwire, Home Run Hero.* New York: St. Martin's Press, 1998, pp. 138, 140, 187.

39. Mays, op cit., pp. 16–18.

40. Ibid.

41. Ibid.

42. Ibid., pp. 23–26.

43. Ibid.

44. Falkner, David. *Nine Sides of the Diamond: Baseball's Greatest Glove Men on the Fine Art of Defense.* New York: Times Books, 1990, p. 203.

45. *San Francisco Chronicle,* June 11, 2003, p. C4. Falkner, op. cit., p. 203.

46. Connor, Anthony. *Baseball for the Love of It: Hall of Famers Tell It Like It Was.* New York: Macmillan Publishing Co., Inc., 1982, p. 86. Snider, Duke, with Bill Gilbert. *The Duke of Flatbush.* New York: Citadel Press, 1988, pp. 70–71.

47. Snider, Duke, with Bill Gilbert. *The Duke of Flatbush.* New York: Citadel Press, 1988, p. 120.

48. Ibid., p. 145.

49. Garvey, Steve, and Skip Rozin. *Garvey.* New York: Times Books, 1986, pp. 199–200.

50. Morgan, Joe, and David Falkner. *Joe Morgan: A Life in Baseball.* New York: W. W. Norton & Co., 1993, p. 68.

51. Rains, op. cit., pp. 165–166.

52. Williams, Dick, and Bill Plaschke. *No More Mr. Nice Guy: A Life of Hardball.* New York: Harcourt Brace Jovanovich, 1990, p. 64.

53. Ibid., p. 72.

54. Ibid.

55. *San Francisco Chronicle,* December 20, 2002, p. C2.

56. Hunter, Jim "Catfish," and Armen Keteyian. *Catfish: My Life in Baseball.* New York: McGraw Hill Book Company, 1988, p. 216.

57. Lyle, Sparky, and Peter Golenbock. *The Bronx Zoo.* New York: Crown Publishers, 1979, p. 132.

58. Roseboro, John, with Bill Libby. *Glory Days with the Dodgers and Other Days with Others.* New York: Atheneum, 1978, pp. 192–193.

59. Robinson, Frank, and Berry Stainback. *Extra Innings: The Grand-Slam Response to Al Campanis's Controversial Remarks About Blacks in Baseball.* New York: McGraw-Hill Book Company, 1988, p. 92–93.

60. Ibid.

61. Honig, Donald. *Baseball Between the Lines.* New York: Coward, McCann, & Geoghegan, Inc., 1976, p. 214–220.

62. Ibid.

63. Wills, Maury, and Mike Celizic. *On the Run: The Never Dull and Often Shocking Life of Maury Wills.* New York: Carroll & Graf Publishers, Inc., 1991, p. 121.

64. Ibid.

CHAPTER TWO: FOCUSING ON THE PRESENT MOMENT

1. *San Francisco Chronicle,* October 24, 1996, p. E5.
2. Shlain, Bruce. *Baseball Inside Out: Winning the Game Within the Game.* New York: Viking Penguin, 1992, p. 35.
3. Davis, Eric, with Ralph Wiley. *Born to Play: The Eric Davis Story.* New York: Penguin USA, 1999, pp. 124–125.
4. Garvey, Steve, with Skip Rozin. *Garvey.* New York: Times Books, 1986, p. 127.
5. Jeter, Derek, with Jack Curry. *The Life You Imagine: Life Lessons for Achieving Your Dreams.* New York: Crown Publishing Group, 2000, p. 126.
6. Koufax, Sandy, and Ed Linn. *Koufax.* New York: Viking Press, 1996, p. 216.
7. Schmidt, Mike, with Barbara Walder. *Always on the Offense.* New York: Smithmark, 1982, p. 20.
8. Wills, Maury, and Mike Celizic. *On the Run: The Never Dull and Often Shocking Life of Maury Wills.* New York: Carroll & Graf Publishers, Inc., 1991, p. 121.
9. Gmelch, George. *Inside Pitch: Life in Professional Baseball.* Washington, D.C. Smithsonian Books, 2001, p. 199.
10. Goldman, William, and Mike Lupica. *Wait Till Next Year.* New York: Bantam, 1988, pp. 175–176.
11. Torre, Joe, with Henry Dreher. *Joe Torre's Ground Rules for Winners.* New York: Hyperion, 1999, p. 111.
12. Stargell, Willie and Tom Bird. *Willie Stargell.* New York: HarperCollins Publishers, 1984, p. 159.
13. Sokolove, Michael Y. *Hustle: The Myth, Life and Lies of Pete Rose.* New York: Simon and Schuster, 1990, pp. 97, 92.
14. Garrity, John. *The George Brett Story.* New York: Coward, McCann, & Geoghegan, 1981, pp. 235–236.
15. Bouton, Jim. *Ball Four Plus Ball Five: An Update, 1970–1980.* New York: Stein and Day, 1981, p. 336.
16. Ibid., p. 428.
17. Oh, Sadaharu, and David Falkner. *Sadaharu Oh: A Zen Way of Baseball.* New York: Times Books, 1984, p. 213
18. Hershiser, Orel, with Jerry B. Jenkins. *Out of the Blue.* Brentwood, Tennessee: Wolgemuth & Hyatt, 1989, pp. 42–45.
19. Ibid.
20. Ibid.
21. Ibid.
22. Ibid.
23. Ibid., p. 206.
24. *The New York Times,* November 3, 1996, p. 28.
25. Wills, op. cit., p. 187.
26. Gmelch, op. cit., p. 135.
27. Ibid.

28. Ibid.
29. Ibid.
30. Ibid., p. 137.
31. Yastrzemski, Carl, and Gerald Eskenazi. *Yaz, Baseball, the Wall, and Me.* New York: Bantam Dell, 1990, p. 12.
32. Ibid.
33. Ibid., p. 176.
34. Ibid.
35. Sokolove, op. cit., p. 56.
36. Linn, Ed. *Hitter: The Life and Turmoils of Ted Williams.* New York: Harcourt Brace & Co., 1993, p. 231.
37. Alexander, Charles. *Ty Cobb.* New York: Oxford University Press, 1984, p. 120.
38. *San Francisco Chronicle,* July, 1992, p. B2. "Dodgers Losing Faith in Darryl Strawberry," by Tim Keown.
39. Ibid.
40. Ibid.
41. Allen, Maury. *Jackie Robinson: A Life Remembered.* New York: Franklin Watts, 1987, p. 180.
42. *San Francisco Chronicle,* March 16, 2002, p. C4.
43. Mays, Willie, with Lou Sahadi. *Say Hey: The Autobiography of Willie Mays.* New York: Simon and Schuster, 1988, p. 236.
44. Drysdale, Don, with Bob Verdi. *Once a Bum, Always a Dodger.* New York: St. Martin's Press, 1990, p. 190.
45. Santo, Ron, with Randy Minkoff. *For Love of Ivy.* Chicago: Bonus Books, 1993, p. 198.
46. Drysdale, op. cit., p. 190.
47. Ibid., p. 191.
48. Gibson, Bob, with Lonnie Wheeler. *Stranger to the Game.* New York: Viking, 1994. pp. 276–277.
49. Musick, Phil. *Who Was Roberto? A Biography of Roberto Clemente.* New York: Doubleday and Company, 1974, p. 122.
50. Schmidt, op. cit., p. 29.
51. DiMaggio, Joe. *Baseball for Everyone.* New York: McGraw Hill, 2002, p. 194–198.
52. Ibid., p. 202.
53. Berra, Yogi, with David Kaplan. *When You Come to the Fork in the Road, Take It.* New York: Hyperion, 2001, p. 18–20.
54. Alexander, op cit., p. 193.
55. Torre op. cit., p. 20.
56. Ibid., p. 20.
57. Rosenfeld, Harvey. *Iron Man: The Cal Ripken Jr. Story.* New York: St. Martin's Press, 1995, pp. 167, 178.

58. Ripken, Cal, Jr., and Mike Bryan. *The Only Way I Know.* New York: Penguin Putnam, 1997, pp. 190–193.

59. Yastrzemski, op. cit., p. 88.

60. Nettles, Graig, and Peter Golenbock. *Balls.* New York: G. P. Putnam and Sons, 1984, p. 59.

61. Snider, Duke, with Bill Gilbert. *The Duke of Flatbush.* New York: Citadel Press, 2002, pp. 86–87.

62. Hunter, Jim "Catfish," and Armen Keteyian. *Catfish: My Life in Baseball.* New York: McGraw Hill Book Company, 1988, p. 136.

63. Gossage, Richard "Goose," with Russ Pate. *The Goose Is Loose.* New York: Ballantine Books, 2000, pp. 113–114.

64. Lally, Richard. *Bombers: An Oral History of the Yankees.* New York: Crown Publishing Group, 2002, pp. 231–232.

65. Gossage, op. cit., p. 117.

66. Lally, op cit., pp. 231–232.

67. Gossage, op. cit., p. 117.

68. Cohen, Joel, editor. *Inside Corner: Talks with Tom Seaver.* New York: Atheneum, 1974, p. 48.

69. Ibid.

70. Koufax, op cit., p. 113.

71. Ibid.

72. DiMaggio, *Baseball For Everyone,* op. cit., p. 203.

73. Gossage, op. cit., p. 321.

74. Ibid., p. 322.

75. *San Francisco Chronicle,* "Notebook," August 28, 2003, p. C4.

76. Horowitz, Mitch. "Barry's Way: Major League Pitcher Barry Zito Gets Creative." *Science of Mind,* Vol. 76, No. 9, September, 2003, pp. 13–25.

77. Torre, op. cit., p. 118.

78. Ibid., pp. 120, 129.

79. Jackson, Reggie, with Mike Lupica. *Reggie.* New York: Villard Books, 1984, p. 194.

80. Lasorda, Tommy, and David Fisher. *The Artful Dodger.* New York: Arbor House, 1985, p. 219.

81. Santo, op. cit., p. 124.

82. Wills, op. cit., p. 132.

83. *San Francisco Chronicle,* May 6, 1994, p. E5.

84. Horowitz, op. cit.

85. Ibid.

86. Ibid.

87. Berra, Yogi, with Tom Horton, *Yogi: It Ain't Over.* New York: McGraw Hill, 1989, pp. 66–67.

88. *San Francisco Chronicle,* June 16, 1995, p. E1.

89. Kuiper, Duane. Interview with J. T. Snow. Fox Sports Net. August 23, 2003.

90. *San Francisco Chronicle,* August 20, 2003, p. C8.
91. Ibid.
92. Baylor, Don, with Claire Smith. *Nothing but the Truth: A Baseball Life.* New York: St. Martin's Press, 1989, p. 131.
93. Morgan, Joe, and David Falkner. *Joe Morgan: A Life in Baseball.* New York: W. W. Norton and Co., 1993, pp. 81–82.
94. Falkner, David. *Nine Sides of the Diamond: Baseball's Greatest Glove Men on the Fine Art of Defense.* New York: Times Books, 1990, p. 281.
95. Jackson, op. cit., p. 208.
96. Lyle, Sparky, and Peter Golenbock. *The Bronx Zoo.* New York: Crown Publishers, 1979, p. 244.
97. *San Francisco Chronicle,* June 16, 1995, p. E1.
98. Ibid.
99. *San Francisco Chronicle,* June 9, 2003, p. C4.
100. Honig, Donald. *Baseball Between the Lines.* New York: Coward, McCann, & Geoghegan, Inc., 1976, p. 233.
101. Ibid.
102. *San Francisco Chronicle,* June 16, 1995, p. E1.

CHAPTER THREE: COMPETITIVE DRIVE
1. Lasorda, op. cit., p. 192.
2. Ripken, Cal, Sr., op. cit., p. 224.
3. Snider, op cit., pp. 61–62.
4. Morgan, op. cit., p. 285.
5. Garvey, op. cit., p. 222.
6. Seaver, Tom, with Marty Appel. *Great Moments in Baseball.* New York: Carol Publishing Group, 1995.
7. Ibid.
8. Sokolove, op. cit., p. 89.
9. Anderson, Sparky, with Dan Ewald. *Sparky!* New York: Prentice Hall, 1990, p. 182.
10. Ibid., p. 186.
11. Ibid., p. 189.
12. Piniella, Lou, and Maury Allen. *Sweet Lou.* New York: G. P. Putnam's & Sons, 1986, p. 102.
13. Ibid., pp. 141–142.
14. Ibid., p. 102.
15. Ibid., p. 146.
16. Ibid., pp. 141–142.
17. Lyle, op. cit., p. 177.
18. Ibid.
19. Feller, Bob, and Bill Gilbert. *Now Pitching, Bob Feller.* New York: Carol Publishing Group, 1990, p. 164.

20. Allen, op. cit., p. 190
21. Ibid.
22. Aaron, op. cit., p. 199.
23. Ibid.
24. Ibid.
25. Robinson, op. cit., p. 29.
26. Ibid., p. 54.
27. Ibid., pp. 34–35.
28. Ibid.
29. Aaron, op. cit., p. 195.
30. Gibson, op. cit., p. x.
31. Ibid., p. xi.
32. Ibid., p. 166.
33. Ibid.
34. Ibid., p. 158.
35. Ibid.
36. Feller, op. cit., p. 185.
37. Ibid., p. 185.
38. Ibid.
39. Morgan op cit., p. 148.
40. Ibid.
41. Ibid., p. 267.
42. Bouton, *Ball Four Plus Ball Five,* op. cit., p. 365.
43. Piniella, op. cit., p. 184.
44. Gossage, op. cit., pp. 161–162.
45. Allen, Maury. *Jackie Robinson: A Life Remembered.* New York: Franklin Watts, 1987, p. 153.
46. Ibid., p. 169.
47. Ibid., p. 166.
48. Ibid., pp. 115–116.
49. Ibid., p. 98.
50. Ibid., p. 120.
51. Ibid., p. 168.
52. Ibid., p. 134.
53. Ibid., p. 165.
54. Ibid., p. 138.
55. Zimmer, Don, and Bill Madden. *Zim: A Baseball Life.* New York: Total Sports, 2001, p. 27–28.
56. Allen, *Jackie Robinson,* op. cit., p. 182.
57. Ibid.
58. Frommer, Harvey. *Rickey and Robinson: The Men Who Broke Baseball's Color Barrier.* New York: Collier MacMillan Publishers, 1982, pp. 186–187.

59. Allen, *Jackie Robinson,* op. cit., p. 242.
60. Aaron, op. cit., pp. 294, 297.
61. Oh, op cit., pp. 252–253.
62. Yastrzemski, op. cit., p. 294.
63. Ibid.
64. Piniella, op. cit., p. 264.
65. Alexander, op. cit., pp. 133, 140.
66. Herzog, Whitey, and Kevin Horrigan. *White Rat: A Life in Baseball.* New York: Harper & Row, 1987, pp. 193–194.
67. Garvey, op. cit., p. 216.
68. Ibid.

CHAPTER FOUR: DEVELOPING CONFIDENCE
1. Feller, op. cit., p. 18.
2. Hershiser, *Out of the Blue,* op. cit., p. 3.
3. Schmidt, op cit., p. 25–26.
4. Lasorda, op. cit., p. 135.
5. Ibid., p. 126.
6. Ibid.
7. Gossage, op cit., p. 67.
8. Stargell, op. cit., p. 118.
9. Morgan, op. cit., pp. 58–59.
10. Robinson, op. cit., p. 25.
11. Garrity, op. cit., p. 244.
12. Lyle, op. cit., p. 200.
13. Berra, *When You Come to the Fork in the Road, Take It,* op. cit., p. 34.
14. Mays, op. cit., p. 72.
15. Ibid.
16. Ibid.
17. Hershiser, *Out of the Blue,* op. cit., pp. 10–13.
18. Ibid.
19. Ibid., pp. 13–14.
20. Lasorda, op. cit., p. 122.
21. Ibid., p. 141.
22. Ibid.
23. Jeter, op. cit. p. 120–123.
24. Ibid., p. 115.
25. Garvey, op. cit., p. 207.
26. Wagenheim, Kal. *Babe Ruth: His Life and Legend.* New York: Praeger Publishers, 1974, p. 69.
27. Aaron, op. cit., p. 71.
28. Torre, op cit., p. 136.

29. Ibid., p. 143.
30. Einstein, Charles. *Willie's Time: A Memoir*. New York: J. P. Lippincott, 1979, p. 146.
31. Greenberg, Hank, with Ira Berkow. *Hank Greenberg: The Story of My Life*. New York: Times Books, 1989, p. 22.
32. Houk, op. cit., p. 179.
33. Lyle, op. cit., p. 11.
34. Garvey, op. cit., pp. 200–201.
35. Morgan, op. cit., p. 166.
36. Koufax, op. cit., p. 87.
37. Carter, Gary, and John Hough Jr. *A Dream Season*. Harcourt, Brace, Jovanovich, Publishers, 1987, p. 65.
38. Ibid, p. 76.
39. Olney, Buster, "New Dimensions to Home Field Advantage." *The New York Times*, May 18, 2003, Sports, p. 4.
40. Ibid.
41. Lally, op. cit., p. 91.
42. Gossage, op. cit., pp. 208–209.
43. Ibid.

CHAPTER FIVE: INTUITION, INSTINCT, HUNCHES, AND GUT FEELINGS

1. Falkner, *Nine Sides of the Diamond*, op. cit., p. 19.
2. Lasorda, op. cit., p. 252.
3. Henderson, Rickey, with John Shea. *Off Base: Confessions of a Thief*. New York: HarperCollins Publishers, 1992, p. 16.
4. Alexander, op cit., p. 189.
5. Sokolove, op. cit., p. 72.
6. Shlain, op. cit., p. 36.
7. McCarver, Tim, with Danny Peary. *Tim McCarver's Baseball for Brain Surgeons and Other Fans*. Random House, 1998, p. 74.
8. Linn, op. cit., p. 49.
9. Berra, *It Ain't Over*, op cit., p. 57.
10. Bouton, Jim. *Ball Four*. New York: World Publishing, 1970, p. 22.
11. Rains, op. cit., p. 102.
12. Bouton, *Ball Four*, op. cit., p. 178.
13. Ibid.
14. Ibid.
15. Hernandez, Keith, and Mike Ryan. *If at First: A Season with the Mets*. New York: McGraw Hill, 1986, p. 156.
16. Ibid., pp. 156, 220.
17. Koufax, op cit., p. 193.

18. Ibid., p. 214.
19. Nettles, op. cit., p. 40.
20. Ibid., p. 88.
21. Wagenheim, op. cit., p. 91.
22. Durocher, Leo, with Ed Linn. *Nice Guys Finish Last*. New York: Simon and Schuster, 1975, p. 55.
23. Hershiser, *Out of the Blue,* op cit., p. 34.
24. Einstein, op. cit., p. 168.
25. Mays, op. cit., p. 15.
26. Einstein, op. cit., p. 168.
27. Ibid., p. 59.
28. Ibid., p. 63.
29. Ibid., p. 156.
30. Aaron, op. cit., p. 270.
31. Ibid.
32. Allen, *Where Have You Gone Joe DiMaggio?,* op. cit., p. 65.
33. Ibid. p. 40.
34. Ibid., p. 159.
35. Ibid., pp. 130–131.
36. Lally, op. cit., p. 34.
37. Williams, Dick, op. cit., p. 132.
38. Ibid., p. 154.
39. Honig, op. cit., pp. 96, 189.
40. Torre, op. cit., p. 173.
41. Ibid., pp. 163, 168–169, 173.
42. Schoendienst, Red, with Rob Rains. *Red: A Baseball Life*. Champaign, Illinois: Sports Publishing, 1998, p. 139.

CHAPTER SIX: MENTAL IMAGERY

1. Lasorda, op. cit., p. 135.
2. Linn, op. cit., p. 192.
3. Ibid.
4. Markusen, Bruce. *Roberto Clemente: The Great One*. Champaign, Illinois: Sports Publishing, 1998., p. 76.
5. Musick, op. cit., p. 284.
6. Houk, op. cit., p. 168.
7. Nettles, op. cit., p. 140.
8. Hershiser, *Between the Lines,* op. cit., p. 63.
9. Koufax, op. cit., pp. 9, 192, 251.
10. Lally, op. cit., p. 268.
11. *San Francisco Chronicle,* April 6, 2002, p. C2.
12. Schmidt, op. cit., p. 19.

13. Morgan, op. cit., p. 205.
14. Falkner, *Nine Sides of the Diamond,* op. cit., p. 16.
15. Morgan, op. cit., p. 205.
16. Mays, op. cit., p. 12.
17. Wills, op. cit., p. 138. (Letter from Rocky Colavito to Neal Vahle, August 12, 2003).
18. Yastrzemski op. cit., pp. 167–169.
19. Ibid.
20. Ibid.
21. Ibid.
22. Ibid.
23. Mays, op. cit., p. 177.

CHAPTER SEVEN: EXERCISING LEADERSHIP

1. *San Francisco Chronicle,* July 13, 2003, p. B7.
2. *San Francisco Chronicle,* September 1, 2003, p. C4.
3. Durocher, op. cit., p. 307.
4. Allen, *Where Have You Gone Joe DiMaggio?,* op. cit., pp. 34–36.
5. Ibid., pp. 40–41
6. Ibid., p. 84.
7. Falkner, *Nine Sides of the Diamond,* op. cit., p. 262.
8. Honig, op. cit., p. 177.
9. Allen, *Where Have You Gone Joe DiMaggio?,* op. cit., p. 90.
10. Houk, op. cit., p. 163.
11. Allen, *Where Have You Gone Joe DiMaggio?,* op. cit., p. 140.
12. Ibid., p. 135.
13. Ibid., p. 151.
14. Ibid.
15. Falkner, *The Last Hero: The Life of Mickey Mantle,* op. cit., p. 100.
16. Allen, *Jackie Robinson,* op. cit., p. 208.
17. Ibid., p. 139.
18. Frommer, op. cit., p. 163.
19. Ibid., p. 238.
20. Ibid.
21. Ibid., p. 185.
22. Allen, *Jackie Robinson,* op. cit., p. 169.
23. Ibid., pp. 242–243.
24. Ibid., p. 13.
25. Durocher, op. cit., p. 308.
26. Einstein, op. cit., pp. 34–40.
27. Ibid.
28. Ibid.
29. Ibid.

30. Ibid., pp. 33–34.
31. Ibid., pp. 33–40.
32. Durocher, op. cit., pp. 431, 307.
33. Honig, op. cit. p. 187.
34. Mays, op. cit., p. 211.
35. Creamer, Robert W. *Stengel: His Life and Times.* New York: Simon and Schuster, 1984, p. 42.
36. Ibid.
37. Ibid.
38. Ibid., p. 243.
39. Ibid., p. 259.
40. Houk, op. cit., p. 236.
41. Falkner, *The Last Hero,* op. cit., p. 157.
42. Ibid., p. 150.
43. Ibid., pp. 161–162.
44. Houk, op. cit, p. 204.
45. Kubek, Tony, and Terry Pluto. *Sixty-One: The Team, the Record, the Men.* New York: Macmillan, 1987, p. 220.
46. Falkner, *The Last Hero.* op. cit., p. 221.
47. Ibid., p. 137.
48. Kubek, op. cit., p. 221.
49. Falkner, *The Last Hero,* op. cit., p. 137.
50. Musick, op. cit., p. 284.
51. Ibid., p. 271.
52. Ibid., p. 284.
53. Ibid., p. 264.
54. Ibid.
55. Ibid., p. 270.
56. Ibid., p. 278.
57. Wills, op. cit., p. 184.
58. Markusen, op. cit., p. 102.
59. Musick, op. cit., p. 303.

CHAPTER EIGHT: YOU GOTTA HAVE FUN

1. Nettles, op. cit., p. 227.
2. Ibid., p. 147.
3. Ibid., p. 219.
4. Carter, op. cit., p. 78.
5. DiMaggio, Joe. *Lucky to Be a Yankee.* New York: Rudolph Field, 1946, p. 72.
6. Winfield, Dave, with Tom Parker. *Winfield: A Player's Life.* New York: W. W. Norton and Co., 1988, p. 228.
7. Rose, Pete, and Roger Kahn. *Pete Rose: My Story.* New York: Macmillan, 1989, p. 14.

8. Sokolove, op. cit., p. 88–89.
9. Ibid., p. 96.
10. Ibid., p. 121.
11. Ibid.
12. Schmidt, op. cit., p. 31.
13. Lasorda, op. cit., p. 176.
14. Ibid., p. 193.
15. Morgan, op. cit., p. 241.
16. Henderson, p. 7.
17. Wagenheim, op. cit., p. 93.
18. Ibid.
19. Ibid.

CHAPTER NINE: WINNING AND LOSING

1. Koufax, op. cit., p. 7.
2. Rosenfeld, op. cit., pp. 3, 4, 189, 199.
3. Houk, op. cit., p. 66.
4. Berra, *It Ain't Over,* op. cit., p. 151.
5. Piniella, op. cit., p. 66.
6. Schoendienst, op. cit., p. 94.
7. Lasorda, op. cit., p. 233.
8. Piniella, op. cit., p. 250.
9. Baylor, op. cit., p. 199.
10. Koufax, op. cit., p. 8
11. Ibid., p. 7.
12. Bouton, *Ball Four Plus Ball Five,* op. cit., p. 64.
13. Anderson, op. cit., pp. 1–2.
14. Ibid., p. 10.
15. Ibid., p. 244.
16. Ibid.
17. Torre, op. cit., pp. 7–9, 281.
18. Ibid., pp. 120–122.
19. Hershiser, *Between the Lines,* op. cit., pp. 51–53.
20. Sokolove, op. cit., p. 90.
21. Schmidt, op. cit., p. 27.
22. Bouton, *Ball Four Plus Ball Five,* op. cit., p. 337.
23. Garvey, op. cit., p. 217.
24. Jordan, Pat. "Winning Used to be Everything." *The New York Times Maga-zine,* July 20, 2003, pp. 24–27.
25. Ibid.
26. Berra, *It Ain't Over,* op. cit., p. 34.
27. *San Francisco Chronicle,* October 18, 22, and 23, 1992, Sports Section.
28. Ibid.

Bibliography

Aaron, Hank, with Wheeler, Lonnie. *I Had a Hammer: The Hank Aaron Story.* New York: HarperCollins Publishers, 1991.

Allen, Maury. *Jackie Robinson: A Life Remembered.* New York: Franklin Watts, 1987.

Allen, Maury. *Where Have You Gone Joe Dimaggio: The Story of America's Last Hero.* New York: E. P. Dutton, 1975.

Alexander, Charles. *Ty Cobb.* New York: Oxford University Press, 1984.

Anderson, Sparky, with Dan Ewald. *Sparky!* New York: Prentice Hall, 1990.

Angell, Roger. *A Pitchers's Story: Innings with David Cone.* New York: Warner Books, Inc., 2001.

Banks, Ernie, and Jim Enright. *"Mr. Cub."* Chicago: Follet Publishing Company, 1971.

Baylor, Don, with Claire Smith. *Don Baylor: Nothing but the Truth: A Baseball Life.* New York: St. Martin's Press, 1989.

Berra, Yogi, with Tom Horton. *Yogi: It Ain't Over.* New York: McGraw Hill, 1989.

Berra, Yogi, with David Kaplan. *When You Come to the Fork in the Road, Take It!* New York: Hyperion, 2001.

Bouton, Jim. *Ball Four:* New York: World Publishing, 1970.

Bouton, Jim. *Ball Four Plus Ball Five: An Update, 1970–1980.* New York: Stein and Day, 1981.

Cepeda, Orlando, with Herb Fagan. *Baby Bull: From Hardball to Hard Time and Back.* Dallas: Taylor Publishing Co., 1998.

Carter, Gary, and Hough, John, Jr. *A Dream Season.* Harcourt, Brace, Jovanovich, Publishers, 1987.

Cohen, Joel, editor. *Inside Corner: Talks with Tom Seaver.* New York: Atheneum, 1974.

Connor, Anthony. *Baseball for the Love of It: Hall of Famers Tell It Like It Was.* New York: Macmillan, 1982.

Creamer, Robert W. *Stengel: His Life and Times.* New York: Simon and Schuster, 1984.

Davis, Eric, with Ralph Wiley. *Born to Play: The Eric Davis Story.* New York: Penguin USA, 1999.

Dickey, Glenn. *Champions: The Story of the First Two Oakland A's Dynasties—and the Building of the Third.* Chicago: Triumph Books, 2002.

DiMaggio, Joe. *Baseball for Everyone.* New York: McGraw Hill, 2002.

DiMaggio, Joe. *Lucky to Be a Yankee.* New York: Rudolph Field, 1946.

Dorfman, H. A. *The Mental ABC's of Pitching.* South Bend, Indiana: Diamond Communications, Inc., 2000.

Durocher, Leo, with Ed Linn. *Nice Guys Finish Last.* New York: Simon and Schuster, 1975.

Drysdale, Don, with Bob Verdi. *Once a Bum, Always a Dodger: My Life in Baseball from Brooklyn to Los Angeles.* New York: St. Martin's Press, 1990.

Einstein, Charles. *Willie's Time: A Memoir.* New York: J. P. Lippincott, 1979.

Falkner, David. *Nine Sides of the Diamond: Baseball's Greatest Glove Men on the Fine Art of Defense.* New York: Times Books, 1990.

Falkner, David. *The Last Hero: The Life of Mickey Mantle.* New York: Simon and Schuster, 1995.

Feller, Bob, with Burton Rocks. *Bob Feller's Little Black Book of Baseball Wisdom.* Chicago: Contemporary Books, 2001.

Feller, Bob, with Bill Gilbert. *Now Pitching, Bob Feller.* New York: Carol Publishing Group, 1990.

Ford, Whitey, with Phil Pepe. *Slick: My Life in and Around Baseball.* New York: William Morrow and Co., 1987.

Ford, Whitey, with Phil Pepe. *Few and Chosen: Defining Yankee Greatness Across the Eras.* Chicago: Triumph Books, 2001.

Frommer, Harvey. *Rickey and Robinson: The Men Who Broke Baseball's Color Barrier.* New York: Collier MacMillan Publishers, 1982.

Garrity, John. *The George Brett Story.* New York: Coward, McCann, & Geoghegan, 1981.

Garvey, Steve, with Skip Rozin. *Garvey.* New York: Times Books, 1986.

Gibson, Bob, with Lonnie Wheeler. *Stranger to the Game.* New York: Viking, 1994.

Glavine, Tom, with Nick Cafardo. *None but the Braves: A Pitcher, a Team, a Champion.* New York: HarperCollins Publishers, 1996.

Gmelch, George. *Inside Pitch: Life in Professional Baseball.* Washington, D.C.: Smithsonian Books, 2001.

Goldman, William, and Mike Lupica. *Wait Till Next Year.* New York: Bantam, 1988.

Gossage, Richard "Goose," with Russ Pate. *The Goose Is Loose.* New York: Ballantine Books, 2000.

Greenberg, Hank, with Ira Berkow. *Hank Greenberg: The Story of My Life.* New York: Times Books, 1989.

Gruver, Edward. *Koufax.* Dallas: Taylor Publishing Co., 2000.

Hall, Donald, with Dock Ellis. *Dock Ellis: In the Country of Baseball.* New York: Coward, McCann, & Geoghegan, 1976.

Henderson, Rickey, with John Shea. *Off Base: Confessions of a Thief*. New York: HarperCollins Publishers, 1992.

Hernandez, Keith, and Mike Ryan. *If at First: A Season with the Mets*. New York: McGraw Hill, 1986.

Hershiser, Orel, with Robert Wolgemuth. *Between the Lines: Nine Principles to Live By*. New York: Warner Books, 2001.

Hershiser, Orel, with Jerry B. Jenkins. *Out of the Blue*. Brentwood, Tennessee: Wolgemuth & Hyatt, 1989.

Herzog, Whitey, and Jonathan Pitts. *You're Missing a Great Game*. Norwalk, Connecticut: Easton Press, 1999.

Herzog, Whitey, and Kevin Horrigan. *White Rat: A Life in Baseball*. New York: Harper & Row, 1987.

Honig, Donald. *Baseball Between the Lines*. New York: Coward, McCann, & Geoghegan, Inc., 1976.

Houk, Ralph, and Robert W. Creamer. *Season of Glory: The Amazing Saga of the 1961 New York Yankees*. New York: G. P. Putnam's Sons, 1988.

Hunter, Jim "Catfish," and Armen Keteyian. *Catfish: My Life in Baseball*. New York: McGraw Hill, 1988.

Irvin, Monte, with James A. Riley. *Nice Guys Finish First*. New York: Carroll & Graf Publishers, Inc., 1996.

Jeter, Derek, with Jack Curry. *The Life You Imagine: Life Lessons for Achieving Your Dreams*. New York: Crown Publishing Group, 2000.

Jackson, Reggie, with Mike Lupica. *Reggie*. New York: Villard Books, 1984.

Kahn, Robert. *The Head Game: Baseball Seen from the Pitcher's Mound*. New York: Harcourt, Inc., 2000.

Koufax, Sandy, with Ed Linn. *Koufax*. New York: Viking Press, 1966.

Kubek, Tony, and Terry Pluto. *Sixty-One: The Team, the Record, the Men*. New York: Macmillan, 1987.

Lasorda, Tommy, and David Fisher. *The Artful Dodger*. New York: Arbor House, 1985.

Lally, Richard. *Bombers: An Oral History of the Yankees*. New York: Crown Publishing Group, 2002.

Lewis, Michael. *Moneyball: The Art of Winning an Unfair Game*. New York: W. W. Norton and Co., 2003.

Linn, Ed. *Hitter: The Life and Turmoils of Ted Williams*. New York: Harcourt Brace and Co., 1993.

Lyle, Sparky, and Peter Golenbock. *The Bronx Zoo*. New York: Crown Publishing Group, 1979.

Mantle, Mickey. *The Education of a Baseball Player*. New York: Simon and Schuster, 1967.

Mantle, Mickey, with Herb Gluck. *The Mick*. New York: Doubleday and Co., 1985.

Markusen, Bruce. *Roberto Clemente: The Great One*. Champaign, Illinois: Sports Publishing, Inc., 1998.

Mays, Willie, as told to Charles Einstein. *Willie Mays: My Life in and out of Baseball*. New York: E. P. Dutton and Co., 1966.

Mays, Willie, with Lou Sahadi. *Say Hey: The Autobiography of Willie Mays*. New York: Simon and Schuster, 1988.

McCarver, Tim, with Danny Peary. *Tim McCarver's Baseball for Brain Surgeons and Other Fans*. Random House, 1998.

Morgan, Joe, and David Falkner. *Joe Morgan: A Life in Baseball*. New York: W. W. Norton and Co., 1993.

Mosedal, John. *The Greatest of All: The 1927 New York Yankees*. New York: Dial Press, 1974.

Musick, Phil. *Who Was Roberto? A Biography of Roberto Clemente*. New York: Doubleday and Company, 1974.

Nettles, Graig, and Peter Golenbock. *Balls*. New York: G. P. Putnam and Sons, 1984.

Oh, Sadaharu, and David Falkner. *Sadaharu Oh: A Zen Way of Baseball*. New York: Times Books, 1984.

Oliva, Tony, with Bob Fowler. *Tony O! The Trials and Triumphs of Tony Oliva*. New York: Hawthorn Books, 1973.

Peary, Danny, editor, *Cult Baseball Players: The Greats, the Flakes, the Weird, and the Wonderful*. New York: Simon and Schuster, 1990.

Piniella, Louis, and Maury Allen. *Sweet Lou*. New York: G. P. Putnam's Sons, 1986.

Rains, Rob. *Mark McGwire, Home Run Hero*. New York: St. Martin's Press, 1998.

Ripken, Cal, Sr., with Larry Burke. *The Ripken Way*. New York: Simon and Schuster, 1999.

Ripken, Cal, Jr., and Mike Bryan. *The Only Way I Know*. New York: Penguin Putnam, Inc., 1997.

Robinson, Frank, and Berry Stainback. *Extra Innings: The Grand-Slam Response to Al Campanis's Controversial Remarks about Blacks in Baseball*. New York: McGraw-Hill Book Company, 1988.

Rose, Pete, and Roger Kahn. *Pete Rose: My Story*. New York: Macmillan, 1989.

Roseboro, John, with Bill Libby. *Glory Days with the Dodgers and Other Days with Others*. New York: Atheneum, 1978.

Rosenfeld, Harvey. *Iron Man: The Cal Ripken Jr. Story*. New York: St. Martin's Press, 1995.

Santo, Ron, with Randy Minkoff. *For Love of Ivy: An Autobiography*. Chicago: Bonus Books, 1993.

Schmidt, Mike, with Barbara Walder. *Always on the Offense*. New York: Smithmark, 1982.

Seaver, Tom, with Marty Appel. *Great Moments in Baseball*. New York: Carol Publishing Group. 1995.

Shlain, Bruce. *Baseball Inside Out: Winning the Game Within the Game*. New York: Viking Penguin, 1992.

Schoendienst, Red, with Rob Rains. *Red: A Baseball Life*. Champaign, Illinois: Sports Publishing, 1998.

Snider, Duke, with Bill Gilbert. *The Duke of Flatbush*. New York: Citadel Press, 2002.

Sokolove, Michael Y. *Hustle: The Myth, Life and Lies of Pete Rose*. New York: Simon and Schuster, 1990.

Stargell, Willie, and Tom Bird. *Willie Stargell*. New York: HarperCollins Publishers, 1984.

Thomson, Bobby, with Lee Heiman and Bill Gutman. *"The Giants Win the Pennant! The Giants Win the Pennant!"* New York: Kensington Publishing Corporation, 1991.

Torre, Joe, with Henry, Dreher. *Joe Torre's Ground Rules for Winners*. New York: Hyperion, 1999.

Tutko, Thomas, and Umberto Tosi. *Sports Psyching*. Los Angeles: Jeremy P. Tarcher, 1976.

Wagenheim, Kal. *Babe Ruth: His Life and Legend*. New York: Praeger Publishers, 1974.

Weaver, Earl, and John Sammis. *Winning!* New York: William Morrow and Company, 1972.

Williams, Dick, and Bill Plaschke. *No More Mr. Nice Guy: A Life of Hardball*. New York: Harcourt Brace Jovanovich, 1990.

Williams, Ted, as told to John Underwood. *My Turn at Bat: The Story of My Life*. New York: Simon and Schuster, 1969.

Wills, Maury, and Mike Celizic. *On the Run: The Never Dull and Often Shocking Life of Maury Wills*. New York: Carroll and Graf Publishers, 1991.

Winfield, Dave, with Tom Parker. *Winfield: A Player's Life*. New York: W. W. Norton and Co., 1988.

Yastrzemski, Carl, and Gerald Eskenazi. *Yaz, Baseball, the Wall and Me*. New York: Bantam Dell, 1990.

Zeligman, Mark, coordinating editor. *George Brett: Royal Hero*. Kansas City, Missouri: Sports Publishing, 1999.

Zimmer, Don, with Bill Madden. *Zim: A Baseball Life*. New York: Total Sports, 2001.

Zukav, Gary. *Soul Stories*. New York: Simon and Schuster, 2000.

About the Authors

Buddy Bell broke into the major leagues with the Cleveland Indians in 1972 at the age of twenty-one, and played for eighteen seasons, mainly with the Indians and Texas Rangers, but also with Cincinnati and Houston. A consistent .290 hitter throughout his career, he amassed 2,514 hits and 201 homers in 2,405 games. Bell was named to the American League All-Star team five times, the first time at age twenty-two with Cleveland, and won six consecutive Golden Gloves as a third baseman. Pete Palmer's Linear Weights, a player rating system, lists him among major league baseball's top four defensive third basemen. *Bill James Historical Baseball Abstract* ranks him nineteenth in the top hundred for all-around play as a third baseman. In *Total Baseball: The Official Encyclopedia of American Baseball,* Bell is listed as one of the four hundred greatest players to play the game.

His career in baseball management includes service as director of the farm system of the Chicago White Sox, 1991–1993; infield coach for the Cleveland Indians, 1994–1995; manager of the Detroit Tigers, 1996–1998; manager of the Colorado Rockies,

2000–2002; and bench coach for the Cleveland Indians in 2003 and 2004.

His father, Gus Bell, had a fifteen-year career as an outfielder in the National League, having been named to the National League All-Star team four times as a member of the Cincinnati Reds. His three sons, David, Mike, and Rick, are currently playing baseball professionally. The Bells are members of one of only three three-generation major league families.

Neal Vahle, Ph.D., has broad experience as an author, editor, and college teacher. He also was a semiprofessional baseball player. Vahle holds a doctorate in American history from Georgetown University and has taught at the American University, the Catholic University of America, and George Mason University. He is the author of three books: *The Unity Movement: Its Evolution and Spiritual Teaching* (Templeton Foundation Press, 2002); *Torch-bearer to Light the Way: The Life of Myrtle Fillmore* (Open View Press, 1996); and *Open at the Top: The Life of Ernest Holmes* (Open View Press, 1993). He has served as editor of *World Affairs* journal, and of *Current* and *New Realities* magazines. Vahle is currently editor of *Unity Magazine,* published by the Unity School of Christianity. Vahle's baseball experience includes several years pitching in high school and college, as well as being paid to pitch in the Minnesota summer leagues. He played baseball full time with major and minor leaguers for the U.S. Army in Europe.

David Bell made his major league debut at third base with the Cleveland Indians at age twenty-two on May 3, 1995. Traded to St. Louis shortly thereafter, he remained with the Cardinals until 1998. He had three productive years with the Seattle Mariners, playing in two American League Championship Series against the Yankees (2000 and 2001). In 1999, his first year with Seattle, he set career highs in both home runs (21) and RBIs (78) and was named Seattle's Unsung Hero. With the San Francisco Giants in 2002 he won the Willie McCovey Award, which goes to the team's most inspirational player. He was the team's top clutch hitter, batting .317 with 50 RBIs with runners in scoring position, and played third base for the team in the World Series. He currently plays for the Philadelphia Phillies, having signed a four-year contract with the club in November 2002.

Mike Bell has had an eleven-year career in professional baseball. He signed out of high school in 1993 with the Texas Rangers, a sandwich pick, thirtieth overall in the draft. An infielder playing primarily third base and second base, Mike progressed through the minor leagues, reaching Triple-A in 1997 at age twenty-two with Oklahoma City, a Rangers affiliate. Drafted by the Arizona Diamondbacks in the expansion draft at the end of the season, he was traded to the Mets in the winter. Playing for the Triple-A Mets farm team in Norfolk in 1999, Mike tore ligaments in this throwing hand in spring training. After surgery on three fingers, he spent an entire season in rehabilitation. He signed with Cincinnati, his home town, in 2000, began the year in Triple-A with Louisville, and was called up to the parent club as an injury replacement in July and again in September. His major league debut was made on July 20, 2000. A home run in a game in September in Milwaukee's County Stadium enabled him to become the fourth member of the Bell family to hit one there—Gus, Buddy, and Dave having also homered there. Mike signed with the Rockies rather than the Reds in the winter because of a desire to play for his father, who was the Colorado manager. Arm and hand injuries again forced him to spend the greater part of the next two seasons in rehablitation. He played for the Diamondbacks Triple-A affiliate in Tucson, Arizona, in 2003 and the White Sox Triple-A affiliate in Charlotte, North Carolina in 2004:

Rick Bell, the youngest of the three Bell brothers, signed with the Dodgers in 1997 as a shortstop after graduating from high school. His professional career, which is now in its seventh year, began in the rookie league in Yakima, Washington. Rick played in Class A in 1998 in San Bernardino, and in 1999 and 2000 with Vero Beach, moving to Double-A in 2001 with Jacksonville, and then to Triple-A in 2002 with the Dodgers' affiliate in Las Vegas. Rick now plays three infield positions: third, second, and first base. The 2004 season marked his third year with Las Vegas.